W9-BTT-630

MAKING WASTE

MAKING WASTE

LEFTOVERS AND
THE EIGHTEENTH-CENTURY
IMAGINATION

Sophie Gee

Princeton University Press

Princeton & Oxford

Published by Princeton University Press, 41 William Street,
Princeton, New Jersey 08540

In the United Kingdom: Princeton University Press, 6 Oxford Street,
Woodstock, Oxfordshire OX20 1TW

LIBRARY OF CONGRESS CATALOGING-IN-PUBLICATION DATA

Gee, Sophie, 1974–
   Making waste : leftovers and the eighteenth-century imagination /
Sophie Gee.
        p.   cm.
   Includes bibliographical references and index.
   ISBN 978-0-691-13984-5 (cloth : alk. paper)
   1. English literature—18th century—History and criticism.
2. Waste (Economics) in literature. 3. Literature and society—Great
Britain—History—18th century. 4. Refuse and refuse disposal
in literature. 5. Great Britain—Civilization—18th century.
6. Consumption (Economics) in literature. I. Title.
   PR448.W37G44 2010
   820.9'3553—dc22   2009032667

British Library Cataloging-in-Publication Data is available

This book has been composed in Adobe Garamond

Printed on acid-free paper. ∞

press.princeton.edu

Printed in the United States of America

10 9 8 7 6 5 4 3 2 1

CONTENTS

ACKNOWLEDGMENTS

Making Waste is based on the doctoral dissertation I wrote at Harvard under the supervision of Barbara Lewalski, Marjorie Garber, and James Engell. I thank them for their mentoring, encouragement, and friendship when I was a student and for ongoing support in later years. Several senior colleagues at Princeton have also given advice and support for which I am very grateful: Claudia Johnson, Susan Wolfson, Oliver Arnold, Jeff Nunokawa, and Nigel Smith.

Fellowships from Harvard and Princeton universities enabled me to research and write this book at home and abroad. A good deal of the work was completed while I was an Ahmanson-Getty Fellow at the Clark Library in Los Angeles; my thanks to UCLA for that award. I thank the Huntington Library in California for a fellowship that supported additional work for the project. Helen Deutsch at UCLA offered much appreciated friendship during that period.

Friends and colleagues in the profession have helped me and guided my work at crucial moments. My thanks to Anna Henchman, Julie Park, Lynn Festa, Cedric Reverand, Cynthia Wall, Jayne Lewis, Dror Wahrman, Jonathan Sheehan, Eduardo Cadava, April Alliston, Diana Fuss, Benj Widiss, Tamsen Wolff, Daphne Brooks, Jeff Dolven, and Tony Miller.

Thanks, finally, to my editor, Hanne Winarsky, my wonderful copyeditor, Vicky Wilson-Schwartz, and the team at Princeton University Press.

An earlier version of chapter 1 appeared as "The Invention of the Wasteland: Civic Narration in Dryden's *Annus Mirabilis*," *Eighteenth-Century Life* 20, no.1 (2005): 82–108. I would like to thank the editors for allowing me to reprint this essay. An earlier version of chapter 3 was published as "Milton's Chaos in Pope's London," in *Science, Literature, and Rhetoric in Early Modern London*, ed. Juliet Cummins and David Burchell (Aldershot and Burlington: Ashgate, 2007).

MAKING WASTE

INTRODUCTION

Making Waste

IN 1772 the Frenchman Pierre Jean Grosley's *Tour to London; or, New Observations on England and its Inhabitants* praised London as Europe's most sophisticated metropolis: well paved, well lighted, convenient and modern. The best passages, however, leave us with an altogether different impression of the capital, a dirty, difficult place, darkened by pollution and contaminated with filth:

> In the most beautiful part of the Strand and near St. Clement's church I have, during my whole stay in London, seen the middle of the street constantly foul with a dirty puddle to the height of three or four inches; a puddle where splashings cover those who walk on foot; fill up coaches when their windows happen not to be up, and bedaub all the lower parts of such houses as are exposed to it. In consequence of this, the prentices are frequently employed in washing the fronts of their houses, in order to take off the daubings of the dirt which they had contracted overnight. The English are not afraid of this dirt, being defended from it by their wigs of a brownish curling hair, their black stockings, and their blue surtouts which are made in the form of a nightgown.[1]

This visitor starts describing one of the most beautiful ecclesiastical monuments in London, St. Clement's Church, but he is diverted by the filth that surrounds it. Waste animates his prose. The "dirty puddle" is a primordial lake, chaotic and unformed, spawning the life of Grosley's

1

tableau. Animation comes from abjection, not from the divine splendor of St. Clement's, which remains static and aloof. The verbs all describe defilement—"cover," "fill up," "bedaub." Dirt, vital and moving, coats the church, the citizens, the coaches and buildings, the elements that would compose a static eighteenth-century London "view"—that pictorial idiom for urban description to which Grosley is paying prose homage. But in this view the splendid buildings, London's ecclesiastical and secular facades, are eclipsed, literally, by a different kind of abundance: proliferating filth. In a contest between the divine splendor and abject surplus, abjection wins out.

The apprentices wash the housefronts each morning to efface its traces, but the very repetitiveness of their task gives it a ritualistic quality—reverent, even—especially in a passage where a description of secular defilement and purification takes over from that of a sacred monument. Londoners "are not afraid of this dirt," and yet their courage depends on their being fortified against it: they are encased in weatherproof armor. This same abjection gives London its life, not just the life-affirming beat that runs through Grosley's prose, but the cultural life of eighteenth-century London too: its fashions, its quotidian rhythms and patterns emerge, in this account, from befoulment. The "foul and dirty puddle" next to St. Clement's Church insists on abjection persisting beside divinity. This proximity of waste to divine splendor is no coincidence of urban geography but paradigmatic, providing vital clues for a literary history of eighteenth-century waste.

A glut of waste matter fills the pages of eighteenth-century literature, not just in minor texts but in canonical works such as *Paradise Lost*, *The Tale of a Tub*, "A Modest Proposal," and *A Journal of the Plague Year*. The waste is nothing if not memorable: Milton's infernal dregs, Swift's odious excrement, Pope's pissing contests, Defoe's corpses. It catches the eye all the more because it is matter that, at the time, was supposed to be ignored. But English writers did not neglect their waste. Dung, guts, and mud, dead dogs and turnip tops, sweep through the pages of eighteenth-century writing—putrid scraps that become perverse signs of metaphoric meaning and successful representation. Bernard Mandeville, praising English prosperity in *The Fable of the Bees*, told Londoners to treasure the dunghills in the streets, the running drains, animals, and crowds of beggars as daily reminders of London's wealth.[2] This book takes Mandeville's adage seriously and asks what, exactly, it meant for eighteenth-century English writing to treasure its waste.

Writers in eighteenth-century London and Dublin who described dust and decay, excrements and rotting corpses, were already reaching toward the psychoanalytic, philosophical, and anthropological insights of Freud, Kristeva, Aurel Kolnai, Mary Douglas, and other twentieth-century theorists of abjection. Without their language or analytical methods, eighteenth-century writers understood waste by way of idioms harvested from material conditions and philosophical and theological debates, finding imagery to describe the phenomenon Kristeva would call the abject, in which looms "one of those violent, dark revolts of being."[3] Twentieth-century waste theory is a subject I return to; here I want to note the overlap between early modern and modern philosophy.

The first chapter of *Making Waste* begins with descriptions of physical waste: the debris that filled the streets of London after the Great Fire. It was oppressive and superfluous, a threat to London's very existence because it took the place of houses and public buildings. It was shocking and traumatic for its citizens. But it also provided rich and promising imagery for literary texts: the literal wasteland of London after the fire evolved into the literary wastelands of modern literature; real debris was converted into the desolate, alienated urban landscape in which urban writing unfolds from *MacFlecknoe* to *The Waste Land*. Real waste thus became valuable in a quite straightforward way: it provided the imagery for describing a new sort of urban consciousness, and it provided the landscape details for a new literary setting. Literary metaphors and figurative language derive from the material conditions of history.[4]

But literal waste, visible and real, transformed by the literary imagination, is not the only sort of reside in eighteenth-century texts. Another kind of waste, which wasn't lying around in the streets, was the subject matter of late seventeenth- and early eighteenth-century philosophical and theological debates about matter, examples of which include the cosmic materials that went unused at Creation, the residues of human digestion, and the terrestrial flesh discarded at the resurrection. Some of this waste was in plain view, to be sure, but it was primarily of philosophical and theological interest, which is to say that it was attended to because it showed what was important and interesting about the concept, the very notion, of waste. The waste matter of eighteenth-century philosophy was usually seen as valuable *because* it was a leftover: a sign that something important had happened, leaving a residue behind.

Waste was a subject of intellectual inquiry for another reason, too: natural philosophers were interested in the problem of how substances were differentiated—why one was waste and another had value—when materially there appeared to be no distinction between them (which is to say, late seventeenth-century science had not yet grasped the difference). The process of differentiation between waste and value happened in places both seen and unseen: the human body in the case of digestion; the cosmos in the case of Creation; the Day of Judgment in the case of resurrection. My chapters on Pope, Swift, and Defoe explain the details of such debates. My larger claim is that the imaginative terms of seventeenth-century philosophy and theology generate literary metaphors for describing distinction. Intellectual debate, as much as material and social conditions, gives writers the language with which they write.

There is yet a third kind of residue, neither material nor "philosophical," which I describe. This is a type of leftover best described as literary, because it is waste that exists only in the pages of literary texts. By this I mean the waste that is the fallout of representation itself, leftovers created by the fact that objects in literary texts have symbolic meaning, meaning differentiated from the natural object itself. Take Sophia Western's muff in *Tom Jones* as an instance of what I mean. At the beginning of the novel the muff is fresh and new, so vivid to the imagination that the reader can imagine the silky feel of its pelt as Tom Jones strokes his hand across its surface. By the end of the novel it is filthy and worn, unwanted and forgotten—but it is nonetheless the symbolic vessel that has carried Tom and Sophia's mutual attraction and affection safely from one end of the novel to the other, in the face of betrayal, indifference, and neglect. The muff is freighted with a complex narrative that outstrips the meaning of the object in itself, which Fielding draws attention to by having the muff look so dejected and un-mufflike by the end of the book. Objects, the vessels of symbolic meaning, become leftovers, kernels of reality that remain behind after fictional meaning has been made.[5] Like all waste, these residues provoke both pleasure and anxiety; they are reminiscent of life and death at the same time. While the waste produced by symbolic meaning takes us far from the literal dust and ashes of postfire London, I am arguing that symbolic residues in later eighteenth-century texts emerge formally from the real debris of Restoration writing.

In the broadest sense the formal connection between fire literature and Sophia's Western's muff is that both are Protestant narratives, with shared assumptions about the relationship of material object to symbolic meaning.[6] All the texts discussed in *Making Waste* belong to the Protestant tradition in the sense that they depend on there being a distinction between objects and their meanings: in Protestant hermeneutics, objects are vessels with symbolic referents, not relics endowed with innate value. But the connection between the literal waste of chapter 1 and the symbolic waste of the afterword is a matter of historical as much as notional continuity. The Great Fire put real waste into eighteenth-century literature, and established the wasteland as a crucial landscape in modern urban writing. As the eighteenth century goes forward, however, literary waste becomes increasingly abstract. Instead of dead dogs and morning toasts, we have muffs and fans; later still we have the circulating objects of it-narratives; and eventually, by the time Austen was writing, for example, we have Fanny Price's topaz cross in *Mansfield Park*, an object which, in being made a leftover by the adulterous and incestuous narratives mediated through it, also makes a leftover of Fanny, the heroine to whom it belongs. My study, which tracks the enormous power and capaciousness of waste in eighteenth-century literature, describes the slow turn waste makes from the literal to the notional, from being the residue created by historical events to being the leftovers created by literary narrative. In each chapter waste is three things at once: it is literal, manifest in material culture; it is philosophically charged, meaningful by virtue of its role in intellectual debate; and it is literary, which is to say that it is created by the very text in which it appears.

While this is not primarily a book about the real conditions of London and Dublin, it is important to point out that in the early eighteenth century waste was both constantly visible and seemingly ineradicable.[7]

When London expanded in the late seventeenth century after the fire and the plague, it was dubbed the "great wen," and an "overgrown monster."[8] At this point it was inconceivable that urban prosperity could exist without the accompaniment of degraded remnants and filthy left-overs. Nobody could get away from dirt, as Emily Cockayne points out in a vivid description of life in the early eighteenth-century capital:

> The poorest were doomed to trudge through the mire, their darned stockings soaking up water admitted through their leaking shoes. Wheels of carriages holding richer citizens splashed the threadbare coats of the street-level poor. However, on a daily basis both rich and poor endured discomfort—the rich in the name of fashion, the poor out of necessity. While the rich donned itchy ruffles and cumbersome wigs for show (scrubbed and powdered by the hired help), the ragtag poor wore patched clothes for warmth and protection.[9]

In everyday culture waste was already metaphorical as much as literal; it described the wasted lives, the waste people, the wasteland, which were vividly present. Cockayne observes that "to some, the destitute and street filth were synonymous—to cleanse the environment the authorities needed to expunge both."[10] The term "slum" was first coined in the early 1700s to describe the festering poorhouses of St. Giles, Whitechapel, and Clerkenwell.[11] Bills of mortality from the Restoration and early eighteenth century show that far more people died in London than were born there. Beggars and cripples lolled in doorways and passages. A visitor to London in the 1730s complained that one needed a servant to walk ahead, sweeping the vagrants out of the way with a broom. Open sewage swilled down the middle of London's streets, animals were slaughtered in the city center, and hogs, dogs, and dead cats were left to rot.

Just how far off England was from anything like modern sanitation in the later seventeenth century is suggested by the fact that when Charles II's court abandoned their temporary apartments in Oxford after the plague, they left piles of feces in the corners of every room and staircase, a common enough practice in the Restoration. People were outraged by it, to be sure, but the proposed solution seems to us absurdly over-elaborate: to build spiral staircases instead of angular ones, so that people couldn't stop in corners to defecate. The notion that people could simply stop defecating in public was not yet self-evident.[12] It was no matter of mere theoretical curiosity but literally true to say that at the beginning of the eighteenth century prosperity and affluence still appeared to be inseparable from their opposites, waste and desolation.[13] Alain Corbin, writing about the French resistance to hygiene in the same period, notes a "loyalty to filth," manifest in riots against cleanliness in the midcentury. Corbin's analysis is that filth had psychological value, untheorized but important:

> A better understanding of this loyalty to filth depends in part on the role played by excrement in infant psychology and the impor-tance of anality in the development of the psyche. It was by odor that the babe in arms experienced the mother's presence, before even seeing her. . . . The odor of the baby's feces was a summons to the mother; in his dealings with her the baby "produces some-thing to smell from below and submits to something to smell from above": breast or bottle.[14]

As I've suggested, twentieth-century theoretical writing helps explain the complex imagery of waste in the eighteenth century by showing why it generates such ambivalence and anxiety in its beholders. The relatively underexamined essay *On Disgust* (1927) by the Hungarian psychoana-lytic theorist and philosopher Aurel Kolnai, takes a phenomenological approach to the experience of disgust, a defense reaction to perceived threats. Kolnai's essay, which established parameters for abjection theo-rists whose work became more famous (Georges Bataille, Jean-Paul Sartre, and Julia Kristeva, among others), demarcates and defines the character-istics of "objects of disgust" and offers a working definition of the abject matter that comprises waste.

Disgusting objects provoke defensiveness by being linked to death and decay. But as Kolnai shows, putrefaction is reminiscent of both death and life and is therefore endlessly ambiguous and confronting. Decay *is* "deathly life":

[S]omething dead is never disgusting in its *mere non-functioning*, for then even fresh meat would be disgusting, which is definitely not the case. Rather, substantial decomposition is necessary, which must at least seem to put itself forward as a continuing process, almost as if it were after all just another manifestation of life. Already here we encounter the relation of disgust to what is positively vital, to what is animated. And indeed there is undoubtedly associated with the extinction of life in putrefaction a certain—quite remarkable—augmentation of life: a heightened announcement of the fact that life *is there*.[15]

Generally, the spectacle of "life in the wrong place," characteristic of putrefaction, is only one of two signs of the disgusting object. As Kolnai observes, abject matter can also be marked by indistinctness or satiation, a quality of oozing diffuseness that makes no distinction between life and death or proliferation and rot: a "soft, gushing type of life which resists all solid formations, all discrimination, selection, all following up towards a goal and towards significance."[16] Indistinctness (as opposed to misplaced animation) is important to my argument because undifferentiated fullness is the material quality that permits waste and valuable abundance to be confused or conflated in literary texts. Each is marked by an "indecent surplus of life" that perversely causes them to resemble one another.

The waste matter in this book includes dirt and refuse, excrement and rotting corpses, but it also includes things that aren't inherently abject: tears, money, books, and paper. These belong to a second category of non-biological, "morally disgusting objects," which are capable of stimulating disgust because they are reminders of the excess and satiation of putrefaction. Objects of moral disgust have "excessive vitality or vitality whose unfurling is misplaced"; they arouse the feeling of "life in the wrong place."[17] Kolnai describes this connection between physical and moral disgust as a "physiological reminiscence," a phrase that resonates powerfully for me because "reminiscence"—a recollection, often imperfect—is almost always present where there is waste: waste consists of leftovers that contain the memory or echo of the matter they used to be. Waste, even if it does not putrefy, is abject because it is characterized by misplaced, animating excess, inflecting it with the physiological reminiscence of decay.

But though waste almost always consists of matter connected to putrefaction, abjection is not enough to classify an object as waste. Waste
is a form of pollution, marked as such by having participated in a process; that process is one wherein substance stops being acceptable or even
valuable and becomes unwanted or taboo. This is important, because as
Mary Douglas pointed out in *Purity and Danger*, pollution exists when a
substance has crossed a border and become threatening to the system to
which it now, improperly, belongs. "There is no such thing as absolute
dirt: it exists in the eye of the beholder," Douglas quips.[18] "Our pollution behavior is the reaction which condemns any object or idea likely to
confuse or contradict cherished classifications," upsetting social, cultural,
and personal stability.[19] Dirt is taboo not for its inherent qualities but
because it is anomalous; it "is that which must not be included if a pattern is to be maintained."[20] And the fact of its being an anomaly itself
signals the presence of a narrative that determines its "proper" place and
polices the boundaries of that location. Dirt exists in the aftermath of a
border crossing.

A crucial argument of this book is that waste is always *made*, not
found—created by political and social processes, and, most importantly,
by language itself. The fact that waste is a product, of language, politics,
and society, means that its appearance in literature always marks the spot
where a troubled process of making has occurred. But it is a process that
readers frequently do not see, because all that remains is a leftover figured as abject matter. In eighteenth-century literary texts, the narratives
connected to waste and its production have often been made to disappear; I rehabilitate them, showing that the appearance and disappearance
of waste narratives is almost always politically motivated. Suzanne Raitt,
a contemporary waste theorist influenced by Freud, Kristeva, and Lacan,
argues that the presence of a narrative of its production is what distin-
guishes waste from all other types of leftover:

> Detritus has its own taxonomy: "rubbish," "garbage" and "litter,"
> for example, construct it as an essentially random, cumulative phe-
> nomenon, a by-product of our daily domestic lives. To call some-
> thing "waste" on the other hand, is to invoke its history. Nuclear
> waste, bodily waste, and medical waste are all the result of specific

processes: they gesture back to the productive economies that generated them. Even in these days of recycling, waste is almost always
disposed of or repudiated, sometimes indifferently, sometimes
contemptuously, and even, on occasion, violently.[21]

My assumption here is that the meanings of eighteenth-century waste
matter are to be found in the narratives, explicit or suppressed, that sur-
round literary leftovers.

The most insidious instances of waste making occur where individuals or groups of people are positioned as abject. Eighteenth-century examples include the edible Irish babies in Swift's "A Modest Proposal"
and the hairy, filthy Yahoos of *Gulliver's Travels*, seen as a contaminated
subspecies by the compassionless Houynhymns. Mary Douglas argues
that persons in a marginal state are vulnerable to being positioned as
dangerous because they are "left out in the patterning of society," safer
when identified as pollution (she uses the example of babies in primitive
societies, reminding us again of Swift).[22] Martha Nussbaum's explanation of the phenomenon is that the feeling of disgust justifies bias and
social exclusion because it is treated as though it were a universal, "true"
emotion. She argues, however, that disgust is "always suspect or prob-
lematic, in need of special scrutiny":

> Because disgust embodies a shrinking from contamination that is
> associated with the human desire to be non-animal, it is more than
> like to be hooked up with various forms of shady social practice, in
> which the discomfort people feel over the fact of having an animal
> body is projected outwards onto vulnerable people and groups.
> These reactions are irrational, in the normative sense, both because
> they embody an aspiration to be a kind of being that one is not,
> and because, in the process of pursuing that aspiration, they target
> others for gross harms.[23]

The most important contribution psychoanalytic theory makes to
my study is to explain why waste simultaneously fascinates and disgusts,
why it elicits simultaneous, competing desires to preserve and discard
it. Kolnai's account is that "in its full intention it is death and not life
that announces itself to us in the phenomenon of disgust,"[24] but that

the announcement of death stimulates aversion through its proximity to life—a proximity that often dissolves into exchangeability. "In the decomposition-products of life not only the withering of life but also the presence of life itself has a disgusting effect."[25] Kristeva extends Kolnai's analysis by claiming that the confusion, or conflation, of life and death is the very confusion of which the abject consists. Abjection is "a border that has encroached upon everything"; "abjection is above all ambiguity."[26] According to Kristeva, abjection is terrifying because it has only the appearance of being an object. In reality it is the boundary that marks the passage from life to death, the very border of the self, and so it threatens the self because it is at once indistinct and alienated from it. "The abject has only one quality of the object—that of being opposed to *I*."[27]

Each of these studies is animated by the perception that the pathology to which waste speaks is a fear of loss. In Freud's analysis, fear of loss, which threatens the very state of being human, drives the desire for cleanliness and order: "dirtiness of any kind seems to us incompatible with civilization," Freud writes. "Order is a kind of compulsion to repeat which, when a regulation has been laid down once and for all, decides when, where and how a thing shall be done, so that in every similar circumstance one is spared hesitation and indecision."[28]

A story from the Renaissance court provides a vivid historical background for my readings of eighteenth-century waste. In the late sixteenth century, John Harington, Queen Elizabeth's godson—a brilliant but eccentric courtier, one of England's most promising diplomats, scholars, and wits—designed an automated water closet. The author of a lavishly produced *Orlando Furioso* translation, as well as poems, essays, and epigrams, Harington seemed destined to become one of England's most important intellectuals. But in 1596 he circulated his long and erudite manuscript, classical in style and full of ornate prose and complex allegory, named *The Metamorphosis of Ajax*. It is a Homeric parody that describes the invention and cultural significance of an automated water closet, and it includes a do-it-yourself manual for building one. Harington's book became one of the most notorious courtly publications to circulate for the next 150 years.[29]

As Harington's Ovidian title implies, the proposal might have effected a domestic and civic transformation. Harington was imagining two fundamental alterations in the fabric of England's social life. First, he pictured a metamorphosis from filth to cleanliness in the realm of domestic hygiene. Second, he imagined a transition whereby effluence stopped being public and became a private, hidden affair. Harington was, in essence, designing domestic privacy, asserting that a person's filth was his own business and that it was no longer something to be shared with others (even if those others were only the servants who emptied the chamber pots).

Harington's treatise includes an apocryphal story about a dung carrier, a hermit, a beautiful woman, and an angel. This dung carrier is walking through a great city in the evening, pushing a steaming barrow full of excrement in front of him. Coming the other way is a hermit, led on his journey by an angel. When the hermit smells the dung cart he retches, stops his nose, and crosses the street to avoid the stench of such a "sour carriage." The angel, who's made of steadier stuff, doesn't blanch. But a few moments later a beautifully dressed aristocratic woman comes rumbling through the street in a fine coach lit by blazing torches, on her way to a forbidden assignation with a gentleman. The angel stops his nose in disgust: this, not the dung cart, is for him the real "sour carriage." Harington glosses the tale cheerfully: "I wish all the readers may find as sure a way to cleanse, and keep sweet, the noblest part of themselves, that is their souls; as I shall show them a plain and easy way to keep sweet the basest part of their houses, that is their sinks."[30] In Harington's allegory the toilet was a figure for cleansing the soul.

But people didn't want to avail themselves of Harington's plan to "keep sweet the basest part of their houses." Like the angel, the sight of real excrement doesn't appear to have offended them as much as the fear of hidden pollutants. The dung cart left human filth openly displayed to public sight; the fine lady conceals her corruption beneath a surface of cleanliness. It seems at first surprising that readers would have found Harington's narrative seditious rather than consoling. But in fact the allegory of the hermit sounds a caution that Harington probably hadn't intended. The fine lady warned, inadvertently, of the social perils of personal hygiene. When filth couldn't be seen, it meant that a much more toxic pollution must be festering out of sight. To put it plainly: people didn't want to seem too clean.

England was in the middle of two centuries of political and religious conflict, seditious intrigue, and insecurity. The objects of persecution and paranoia were alternately Catholics, Puritans, royalists, republicans, and again Catholics. Political sectarians and religious dissenters were treated as the nation's excrement and flushed away. England's political elite and uneducated masses alike were worried about the existence of hidden menaces and festering traitors: no one was entirely safe in a world where political and religious boundaries were constantly shifting. When Harington described a contraption that made unwanted effluence disappear, and when he implied that his treatise was social allegory, it is hardly surprising that English courtiers were wary of his reforms, nor that subsequent generations remained suspicious of the hygienic efficiency he proposed. He seemed to promise exactly the kind of political cleansing that England had learned to dread.

The automated toilet of Harington's invention would have been far more than just a domestic gadget. The subtext of *The Metamorphosis* was that the efficient disposal of excrement was an allegory for England's social and political hygiene too. Harington's book met with a storm of criticism and anger. The court regarded his proposals as outrageous, and the treatise cost him his favor with the monarch.[31] But while critics have argued about the precise nature of Harington's political and rhetorical blunders in writing the treatise, nobody has taken seriously the role played in the furor by the subject matter itself: the suggestion that toilets should flush. It is crucial to note that the Elizabethan court rejected Harington's proposal: there was something perversely undesirable about the idea of making waste disappear.

English society did eventually become less filthy. There still were no automated water closets, but eighteenth-century writers, politicians, and philosophers set out to create social and intellectual institutions that might conceivably efface England's polluted, uncivilized past. The coffee-house, the periodical, the public ball, the private assembly: these embodied the awakened ideal of a polite society—and the hope that public civility could cover over private conduct, to be penetrated only by the all-seeing gaze of the eighteenth-century novel. This, at least, was the idea.[32]

As scholarship has shown, the cult of English politeness was not as dedicated to civility and regulation as might initially appear to be the case—and it certainly did not secure them. When Ned Ward, the grubby, irreverent, scatological satirist, parodied the emerging cult of politeness at the beginning of the eighteenth century, he showed that abjection and civility were much harder to keep separate than people realized; he perceived what Kolnai would call the "physiological reminiscence" between them. In 1709 he printed a collection of satiric essays, *A History of the London Clubs*, including a sketch called "The Farting Club," a satire on private clubs. In Ward's travesty, a group of gentlemen (a "perfumed assembly") gather weekly to host a farting contest: "The Liquors that they usually drank to Tune their Merry Arses, were new Ale and Juniper Water, till everyone was swell'd like a blown Bag-Pipe, and then they began to thunder out whole Volleys like a Regiment of Train'd Banks . . . till the Room they sat in stunk ten times worse than a Tom-Turd Man's Bucket."[33] When their farting becomes too vigorous, performers are sent into the next room to have their breeches examined by the lady of the house, lest the "nasty Bird had befoul'd his own Nest." In Ward's satire, it is a sign of gentlemanliness that these farters check their breeches, and a sign of the artifice of politeness that they are holding a farting contest at all. The habits of civilized society—fine clothes, elaborate manners, complicated social rituals—are visions of excess, like the farts themselves. It's easy for Ward to substitute a farting competition for the activity that normally goes on in private clubs because both are superfluities: literally and figuratively hot air.

Jonathan Swift's description of a chamber pot opens up the unstable meanings of literary waste in the period still further. There are many brimming chamber pots in Swift; this one is from *Directions to Servants*, his parody of a housekeeping manual. Mockingly encouraging servants to behave negligently, Swift's pompous speaker imagines a scene in which a maid exposes her mistress's excrement to a party of arriving guests:

> I am very much offended with those ladies, who are so proud and lazy, that they will not be at the pains of stepping into the garden to pluck a rose, but keep an odious implement, sometimes in the bed chamber itself, or at least in a dark closet adjoining, which they make use of to ease their worst necessities; and you are the usual carriers away of the pan, which maketh not only the chamber, but

even their clothes offensive, to all who come near. Now, to cure
them of the odious practice, let me advise you, on whom this office lieth, to convey away this utensil, that you will do it openly,
down the great stairs, and in the presence of the footmen; and, if
anybody knocketh, to open the street door, while you have the
vessel in your hands.[34]

The joke is that if servants behave badly enough, they will be saved the
trouble of working at all. But it's more complicated than that, as it always
is with Swift. What we're seeing is another instance of people holding on
to waste. It's treated like a precious substance: first saved in a porcelain
receptacle and then displayed, ceremonially, if maliciously, to visitors.
Excrement is two things at once: a leftover so secret that it must be produced somewhere unseen (a dark closet) but also the object of ceremony.
Even though this is a joke, the joke turns on the fact that filth and splendor are alike. The servants themselves are muckrakers, to be sure, but they
are also officeholders, "carriers away of the pan," the persons "on whom
this office lieth." There's even a quasi-liturgical feel about the ritual, a
hint—underscored by Swift's calling the pot a "vessel"—that the turds
have become, in the servants' hands, sacred objects.

On the one hand, a private residence is a place where shameful and
pleasurable acts can be conducted in secret (the excreting and fornicating
that go on in the bedchamber), but on the other hand it is where visitors
get to see evidence of a family's prosperity and success (the files of footmen, the formal opening of the door by a servant). The juxtaposition is
contained in the spectacle of the chamber pot, and the guests are shown
the turds as though they were canapés, little signs of hostly generosity.
The servants bear the utensil "in the presence of footmen," as at a dinner;
in a small household these might even be the same servants who serve
food, as detailed in other sections of the *Directions*.

The scene is already doing what we know novels were about to do: the
narrator penetrates private spaces—in this case both domestic and digestive interiors—to emphasize the formal power of literature to cross social
and architectural boundaries. And in crossing boundaries, it causes confusion. Domestic waste gets glorified, converted into something magnificent and ceremonial, and yet it remains abject and taboo. Part of Swift's

joke, indeed, is that people go to visit one another's houses precisely because they are hoping to take a peek at others' secret shame—to see their excrement. These visitors must, after all, already know what they will find behind their friends' closed doors, since they share the same dirty secrets. Waste inhabits both sides of the boundary between private production and public display.

Whenever there is a remnant, a leftover, there is also abundance. In the instance of the Great Fire, the debris of burnt-out London supplied the imagery for describing a new kind of urban experience: degraded, alienated, but profoundly resonant and meaningful. But waste signified something more complicated too, as this example from Swift reveals. It is the remnant that marks the place where meaning has been generated. The turds are carried as if in a sacred vessel, but here the sacramental offering is not glorious but repulsive, base matter being treated as though it were divine. The scene models a parody of the sacrament that Swift will repeat in *A Tale of a Tub*, in *Gulliver's Travels*, and in his patriotic polemics: one of his most common satiric tricks is to describe abject matter that gets mistaken for something precious. In *A Tale of a Tub*, the parody is explicit: the brother Peter carves a loaf of bread, declaring that it is a haunch of flesh. In *Directions to Servants*, the abjection of ordinary matter is emphasized in the process of turning it into a secular offering. Transubstantiation isn't only at issue in church; it can happen in literary texts as well, where the metamorphosis of base matter to splendid abundance is always at stake in the process of making literary meaning.

The first two chapters of *Making Waste* are about literary wastelands, the landscape in which remaindered matter is most visible. Like waste itself, wasteland has a paradoxical volatility. It is filled with debris, but described as though it were empty; it often has enormous value, both cultural and commercial, but it gets talked about as though it were worthless. Wasteland began as a biblical setting, but it became a seventeenth- and eighteenth-century literary landscape via *Annus Mirabilis* and *Paradise Lost*.

It is not only theoretically but also historically appropriate to begin a full-length study of waste with the wasteland setting. The term "waste" was first introduced into English writing in 1267 with the Statute of Marlbridge, which established the wasting of property, whether land or goods, as an actionable offense. The statute set out to protect property from being made valueless as a result of negligence or malice. The creation of wasteland was one of the earliest offenses to be addressed by English statute law, establishing it as the most threatening and potentially dangerous of England's literal and literary landscapes.

In the chapters that follow, I describe the degraded matter with which literary wastelands are filled. For Pope, Grub Street, filled with the debris of thousands of hack publications, was a secular reincarnation of Milton's wasteland in Chaos. Swift's wastelands are mostly Irish, saturated with goods that the English deem valueless: coinage, manufactures, and, notoriously, the babies of the Irish poor. In Defoe's case, waste takes the form of bodies, too, the corpses that turned London into a ghastly desert during the Great Plague.

On the one hand, publications like the *Tatler* and the *Spectator* took it upon themselves to clean up English culture, and to usher in a new age of sophisticated, civilized living. Addison and Steele eschewed embarrassing and hard-to-explain residues; in their account of civic culture, all aspects of daily life ought to yield valuable social meaning. Similarly, the literature of sentimentality and sensibility generated novels, essays, and poems that were frequently eccentric and strange, but nonetheless emphasized the essentially generative, recuperative power of literature. If everything, and everybody, could be sympathized with and felt for, nothing need remain behind. Take, for instance, the bizarre eighteenth-century genre of "it-narratives": stories in which inanimate objects acquire feelings and rational powers. No object, however base, need be relegated to the category of uselessness.

But Swift and Pope and the other writers in this book would not accept this. They insisted on the debasement and abjection of waste matter, refusing to concede that literature could recuperate everything. They insisted, in other words, that writing plays a crucial role in preserving waste, not eliminating it. This turns out to be for an important reason. The largest claim of this book is that writers who preserve the abjection and debasement of filth show us something absolutely fundamental about literature itself. Material leftovers and abject residue are signs of the peculiar transformations that take place in literary texts; perversely, they show us that meaning has been made.

1

The Invention of the Wasteland

CIVIC NARRATIVE AND DRYDEN'S
ANNUS MIRABILIS

DURING 1665, the plague evacuated London's streets and public buildings. Then in September 1666, as citizens were returning to the capital and resuming normal life, the Great Fire razed central London in four days.[1] The city was debilitated, its streets filled with blockages and displaced persons, its buildings in ruin, its crowds dispossessed: "[T]he people who now walked about the ruines, appeared like men in some dismal desart, or rather in some great Citty, *lay'd waste* by an impetuous and cruel Enemy,"[2] wrote John Evelyn, the celebrated seventeenth-century diarist. Evelyn was giving a term to the new geography of postfire London: it was a wasteland. Evelyn used waste to convey a calamity of biblical dimensions, an imagined apocalypse that had suddenly become actual. The word took hold; waste, wasteland, and its affiliated terms (vast, devastation) became catch-cries in the fire's aftermath. Evelyn probably used the word on impulse, as he searched for an adequate phrase in the vocabulary of disaster. But unwittingly he stumbled upon what was to become one of the most resonant images in the history of writing about London. Something about a landscape of waste described London with uncanny precision. As Evelyn pointed out in the same diary entry, the landscape was both "desert" and "city," filled with people but giving out the sense of emptiness, of void.

Descriptions of wasteland would become central to writing on the Great Fire. The image dominates sermons, poems, civic treatises, and official proclamations from the period. Nathaniel Hardy described the "houses of God . . . burnt up, and *laid waste* in the City," in a sermon at St. Martin in the Fields; William Sancroft, in a sermon preached before the king, spoke about "the earth wasted, and utterly spoiled, and turn'd upside down." As late as 1668, Thomas Jacomb, a nonconformist divine, pressed for the "reedification" of "*waste and desolate* Habitations."[3] Samuel Rolls, an advocate of commercial growth through urban expansion, like-wise wrote a treatise in 1668 urging "that the *now wast, and desolated* City of London should be reedified."[4] The wasting of London was attributed variously to religious and secular causes: the restoration of Charles II, increased religious toleration after 1660, liberty and license in the cap-ital.[5] But as these quotations makes clear, wasteland was imagined as an apocalyptic site of judgment and collective ruin. Biblically speaking, wasteland is a place of residue, spiritual and moral as well as material.

But the fire had outstripped even the Bible, turning London into a literal desert. This was no longer the terrain of literary conceit or biblical allegory. All of a sudden, real waste threatened to overwhelm England's once thriving capital. After the fire, the imagery and language used to describe biblical wasteland doubled as a way to convey the imperilment, commercial and psychological, of modern life. Such a transition from the biblical to the real had always been at issue in early-modern London: as Nigel Smith points out, people lived with the sense that fire was im-minent throughout the seventeenth century, and "we should not be sur-prised that the rhetoric of many sermons suggested that the Apocalypse had all but arrived with the fire."[6] In 1666 Dryden and other secular writ-ers had, at last, a new way to describe modernity: an alienated, precarious landscape that, rather than trying to escape, they gladly embraced. Even though Londoners did try to mend the city after the fire, the notion that they were living in a desolate landscape was never eradicated.

Wasteland is one of several eighteenth-century literary tropes to be drawn from the Bible.[7] As Michael McKeon and J. Paul Hunter have shown, early novels borrowed heavily from biblical and religious texts because such antecedents enabled novels to register as "real" or at least trustworthy—they included redemption and conversion narratives,

providential stories, as well as guide literature and "occasional meditations."[8] Wastelands, both urban and "desert," were already established as
settings through which to explore selfhood, nationhood, and communal
life. But the convergence of lived experience and biblical narrative gave
wasteland a virtually unprecedented literary power. It was a believable
setting because it was real, and it was symbolically resonant because it was
biblical. "Urban life is neurotically, nauseatingly close, exaggertedly so in
the concertina-ed dwellings that artisans (nonconformists among them)
inhabited. No wonder it felt on the edge of time: just about ripe for a
Second Coming," Smith writes.[9] Aptly enough, Simon Ford, a Puritan
minister (later a conformist) proclaimed in his postfire poem "London's
Resurrection" that "waste is merit." Precisely so. Theologically speaking,
the value of wasteland was clear. Desolation is the condition of salvation;
without waste, resurrection is impossible. "On the one hand, fire is the
ultimate means of destruction, a wholly uncontrollable force. On the
other hand, it signifies the power of purification. Fire cleanses the elect,
burning away the tainted dross in the world."[10] The surprise is that this
was to hold true for secular writing, too. We might expect that, in reality,
waste wouldn't seem meritorious at all. People would just want to clean
it up and make it go away. But the idea that "waste is merit" proved
compelling. Now that they had their real-life wasteland, English writers
were not going to tidy it away.

I

After 1666, the landscape features that would define the new geography
of London were the same rubble, rubbish, and dust that had defined the
wastelands so prominent in Puritan pamphlets of the 1640s and 1650s
prophesying millennial violence and the last days.[11] The civic and commercial disaster in London could be explained in terms of apocalyptic
imagery, but its primary significance lay in its real, massive impact on the
rhythms of London life. Sancroft, dean of St. Paul's and later the arch-
bishop of Canterbury, could hardly credit that so familiar a phrase, "we
are but Dust and Ashes," could have been so vividly realized: "not only
Dust in the course of ordinary Frailty, but Ashes too in the merit of a

far sharper Doom; perceive that God should bring us to Dust, nay, even turn us to Ashes too, as our Houses," he declaimed.[12]

Edward Stillingfleet, an Anglican divine who was to become archdeacon of London,[13] also recognized that the imagery of biblical apocalypse had been matched by the real. Like the stricken inhabitants of Sodom and Gomorrah, Stillingfleet points out, Londoners had no time at all to flee, either:

> Surely that [force] was very great which consumed four Cities to nothing in so short a time, when God *sis pluere Gehennam de caelo* as one expresses it, rained down *hell-fire upon* Sodom and Gomorrah. And this is that which some think is called *the vengeance of eternal fire, which all those in* Sodom *and* Gomorrah *are said to suffer*; i.e. a Fire which consumed, till there was nothing left to be consumed by it.[14]

Stillingfleet, like Evelyn, noticed that emptiness is the defining characteristic of wasteland. "Consumed, till there was nothing left to be consumed by it."

The emptiness of Stillingfleet's wasteland, though, isn't only a sign of the moral desolation like the judgment that afflicts Sodom, Gomorrah, and Jerusalem. It is, rather, made richer and more complex by the secular, commercial echo in the midst of his biblical imagery; it is a symptom of the real. The image of consuming fire leads the listener associatively to another kind of consumption; London has consumed, commercially as well as morally, until there is nothing left. The familiarly dire images of hellfire and vengeance in Sodom and Gomorrah become vividly real in Stillingfleet's sermon as he describes a wasteland that is recognizably commercial in character: "Look now upon me [London], you who so lately admired the greatness of my trade, the riches of my merchants, the number of my people, the conveniency of my Churches, the multitude of my streets, and see what desolations sin hath made in the earth."[15] "Desolations" is the crucial word here. We get the despair and moral regret that the congregation ought to feel, but we're also reminded that postfire London is a wasteland because it is a commercial capital, stripped of its capacity to function. Robert Elborough, another prominent Anglican cleric, works through the same set of associations when he asks his congregation, "what are become of your Houses, Shops, Goods, Estates and Warehouses, when you could not keep them from being destroyed, and they could not keep your houses from being consumed?"[16]

Speaking in his powerfully titled sermon *Lex Ignea; or, The School of Righteousness*, Sancroft also read the disaster as a replication of God's judgment on Jerusalem, since phrases describing the disaster in the Bible map onto the actual circumstances exactly:

> [The] *City of Confusion*, which *is broken down*, a City turn'd *Chaos again . . . the City turn'd into a Heap*, or a Ruine . . . into one great sepulchre to it self, buried in its own Rubbish, [Isaiah] Cap. xxv. 2. . . . *The City desolate, and forsaken, and left Wilderness, and Desart all over*, [Isaiah] *Cap. xxvii, 10*. Are but so many variations on the same phrase, and signifie all the same thing, the *burning of Jerusalem by Nebuchadnezzar, or Tartar*, or (as some will have it) by both.[17]

But when the words "confusion," "broken," "chaos," heap," and "ruin" are no longer merely the rhetoric of millennial sermon-writers—when the city is literally "buried in its own Rubbish"—the power of wasteland as a secular, literary landscape begins to make itself clear. It is a glut of worthless matter, a chaos of rubbish and ruin, and yet it is literally formed from the abundance that was once so prized: prosperous trade and prolific commerce. Even though the wasteland is a void, it teems with ghastly surplus.

Divines talked about the wasted cities of the Bible for the obvious reason: it was their job to make people draw connections between their own lives and biblical catastrophes that, most of the time, seemed remote. Although Stillingfleet, Sancroft, and others appeared to be intoning biblical commonplaces, they also laid the foundations for a new kind of urban writing. In this new discourse, desolation is a form of despair that is secular, psychological, and commercial in character, and the most desolate of landscapes, wasteland, is also disconcertingly full—of people, goods, and ruins in profound disorder. Disorder becomes a condition that writers are fascinated by. The image of wasteland emerges, in other words, as a rich, symbolically complicated terrain—as it turns out, a terrain that will be a central feature of urban writing for the next three hundred years. In this chapter we watch as a group of early modern writers feel their way toward the wasteland that T. S. Eliot would eventually realize as the most desolate, and yet compelling, of all literary landscapes.

When John Evelyn describes the burning city of London he turns to the Bible, but not for the precise political and religious implications of his imagery so much as for the broad symbolic framework that the imagery of biblical apocalypse imparts to the modern setting. He uses the biblical imagery to express the fact that the Fire had literally wiped away early modern London, displacing an internationally renowned metropolis with a wasteland: "[T]hus I left it this afternoone burning a resemblance of Sodom, or the last day: It call'd to mind that of 4 Heb. *non enim hic habemus stabilem civitatem*: the ruins resembling the picture of Troy: London was, but no more."[18] Evelyn might begin by making a typological comparison between London and Sodom and a mythological comparison with Troy. But Sodom and Troy ultimately give Evelyn the images he needs for a realist description of the city: "London was, but no more," which sounds rhetorical but is literal. By declaring that London is "no more," Evelyn makes it clear that the wasteland is important because it is a void, an evacuated geography, and a new, empty literary landscape that needed to be filled in by an entirely new set of literary images and devices, hitherto unexplored.

The emptiness that all these writers comment on is, perversely, what gives wasteland its value. Being empty, it opened the way for new kinds of writing. Cynthia Wall points out that "over and over again, the city is called a 'heap,' shapeless, prostrate, its indistinguishability its distinguishing mark.... Language itself seems collapsed, the familiar discourse inadequate to express the cultural and spiritual horror."[19] Wasteland reflects both spatial void and psychological emptiness—exactly what English writing, urban, often disaffected, self-consciously modern, turned out to need.

The terrain of psychic distress and disorientation counteracted other emerging literary settings—the private closets and domestic spaces of words—places that functioned to celebrate psychological autonomy and self-determination. In J. Paul Hunter's account of the origins of the novel, "the validation of individuals, not necessarily trained individuals, as observers and interpreters" is at the heart of the genre's rise, and "once unleashed, the power of the individual was impossible to control."[20] Autonomous individual readers are commemorated by the intimate spaces and modes of writing (diaries, letters) of early novels. But the opposing phenomena of psychological peril and personal alarm, symptomatic of self-determined but frequently disoriented individuals in urban society, relied upon a different Protestant trope: barren desert. Wasteland would figure a dark side to Ian Watt's claim that "modern realism . . . begins from the position that truth can be discovered by the individual through his senses," a position established by Descartes and Locke.[21] Desolate urban landscapes expressed the reality that individuals confronted disorientation and confusion as much as they experienced enlightenment—a reality that would help carry novels from the Whiggish optimism of the early eighteenth century to the epistemological crisis of literary modernism.

Stillingfleet's sermon on the Great Fire captures this vividly, describing the psychological alienation and alarm that wasteland inspires: "And no kind of Judgments are so dreadful and amazing, as those which come most unexpectedly upon men; for these betray the succours which reason offers, they insaturate men's councils, weaken their courage, and deprive them of that presence of mind which is necessary at such a time for their own and the public interest."[22] Amazement, weakness, deprivation are the psychological debris which fill in the "desert" terrain of urban wastes; insaturation and betrayal of reason describe a newly disordered, confused mode of apprehension with which people responded to ruined and displaced urban space. This literal apocalypse gave modern writers a new landscape, characterized by physical and psychological confusion and alienation, by an incoherent abundance of people and matter, and by a sense of profound void. As Stillingfleet and Evelyn tell us, wasteland is a nothingness, and yet it is uncomfortably full. The glut of ash and debris had, days before, been an abundance of prosperity. This literal wasteland forced observers to recognize that unwanted remnants and glorious surplus were, literally, one and the same. Because waste was debased it had value: it was an expressive term for psychological imperilment.

John Evelyn's walk through London the day after the fire describes an abundance of material waste that has taken the place of known streets and passages:

I went this morning from Whitehall as far as London bridge, thro the late Fleete-streete, Ludgate Hill, by St. Pauls, Cheapside, Exchange, Bishopsgate, Aldersgate, & out to Morefields, thence thro Corne-hill, &c: with extraordinary difficulty, clambering over mountains of yet smoaking rubbish & frequently mistaking where I was, the ground under my feet so hott, as made me not onely Sweate, but even burnt the soles of my shoes & put me all over in Sweate.

The bie-lanes and narrower streetes were quite fill'd up with rubbish, nor could one have possibly known where he was, but by the ruines of some church, or hall, that had some remarkable tower or pinnacle remaining.[23]

The geography Evelyn describes is vast, oppressive, and unexplored. He is alienated, like an explorer, clambering, lost, sweating, and the blockages he confronts are monumental: mountains of rubbish, streets "quite fill'd up." Curiously, for so self controlled a diarist, Evelyn allows his subjectivity to slip into generality: "I" gives way to "one," which is displaced by "he." He navigates by way of ruins, and he conveys in this passage a sense of discovery as well as of loss. The city which in a previous entry was "no more," "lay'd waste," is being mapped, or filled in, with the physically and psychologically disorienting landscape of waste itself—debris, dust, rubbish, and ruins. Emptiness, or void, gives rise to a mode of narrating: a surplus of unstable impressions and descriptions without neat narrative trajectory.

Using the image of urban desert to describe the effect of calamity on the city's economy, Samuel Pepys' description of the dispossessed geography of London admits frankly that the wasteland is more powerful as an image of commercial disruption than of moral or religious failure:

I walked into the town and found Fanchurch-street, Gracious street, and Lumbard St all in dust. The Exchange a sad sight, nothing standing there of all the statues or pillars but Sir Tho. Gresham's picture in the corner. Walked into Moorfields (our feet ready to burn, walking through the town among the hot coles) and find that full of people, and poor wretches carrying their goods there, and everybody keeping his goods together by themselves.[24]

Through its grand elegiac phrases—"all in dust," "poor wretches," "our
feet ready to burn," and the grandiose "nothing standing there of all the
statues and pillars," Pepys' description recalls the fall of Troy and the destruction of biblical cities. But Pepys makes it clear that his investment in
all of this is not the similarities of biblical to classical apocalypse; rather,
he sees in the ruins of London a crippled economy, still trying to engage
in exchange and circulation. The wretches "carrying their goods" into
Moorfields denote a distorted marketplace, full of people and goods but
"everybody keeping his goods together by themselves." This phrase is the
centerpiece of Pepys' description, the circumstance that makes him so
especially sad to witness the dust of the streets and the "nothingness" of
the Exchange, for these sights represent the disruption of exchange, commercial and social. Pepys' wasteland is a commercial void, peopled by a
dispossessed (but possessing) crowd in whom, he seems to acknowledge,
London's precarious civic culture must once again be founded. As Blair
Hoxby points out, the refocusing of imagery from the apocalyptic to the
commercial attempted to create national recovery: "The Restoration's
politically inflected discourse of work, building, and production, which,
flourishing after the Fire of London, looked to the world of goods for
things beneath dispute [was] therefore suitable as the basis for a society otherwise riven by religious and political differences."[25] The "poor
wretches" are a reminder of vagrant groups which shaped the social fabric
of London's population, disparate and resistant to assimilation.[26] Pepys,
like other contemporary writers, represents a modern city laid waste—a
commercial and psychic wasteland. Until now, wasteland had always
been a place apart, where people hoped never to be. When the fire swept
through London, the capital of England became the wasteland that had
always been imagined elsewhere.

II

This was the landscape that Dryden inherited for his great secular poem
about the Fire, *Annus Mirabilis*. In describing the ravishing of London by consuming flames (and this after a year of financially crippling
war), Dryden gives us a wasteland that has all the properties of Sodom,

Gomorrah, and Troy, and yet it is, unmistakably, the setting for a new kind of urban writing. To argue that *Annus Mirabilis* is concerned with wastefulness, in either a commercial or an apocalyptic sense, goes against the grain of Dryden's own claim, that the poem was intended to celebrate Charles II by describing his management of war with Holland, his relationship with Parliament, and his response to the Great Fire as strategic triumphs, brilliant recoveries from potential disaster. Nonetheless, the celebratory register of Dryden's poem is arrested at key moments, in destroyed fleets and damaged merchandise, in the expenditure of Dutch resources in their bid to dominate international trade, and in the wasted city of London after a four-day fire. The climactic scene of the poem stages the dreadful transformation of London into a ruined geography, hopelessly reduced: "shr[u]nk like Parchment in consuming flame" (1064).[27] London's public spaces, in which the final scenes of the poem play out, is dispossessed, "half in rubbish [lying]" (1119). What happens to London in *Annus Mirabilis* mirrors the records of Pepys, Evelyn, and others; the city becomes a waste place, a scene in which devastation literalizes biblical apocalypse and so reshapes the expressive significance of wasteland in modern urban writing. Although Dryden is preeminently a poet, his realism often takes him close to the novel, especially in the references to urban degradation, culminating in the morning toasts of *MacFlecknoe* (1682).

In Dryden's slickly performed panegyric, London's contamination with the debris of rubbish, dust, and ashes gets recuperated through the poet's adept use of a "phoenix" conceit: Charles II's capital will rise from its ashes, more splendid and more powerful than before: "She shakes the rubbish from her mounting brow" (1174), and "New deifi'd she from her fires does rise" (1178). But for all Dryden's assurances that the remainders of the fire will be eliminated, *Annus Mirabilis* leaves the reader with its own residues, or loose ends. The poem closes in ruin, with only the promise of restoration dangled reassuringly before the reader's eyes. Material remnants, the waste matter of England's war and London's fire, are always left over in the poem, the tangible evidence of failures that are never quite eradicated by Dryden's rhetorical polish. And the point is that Dryden chose to celebrate Charles II through such a poem, one where gain and success are asserted in the face of concrete evidence to the contrary, where waste is used, perversely, to prophesy long-term triumph.

The disaster of the fire, actually witnessed by Dryden's readers, signaled not only symbolic failure but, more vividly, economic disaster, a real threat to the survival of Charles's government. Dryden's portrait of Charles II's leadership in the opening sections of the poem explores the financial and diplomatic risks involved in war with Holland, anticipating the explicit thematization of waste in the section on the fire. If it was not fully recognized that the wars with Holland had been fiscal and administrative calamities, it was certainly widely suspected, for satires on Charles and his ministers were in private circulation, including the infamous "Painter" satires written after Waller's 1665 panegyric on the English victory at Lowestoft, "Instructions to a Painter."[28] Charles II's government depended on both martial and commercial success. Blair Hoxby argues that "the Rump [Parliament] not only won a reputation for championing the cause of English commerce but forced Charles II to live up to that example by reimagining his empire in terms of trade rather than dominion. His royal entry suggested that such an empire could be achieved only through the coordinated exertions of Crown and City, force and commerce."[29]

This is, in other words, a worldly poem, where waste is understood in primarily commercial and political terms. Dryden's interest in the financial importance of London's recovery from the fire, his perception that London was significant as the economic center of England, and his recognition that war with Holland must ultimately be a lucrative exercise are revealed in his prophetic description of London's emergence from the ashes:

> Methinks already, from his chemic flame,
> I see a city of more precious mould;
> Rich as the town which gives the Indies name,
> With silver paved, and all divine with gold.   (1169–72)

Images of balance, loss, and gain, which imply the assumption of risk, show us that when Dryden celebrates "restoration" in the poem, he is talking about commercial, rather than moral or religious, recuperation.

"With the Second Anglo-Dutch War, efforts to articulate what was in the public's interest and what could be expected of an able government were increasingly expressed in terms of trade supremacy and fiscal responsibility, while the information that was required for such public debates was often supplied by the financial markets rather than the Crown or Parliament."[30] It was well known that Charles could not afford to let his expenditure on the war go to waste, as Dryden makes clear in stanzas 10–13 where he describes the level of risk which the king has assumed:

10

This saw our King: and long within his breast
His pensive counsels ballanc'd too and fro;
He griev'd the Land he freed should be oppress'd,
And he less for it then Usurpers so.

11

His gen'rous mind the fair Idea's drew
Of Fame and Honour which in dangers lay;
Where wealth, like fruit on precipices, grew,
Not to be gather'd but by Birds of prey.

12

The loss and gain each fatally were great;
And still his Subjects call'd aloud for war:
But peaceful Kings o'r martial people set,
Each others poise and counter-balance are.

13

He, first, survey'd the charge with careful eyes,
Which none but mighty Monarchs could maintain;
Yet judg'd, like vapour that from Limbecks rise,
It would in richer showers descend again.   (37–52)

We are dimly aware that this passage takes up Charles II's perspective (we perceive the calculations being made through the monarch's eyes), but Dryden masks the subjective point of view through assured tone and confident declarations, suggesting that Charles is not fully aware of his own uncertain situation. On the one hand, the words "balance," "fair," "poise," "careful," "survey'd," and "judg'd" reveal that Charles sees himself as a clever calculator; his "pensive counsels" and thoughtful balancing of ideas describe the manner in which Charles assesses the level of English risk involved in continuing the war. The quasi-economic meaning of "balance" reveals that Charles's ministry is calculating in the attempt to balance risk against reward. But the image of the bird of prey suggests that Charles is rapacious in his ambitions. Charles fancies that he understands the scale of risk involved in pursuing international trade interests through war: "wealth, like fruit on precipices, grew," and he values the possible gains generously. If the sums involved do not match his greedy projection, the waste of English resources will be the more pronounced ("the loss and gain each fatally were great"). The curiously mixed metaphor of the bird of prey plucking fruit is presumably designed to strike the reader with the fiscal daring—and potential miscalculation—in Charles's judgment that England's investment in war "would in richer showers descend again."

The point is that waste is understood by Dryden as the possible outcome of risky, financially unsound calculation. This poem has moved far from the wastelands of the fire sermons, where desolation is a sign of divine judgment. Nonetheless, when Dryden tells the story of London's devastation and commercial loss, it is still through the imagery of apocalyptic ruin, familiar from religious texts of the Civil War period.[31] In the climax of the poem, the fire is a prodigious monster, consuming the city with voracious, apocalyptic energy. But the worldly imagery relating to financial loss and gain, possession and dispossession, that preoccupied other sections of the poem have an ironic, cooling effect on the grandiose drama of the episode. Dryden's imagery generates a simultaneously biblical and commercial narrative, using the spectacle of ruin—biblical in proportion but now realized—to reflect his own shift as a public poet from assured celebration to historical inquiry, from epic to history.

When Dryden figures the fire as a prodigy, he uses the language of radical religious pamphlets and their counterattacks:

217

In this deep quiet, from what source unknown,
Those seeds of fire their fatal birth disclose:
And first few scattering sparks about were blown,
Big with the flames that to our ruin rose.

218

Then, in some close-pent room it crept along,
And, smouldering as it went, in silence fed:
Till the infant monster, with devouring strong,
Walked boldly upright with exalted head.

The fire sires its own offspring, but is simultaneously a pregnant mother and fertile embryo: "those seeds of Fire their fatal birth disclose." It remains perpetually impregnated, however, "big with the flames that to our ruin rose," mimicking the grotesque births and monstrous deformities associated with apocalyptic polemic. It lays waste with greedy and insatiable precocity; an "infant monster, with devouring strong," it leaps through the city with "inrag'd desire." The monster fire rushes down narrow streets like an angel cast out of heaven: "to either hand his wings he opens wide," and it metamorphoses from grotesque mother to an imperial power creating its own colonies of flame (935–36).

Dryden's title for the poem had signaled that he would tease at the imaginative possibilities of radical imagery, and the figuring of the fire as "dire Usurper" (849) sustains both the apocalyptic tone of dissenting literature and the parodic grotesquerie of counterattacks upon it. The fire is at once a vengeful army destroying the institutional icons of Charles's authority (236ff.) and a feeding, frenzied beast.[32] The ambiguous recycling of imagery from religious pamphlet wars has a very deliberate effect. Dryden's recognizable but confused borrowing from dissenting texts shows that violent, apocalyptic imagery survived during the Restoration as a vocabulary for social disruption and cultural threat (note that the fire is of dubious social origins, "in mean buildings first obscurely bred" [858]). For Dryden, the prose of political pamphlets communicated imperilment and vulnerability, individual and collective.

The hint is made explicit at line 889, when "the Ghosts of Traitors from the Bridge descend, / With bold Fanatick Spectres to rejoyce." The "traitors" are the rebels of the failed republican revolution, but the violent wasting, usurpation, gluttonous feeding, and unopposed armies, and the highly nuanced distinctions which gave each of these images partisan meaning in the 1640s and 1650s, are collapsed in *Annus Mirabilis* to invent a new imagery of threat and disruption. By retaining its link to apocalyptic pamphlet literature, a wasted city connotes violent discontent, schism, and cultural dysfunctionality. Dryden's title, *Annus Mirabilis*, inverts those of three dissenting *Mirabilis Annus* tracts, pamphlets that used figures of judgment and apocalypse to signal a second revolution in post-Puritan England.[33] It is worth pausing on Dryden's image of treasonous ghosts here. History, both the history of seventeenth-century schism and the wastelands of biblical narrative, haunts Dryden's poem like troublesome apparitions. The past provides its own leftovers, literary and political remnants that eighteenth-century writers, following Dryden, must somehow rehabilitate and turn to account. Like other waste products, history attains value and yet remains simultaneously haunting, never entirely recuperated even when it is virtuosically recycled.

The imagery of prodigious monstrosity, which reminds us of epic and biblical apocalypse narratives, is interwoven with a story of civic and domestic activity reminding us that Dryden's setting is the site of much eighteenth-century fiction, where literal conditions supply an expressive register for psychic peril. When the Fire breaks out, "the diligence of Trades and noiseful gain, / And luxury, more late, asleep were laid" (861–62); a "waking lover" happens first to see the blaze; and later, amid the ruins, "sad parents watch the remnants of their store" (1032). Wasteland has become the dispossessed geography of modernity, the site of psychological and cultural desolation.

To convey the impact of the fire on London's commercial and trading interests, Dryden uses images of worldly goods and financial calculations. At line 842 Dryden uses the word "ruine" to describe the decimating effect of the blow fate deals to London in the fire: "Each Element his

dread command obeys, / Who makes or ruines with a smile or frown."
"Ruine" seems, on the face of it, to be a word chosen out of rhetorical
interest—a flourish intended to imply the demise of civilization in the
burning of London. But the ruins will have a more practically debilitat-
ing effect than to announce symbolically the collapse of Stuart culture.
And Dryden has in fact used the verb ruin four stanzas earlier, to describe
the pragmatic threat to the English woolen trade posed by European
manufacturing techniques:

> Some English Wool, vex'd in a Belgian Loom,
> And into Cloth of spungy softness made:
> Did into France or colder Denmark doom,
> To ruine with worse ware our staple Trade   (825–28)

"Ruine" has been folded into the vocabulary of economic competition,
and thus in the line about fate it suggests a pun on financial and physical
ruin, implying that the real cost of physical devastation will be the collapse
of London's precarious financial system. Dryden's interest in the economics of ruin is implied in the later suggestion that the wasting of London
ironically makes restoration and enlargement possible: "this benefit we
sadly owe the flame / If only ruin must enlarge our way" (1107–8).

The fiscal preoccupation that characterizes the whole poem supplies
a narrative for the escalation of the disaster: the fire cunningly takes ad-
vantage of the fact that "the diligence of Trades and noiseful gain, / And
Luxury, more late, asleep were laid" to transform itself into the guise of a
"rich or mighty Murderer." The implication is that the fire will butcher
the city's economic institutions, which is, indeed, what happens:

> One mighty Squadron, with a side wind sped,
> Through narrow lanes his cumber'd fire does haste:
> By pow'rfull charms of gold and silver led,
> The Lombard Banquers and the Change to waste.   (941–44)

The fire's destruction of London's institutional landmarks is figured as
criminal activity, for the flames break out of prison: "so scapes th'insulting
fire his narrow Jail." Dryden implies, moreover, that the fire escapes by

buying his way out of London's corrupt prison system, for he breaks from his prison bars "with gold." The fire is a tax evader: "who, fresher for new mischiefs does appear, / And dares this world to tax him with the old"; a few lines later he is a developer and entrepreneur who "O'er-looks the neighbours with a wide survey, / And nods at every house his threatening fire." Such worldly imagery emphasizes Dryden's turn to a pragmatic analysis of the sources of security and threat for the Restoration government.

Indeed, the wasting of London in 1666 threatened not only Charles II but Dryden himself, for as a public and professional poet he relied upon a functional, populated, and solvent capital. He needed subject matter that would prove enduring, so in writing about waste he places his own poetic reputation at risk—just as he would subsequently do in printing *MacFlecknoe* and *Absalom and Achitophel*.[34] *Annus Mirabilis* imperils the public poet in search of a patron by predicating Charles's success on a collaboration among the citizens of London, its technological and economic institutions, and volatile Restoration parliaments. Poetically, the spectacle of waste reflects the threat of failure and obsolescence that nags at professional writers in the Restoration, whose work reveals the unstable narrative modes and sense of a creative void that arise when conventional genres and forms seem no longer adequate.

For all Dryden's classical framing devices, the image of the burnt-out city in *Annus Mirabilis* was vivid and real: it synthesized the material and ideological failures of Restoration urban culture. The paradoxical appearance of failure in a work devoted to the commemoration of success, and itself so ambitious, is interesting for it suggests that waste is the trope for the residual failure or loss that is a part of any project, however successful.[35] Writing that engages explicitly with waste recognizes its inevitability; it is the aftermath, deflated or grotesque, of any investment of human energy. Dryden's poem concludes by reminding us that his theme is trade; in the final stanza, a utopian vision of steady breeze and stable commerce conveys an imagined setting in which both physical and fiscal wastage are in abeyance: "A constant trade-wind will securely blow, / And gently lay us on the spicy shore" (1216–17).

Annus Mirabilis is a poem about greed, and the mania of greed—the delusion that one can have all and waste nothing. It is a poem about ambition, and the illusion of the ambitious that success is without cost. It trades in the grubby imagery of war and financial calculation and in the poetics of opportunism, and so the worldly fears of failure and waste are bound into its imagery. The poem's worldly knowledge—its topical references; its self-consciously modern vocabulary; its themes of chance, opportunism, risk, and calculation—is more vividly alive than the formal conventions and historical allusions on which the narrative seems at first to be structured. Dryden shows us that waste and failure threaten the Restoration simply by virtue of their presence in urban life; they affect not only political ideology but the economic and civic framework on which political stability is founded. He shows us that waste and loss are ineradicable residues of economic modernity, based as it was on risks that were inadequately understood, uncertain trading conditions, and unstable politics.

We might expect that the literalization of biblical apocalypse in the heart of London would persuade people that God's wrath was real, that their immorality had been punished. But this isn't what happened. Instead, people used biblical apocalypse to describe a modern, commercial wasteland. But it was a wasteland that inherited the symbolic force of its biblical antecedents. And, as we have seen, the perverse truth about biblical waste is that it has value. Far from being unmentionable, biblical waste has immense power, so instead of wanting to abolish its traces, writers set out to memorialize the landscape that embodied a most surprising truth: that waste was valuable in literary as well as religious texts.

III

London had been turned into a waste that threatened England's prosperity and success. Practically speaking, the way forward was self-evident: to clear the rubble away and make sure it didn't happen again. And on one level that is what happened. Plans for rebuilding call explicitly for the need to eliminate wasteland, and with it to eliminate the emptiness and attendant desolation that made postfire London so frightening.

Generally speaking, responses to the fire recommended that waste must be contained, debris eliminated, and London turned into a clean, unobstructed urban space. The idea was that waste must be minimized and convenience maximized. Westminster proclaimed that "rules and directions for rebuilding cannot yet be given, but the inconveniences of hasty and unskilful buildings must be avoided," and again in the *London Gazette* of September 15, 1666, recommended that "no streets, especially towards the water, be so narrow, as to make the passage uneasie or inconvenient; nor any allies or lanes errected, but on necessity." After all, waste was the wrong kind of excess, and by taking it outside the city, the hope was that the only kind of surpluses to fill London would be the income from trade, manufactures, and commerce, and the productive, bustling workforce that went with them. The strict separation of wasteful excess from valuable surplus was an understandable impulse, even if it turned out to be impossible, or even undesirable. Eventually, the idea that value and waste, like loss and gain, are dialectically related was theorized. Bataille explained it in the following terms: "wealth appears as an acquisition to the extent that power is acquired by a rich man, but it is entirely directed toward loss in the sense that this power is characterized as the power to lose. It is only through loss that glory and honor are linked to wealth."[36] In 1666, when the insight had not yet been formulated, civic planners at first followed their common sense and tried to make debris disappear.

It was common for texts to recommend making London empty, making waste go away. "All Church-Yards, Gardens, and unnecessary *vacuities*; and all Trades that use great fires, or yield noisome Smells," shall be removed "to places out of the Town," recommended Christopher Wren.[37] But the problem was that real void, clear space, was antithetical to London's vibrancy and life. John Milward, MP, recognized that a certain teeming fullness was essential, or "the merchants and wealthiest of the citizens would alter the course of their life and trade and remove themselves and estates into other countries and so the City would remain miserable for ever."[38] It seemed that a fear of wasteland might cause people to forget the absolute dependence of a commercial economy on concentrated public space. Samuel Rolls urged: "Tell us not of the Suburbs, Citizens know how inconvenient they are for their busines, over what the City is; and besides, both together are little enough for traders . . . ; they durst not go after the declining Sun, lest they themselves should decline also in their trade and busines."[39]

It was obvious that if London was really cleared out, made empty, it would suffer a fate far worse than the fire: it would experience economic collapse. For better or for worse, Londoners needed to learn to tolerate chaos because new financial systems, communications, the urban media—modernity, in other words—depended on intense population. Excess and surplus, both good and bad, had become the defining traits of a modern city.

Roy Porter makes the case that the ambitions of the fire's aftermath were doomed: "the dreams of Wren and Hooke to redesign the City after the Great Fire on a noble ground plan had been lost . . . and the urban jungle closed in. Open spaces and gardens were overrun by new houses, huts and hovels making up De Quincey's fearful 'Sphinx's riddle of streets'; the rookeries of courts and blind alleys shut out light and air and thus became the breeding-grounds of flyblown noisomeness and disease."[40] For reasons both practical and symbolic, Londoners maintained a loyalty to filth that postfire planners had not considered. William Hogarth's images of eighteenth-century London streets in *The Times of Day* (1736), *Beer Street*, and *Gin Lane* (1751) or Ned Ward's descriptions of a City that smelled of "stale sprats, piss and irreverence" (*London Spy*, 1703) suggest that even if London was in better physical shape after the fire than before, urban filth was treasured as a literary trope. Alain Corbain argues, moreover, that the compulsion to separate putrefaction from the realm of the living was largely a later eighteenth-century preoccupation; olfactory offense was tolerated in the early part of the century.[41] Roy Porter also finds plenty of evidence that Georgian London was still a hellish place: "London as diseased, parasitic, and contagious echoed down the century, with its connotations of sterility and death. For London tainted all it touched, sucking in the healthy from the countryside, and—as the Bills of Mortality proved—devouring far more than it bred."[42]

Even insofar as the redesign of London after the fire did produce a grander, more orderly and hygienic city, the new public spaces became theaters for the more obvious display of waste and filth. This was not only true of London's literal pollutants—the piles of garbage and filth left in the public spaces outside residences and in communal squares— but also of London's waste people, whose destitution became, paradoxically, more visible after the Restoration, bringing into being the city of beggars and vagrants that Hogarth would memorialize. Tim Hitchcock explains that the wide streets, open squares, and formal railings built in the late seventeenth century, accompanied by the spread of London's residential areas into the West End, "created poorly policed public areas" where beggars would set up camp and never move on. Wren's vision paradoxically brought into being a new kind of encumbered modernity, public streets, for which nobody felt custodial responsibility: "stationary public begging became increasingly detached from traditional notions of Christian charity; becoming more obvious, possibly more offensive, and probably more centralized on newly 'public' spaces. At the same time it became less clearly the responsibility of individual householders and parish communities."[43]

In reality it is difficult to assess how filthy London was, that is, whether its filth exceeded reasonable levels for a city of its size. In 1671 the Sewers and Streets Act was passed, and commissioners were able to impose taxes upon the residents of the City of London to finance paving and cleansing. Scavengers, rakers, and carters were employed to clean, the streets. Newly paved streets were easier to clean, and laystalls were probably adequate.[44] Eighteenth-century London did possess a pre-Chadwickian "public sickness" movement, a genuine concern about the perils of urban dwelling.[45] But Emily Cockayne begins her catalogue of London's filth by observing that "travelers hoping to find London streets paved with gold were disappointed. In reality, if paved at all, the streets were clad with stone and coated with dirt and mire."[46] Legislation requiring citizens to pave the streets in front of their residences and keep them clean was often ignored, and there was inadequate water supply and drainage.[47] Cockayne shows, indeed, that holding on to waste matter was not by any means a merely literary or imaginative event:

> Many waste products did not make it on to the piles. . . . Neighbours would have salvaged large pieces of wood, cinders and building material. The pig, described by Gervase Markham as the best scavenger, "for his food and living by that which would also rot in the Yard," consumed much waste vegetable matter. The "black contaminated sulphurous substance called Greaves" left at the bottom of the tallow-chandlers' melting coppers could be fed to dogs.

Fat that was cut from meat or that melted out during cooking was sold to tallow-chandlers to make candles. Barges carrying London's refuse away were often refilled with bricks for the return journey. These bricks were in part made from reusable particles from the refuse, such as grit and ashes riddled from the street sweepings.[48]

The idea that filth might have value, that waste should be kept close to hand, is a reflection of the real conditions of eighteenth-century London as much as of its literary sensibilities.

It turned out to be important that Dryden's model for urban apocalypse of the kind that devastated London in 1666 was originally biblical. Religious narrative insists on the very idea that these overly ordered, civic reactions to the disaster resisted: that wasteland cannot, indeed should not, be built upon and forgotten. Even if wasteland is rehabilitated, it must, theologically speaking, be memorialized. When Thomas Jacomb published a treatise in 1667 about the rebuilding of London, he wrote:

> Isa. 61.4 They shall build the old wastes, they shall repair the waste Cities, the desolations of many generations Jer. 30. 18. Thus saith the Lord, Behold, I will bring again the captivity of Jacobs tents, and have mercy on his dwelling places; and the City shall be builded upon her own heap, and the palace shall remain after the manner thereof, &c. Amos. 9.14. They shall build the waste cities and inhabit them.

As Bataille would explain, there is, indeed, a crucial relationship between experiencing loss and professing piety: "sacred things are constituted by an operation of loss: in particular, the success of Christianity must be explained by the value of the theme of the Son of God's ignominious crucifixion, which carries human dread to a representation of loss and limitless degradation."[49] An "operation of loss," expenditure on a massive scale, is what marks the Great Fire of 1666 as a sacred event. But it also explains why descriptions of London as Jerusalem, Sodom, or Gomorrah provide writers so readily with the imagery for secular wasteland. This is the crucial point: waste always retains its theological significance, because it is matter that we desire, simultaneously, to retain and to eradicate. This is the paradox of waste that secular descriptions of wasteland inherit from their biblical antecedents.

When London was described as a wasteland in 1666, then, the general assumption was that the laying waste of London would end in glorious regeneration. But it happened much more slowly and haphazardly than Wren and Evelyn and the other planners had imagined. Instead of a new Rome, built upon generous, broad avenues and vast public piazzas, came a teeming city not so unlike its precursor, and instead of a cleaned up city whose social and commercial centers were free of waste came the confused, filthy London of the *Dunciad* (first edition, 1728) and *The Beggar's Opera* (1728). Simon Ford's claim in 1666 that "waste is merit" was more revealing than it had seemed; the citizens of London were becoming attached to their wasteland. Evelyn's crucial perception, which began this chapter, was that "the people who now walked about the ruines appeared like men in some dismal desart, or rather in some great Citty." He saw, in other words, that desert and city—wasteland and populous center—are related not by opposition but by uncanny similitude.

2

Wastelands, *Paradise Lost*, and Popular
Polemic at the Restoration

THE hybrid wasteland of *Annus Mirabilis*, partly drawn from the Bible, partly a reflection of reality, created a new literary terrain: a setting in which personal and social desolation became themes in modern secular writing. Dryden's wasteland figured political and cultural disaffection, and yet, like the sacked cities of the Bible, its strange, alienated landscape commanded memorialization. Once invented, this hybrid wasteland became the landscape through which writers articulated a sense of belonging and yet being alienated—the landscape in which modern literary selfhood would come of age. Living amid leftovers was to become perversely pleasurable, and English writers would preserve the wastes among which they happily, and discontentedly, existed.

The urban wasteland of Dryden's poem is only half the story, however. The rural wastes of agricultural England were also crucial to the late seventeenth-century imagination, and wilderness took on complex literary value in *Paradise Lost*, the poem that probably had most influence with eighteenth-century readers. Milton's epic is set amid wastelands, and not just in the places we might expect, Chaos, Hell, and the Limbo of Vanities, but also in Eden and Heaven, landscapes from which waste (at least in a pejorative sense) seemingly ought to be excluded. And while Milton sets out to "justify the ways of God to men," he pays scrupulous attention to God's dregs and discards: substance that has no value takes up almost as much of the poem as the matter that does. By working the expressive possibilities of wasteland into *Paradise Lost* as rigorously as he does, Milton plays a key role in establishing waste as one of the most resonant tropes for eighteenth-century English literature.

The publication of the first, ten-book *Paradise Lost* (1667) was in the same year as *Annus Mirabilis* and most of Milton's poem had been written long before Dryden put pen to paper. Both texts emerge from the context of republican revolution—Dryden's in praise of its defeat, Milton's in ambiguous lament. Blair Hoxby pairs them because "they both engage the Restoration regime's ideology of trade and because it is partly by way of their strikingly opposed representations of force and commerce that they ask to be read in, and understood against, the heroic tradition."[1] Milton and Dryden were vexed by the same paradox, that where there is excess, there is, simultaneously, desire and despair. For Milton these are resolvable anxieties, but Milton's philosophical solution to the problem of waste is never entirely effaced at the poetic level. In other words, anxiety about waste—an unresolved desire for and fear of excess—haunts his writing, creating literary echoes and affinities among scenes and sequences that are morally, theologically, and philosophically incompatible.

For Milton, waste is a potentially confusing and negotiable category because it is a form of abundance. Milton was, after all, writing about the grandest kind of abundance there is: divine creation. Like abjection, luxurious excess is at once alluring and alarming, threatening to decline into putrefaction but also a source of life, energy, and renewal. Degraded leftovers in *Paradise Lost* are as cosmically significant as their much more glorious counterparts because in Milton's republican imagining of the cosmos, waste and abundance are equally necessary as markers of a theologically and philosophically coherent universe. In Milton's cosmos, precious matter can be degraded (the gemstones of Hell, for instance), while abject remnants (fallen fruit in Eden, for example) can be glorious. In the secular environment of *Annus Mirabilis*, the negotiation between expanding and containing waste is subject largely to urban planning, which often clashes awkwardly with practical reality. But Milton's politics and theology do not permit regulation through a secular alliance of the practical with the planned. The regulation of excess—and the creation of waste—are subject to strict Miltonic morality. The value of matter in Milton's universe is neither inherent nor arbitrarily created; it is acquired through a process of choice, which makes little sense from a modern scientific standpoint, but is founded on Milton's philosophical and political arguments for the importance of free will. The moral terms of Milton's theology and politics are frequently at odds with a reader's expectations of how waste and excess come into being and what they mean. Miltonic waste is often surprising, counterintuitive, perplexing. It shows, above all, that waste can be made by literature itself: Milton's language and moral philosophy are what separate diabolical waste from divine abundance.

Several debates taking place in late seventeenth-century England engaged with the troublesome relationship of waste to value. They included the controversy over the place of excess in commercial exchange, confusion about the status of wasteland and wilderness in England's rural areas, and theological arguments about the nature of abject matter. Milton, acutely aware of the financial revolution through which he was living, explicitly interested in the politically fraught terrain of wasteland, and heretically engaged with the theology of abject matter, paid a vital contribution to all three. In *Paradise Lost* and in other writings, Milton's account of the relationship between glorious surplus and degraded excess would set the terms for eighteenth-century texts taking on the fraught questions of what waste and value were and how they were created.

I

A Masque Presented at Ludlow Castle [*Comus*] (1634) is the earliest of Milton's texts explicitly to stage an encounter with the spectacle of excess and the meaning of waste. I glance at it before proceeding to *Paradise Lost*, because Comus's appetite for surplus is echoed not only in Satan's desire for "more" (more territory, more power, more pleasure) but also in Eve's. Some of the most difficult, ambiguous sequences in *Paradise Lost* work off the imagery of excess and waste that Milton introduces in *A Masque*, but, unlike this early work, the problems such imagery poses are never entirely resolved. After pursuing the virtuous Lady (the chaste heroine of the drama) through a wild wood and several pastoral scenes, the enchanter

Comus conjures a Spenserian temptation setting, a "stately palace" where
the Lady is set in an "enchanted chair" in the manner of a character from
The Faerie Queene. Comus attempts to seduce her with promises of luxury
and pleasure, summoning a *carpe diem* argument about the need to enjoy
nature's bounty and prevent abundance from going to waste:

> Wherefore did Nature pour her bounties forth,
> With such a full and unwithdrawing hand,
> Covering the earth with odors, fruits, and flocks,
> Thronging the seas with spawn innumerable,
> But all to please and sate the curious taste?
> And set to work millions of spinning worms,
> That in their green shops weave the smooth-haired silk
> To deck her sons, and that no corner might
> Be vacant of her plenty, in her own loins
> She hutched th'all-worshipped ore and precious seams
> To store her children with; if all the world
> Should in a pet of temperance feed on pulse,
> Drink the clear stream, and nothing wear but frieze,
> Th'All-giver should be unthanked, would be unpraised
>
> (710–23)

The Lady should sleep with Comus because God did not make pleasure
and beauty to go unused, the Enchanter argues. *Not so fast*, the Lady
replies, and maintains her chastity. But if Comus's seduction fails in this
scene, Milton's does not. It is all but impossible not to be enraptured by
the glorious images of his lines. How adeptly Milton progresses through
assonances formed of the circular, open, sensuous, and yet reassuringly
enclosed sound of *o*, conveying a tumbling together of great bounty.
Barely have we registered "pour" than the aural echo takes us to "forth";
we tumble to the alliteration in "full" and the assonance in "unwithdrawing." The *o* pattern greedily draws in "odors," "flocks," "thronging,"
"spawn," while the alliteration pulls in "fruits." New alliterations arise,
confusedly mingled with the assonance: "seas," "spawn," "please," "sate,"
"taste," "set," "spinning," "worms," "shops," "smooth," "silk," "sons,"
"loins," "seems," "store" (all working off the insinuating hiss of *s*), while

"work," "worms," and "weaves" establish a sequence of intertwined assonance and alliteration that subsequently gather up "no corner," "own loins," and "worshipped ore." We realize, too late to resist the seduction, that the rolling, open *o*'s create a sameness, a surfeit that overspills boundaries and contained forms. The paradox "vacant plenty" is itself an excess, since the experience of plenitude that anticipates the vacancy of death already saturates every phrase.

By the time Comus describes his vision of unused luxury as "waste fertility" (729), we can beat Milton to its implied inversion: this isn't just waste fertility but fertile waste. There is repugnance in so much plenitude and vigor, and there is an unpleasant vigor in so much that is repulsive. Aurel Kolnai writes of "extreme propagation and growth" that "there is here an intention of a rapidly encountered death, an over-accentuation of the rise and fall of life. . . . In all this shortness and abortiveness of life, coordinated with frenetic rapidity and furious zest for life there is something disgusting."[2] Comus's lines are more voluptuously compressed than in the later description of Edenic abundance in *Paradise Lost* that echoes them, and the reader here feels suffused with overwhelming pleasure and surfeit; keeping up with it is exhausting and anxiety-inducing. The images slip by too quickly, each one too gorgeous; and the reader's enforced abandonment of each, unused, as she gallops through the lines, makes them seem like splendor that is already rotten, like the image of silk that we know is extruded from the worms' digestive tracts. Through an excess of life Milton conjures a parallel vision of putrefaction, of waste. He need not make that putrefaction explicit, because the undifferentiated sameness of Comus's glorious spoils have the blurred formlessness of rot. Seduction—the reader's seduction by Comus's fabulous imagery—is experienced as something very like disgust, in the impossibility of keeping one image separate from the next, in the sense of mounting panic as deformed abundance pours, liquid and unformed, into the next.

Milton reuses the argument in *Paradise Lost*, when Eve asks Adam about the potential "waste fertility" of the stars: "But wherefore all night long shine these, for whom?" (4.657ff.). Adam replies: "These then, though unbeheld in deep of night, / Shine not in vain. Nor think, though men were none, / That Heaven would want spectators, God want praise"

(4.710–12). Not only does Eve's "wherefore" echo Comus's, but Adam's answer echoes the double negatives of Comus's speech, repeating the sense that plenitude is vexed by its proximity to negativity and emptiness. Thus Comus's "unwithdrawing," "unthanked," "unpraised," is matched by Adam's "unbeheld," "shine not," "nor think." Even when the problem of excess is understood correctly, as in *Paradise Lost* (God has adjusted the universe to absorb all seeming excesses, even when to humans they seem wasted), the relation of plenitude to vacancy remains, poetically speaking, as a problem.

Blair Hoxby argues that Comus's argument represents a seduction by economic language, and that the whole performance reflects Milton's engagement with contemporary economic theory.

> The Lady's distrust of Comus and her annoyance at having acted upon false information are crucial not only to the masque's larger themes of faith, trial, and virginity but to its inset drama of economic models because belief is the sine qua non of what we now call the 'multiplier effects' of the sort of dynamic economy that Comus celebrates—its ability to generate new wealth through a series of transactions. It is no accident that terms like credit, trust, security, good will, assurance, and faith enjoy such prominence in the economic lexicon.[3]

Part of the anxiety of the new economics of late seventeenth-century England was that they made value negotiable, a matter of fluctuation and substitution rather than of assigned, inherent "worth." The problem of value (and its opposite, waste) is a problem that Milton sets out to correct in all his writing, insisting that real value, real worth are moral, not marketable, phenomena.

When the Lady replies to Comus, she corrects his account of plenitude, explaining that the best way of dealing with excess is to create even distribution of spoils, such that neither luxury nor want exists:

> If every just man that now pines with want
> Had but a moderate and beseeming share
> Of that which lewdly-pampered Luxury

Now heaps upon some few with vast excess,
Nature's full blessings would be well dispensed
In unsuperfluous even proportion,
And she no whit encumbered with her store;   (768–74)

Plenitude and waste need not go hand in hand—need not provoke either
Comus's fleshly lust nor Eve's anxious helplessness—if excess is dispensed
evenly. These lines correct Comus's poetics, too, eliminating assonance
and reducing alliteration, except in the couplet where she recapitulates
Comus's argument: "of that which lewdly-pampered Luxury / Now heaps
upon some few with vast excess." Here the "vast" of "vast excess" echoes
the "waste" of "waste fertility," creating a paradox (empty excess) that looks
like a redundancy (surplus). The Lady's answer comes as a relief, inter-
rupting Comus's disturbing vision, but the relief is only temporary. When
the Lady describes a balanced distribution of spoils, she calls it "unsuperfluous"—the word "superfluous" is negated, but not effaced entirely.
The problem of excess persists, Milton recognizes, and wherever there is
excess there is the anxiety that desire and disgust, simultaneously pro-
voked, arouse. Milton leaves behind the simple allegorical temptation that
Comus presents, but he cannot leave behind the problem that excess both
allures and alarms. The turning point in *Paradise Lost*, arguably its most
important crux, unnervingly revisits this scene from *A Masque*, as Eve attempts to puzzle out the phenomenon of superfluity in Paradise.

By the time Comus's arguments about wasted plenitude reappear in *Paradise Lost*, however, they are merged with a real-life debate about the status
of rural waste in England. In the context of seventeenth-century debates
about land reform and enclosure, the idea of confining and eradicating
waste became a figure for national and moral self-regulation. The practice
of enclosing common land for private use was highly contentious because
it had the effect of dispossessing the rural poor, eliminating commons, and
destroying the traditional agricultural habits and culture of early modern
England.[4] In the eighteenth century, parliamentary enclosure sealed the
fate of much common land, but at the time Milton was writing *Paradise
Lost*, enclosure was mostly "by agreement," which is to say that it relied
upon political and polemical persuasion to achieve its aims. "Wastes"

were the places that enclosure polemicists had traditionally focused their attention on, since they were among the last unused tracts of country in England.[5] Technically, waste was a topographic category distinct from common, but in the mid–seventeenth century common was often erroneously referred to as "waste," to explain and justify its enclosure. The interesting thing about waste in the enclosure debates is that it attracts attention because it's a form of excess—land that is presently valueless, but whose value can be established through the "improvements" that enclosure promises. "Waste is largely defined in the early modern period by what it is not, or is not *yet*. Specifically, it is seen as land not yet under the plough, arable land-in-waiting . . . From a legal pespective, waste (as opposed to barren) ground is fertile, although the fertility has not yet been channeled into agriculture, writes Karen Edwards."[6]

Enclosing land was meant to enable the rise of a new rural gentry and encourage the transfer of local, rural power away from those large landowners traditionally in authority.[7] In the mainstream republican politics of the civil war, wasteland was regarded as an obstacle to progressive rural change, and enclosure was seen as a path to economic reform. But even when major radical figures such as Gerard Winstanley opposed enclosure, they too made use of the term "waste" to argue for improvement—in Winstanley's case, to claim the land on which the Diggers would establish their agrarian commune.[8] In order to be improved, however, wastelands first had to be made.

In a pamphlet called *Wasteland's Improvement* (1653), for instance, written at the height of revolutionary turmoil, the polemicist argues for enclosure by insisting that the abolition of wasteland can bring wholesale political order to England, making the countryside safe for its inhabitants to live and work upon. The argument is made though the image of an overgrown tree: "[B]etter it is to lay the axe to the root, than (by imploying souldiers to thief-catching) to be always lopping the branches; which if the root remain, wil upon every occasion grow again notwithstanding, and may in time make Englands wasts a receptacle and harbour for troops of assassinating rogues like the Tories in Ireland, and the Moss-Troopers in Scotland."[9] Land enclosure, says the author, is necessary because waste is a "receptacle and harbour"—not only wild, but dangerously empty—waiting to be filled with assassinating rogues who breed political dissent and threaten England's national security. The term "receptacle" reminds us that etymologically waste is empty—a vessel, waiting to be filled. And we see that it is empty in an economic sense, as well as being the terrain of political dispossession, occupied by seditious waste-people. Like London after the Great Fire, the important point about rural wasteland is that it is simultaneously empty and full, and this makes it a landscape that can accommodate very complicated, often contradictory narratives.

The enclosure movement continued from the fifteenth century until the nineteenth, generating pamphlets, essays, poems, and polemics for and against. The variety, rhetorical complexity, and political diversity of writings about enclosure reveal that the oppositional imagery of enclosed and open fields enabled writers to map out a narrative of England's national destiny through an argument about the benefits or detriments of enclosure. Radicals as well as royalists argued about enclosure, including Gerrard Winstanley and the Diggers, Samuel Hartlib, the Levellers, and Milton himself, who wrote in a (probably) unpublished essay that "England had many hundreds of acres of waste and barren lands, and many thousands of idle hands; if both these might be improved, England by God's blessing would grow to be a richer nation than it now is by far."[10] As Karen Edwards has shown, despite the range and political diversity of arguments, enclosure polemic was united by one point of common agreement: that waste should be brought under cultivation, whether in common or in private.[11] Rachel Crawford argues convincingly that the symbolic narrative of enclosure was more powerful than its literal effects—"enclosure alone cannot account for the economic, social and technological changes which accompanied the transformation from an open- to an enclosed-field system"—and she shows the range of political, social, and cultural idealization that could be communicated by writing about enclosure.[12] The sample of enclosure polemic in this chapter is both specifically directed and entirely generic, using imagery common to virtually all writings on enclosure in the period, even when these made very different political arguments.

When pamphleteers made waste, they changed it from a term that described a specific geography to a pejorative word that made commonly held land look valueless. The word "waste" connoted all kinds of degeneration and worthlessness, not just of land but of people. It included low-lifes who got referred to as waste-people: beggars and vagrants, prostitutes, Puritans, Catholics, Irish peasants, promiscuous women, thieves, and murderers. Even in texts written in vocal opposition to enclosure—in More's *Utopia*, in Winstanley's tracts, and later in Goldsmith's *The Deserted Village*—land reform is still discussed in terms of eliminating wasteland.[13] Thus Thomas More invoked its specter in his attack on enclosure: "And if enough of your land were not wasted on ranges and preserves of game, those good fellows turn all human habitations and all cultivated land into a wilderness [of enclosed pasture]."[14] Whenever there was waste, it indicated that all was not well in agrarian England.

Andrew McRae, along with other scholars of English georgic, points out that in the country, just as in the city, wasteland is not "an unproblematic reflection of material conditions," but rather a calculated representation of a particular vision of England's landscape.[15] Wasteland, to use a phrase of McRae's, was a "site of struggle," a struggle that was both political and literary: a battle as to what waste would mean. Polemicists who favored land enclosure traded on the fact that people were both frightened by the emptiness of waste and yet powerfully attracted to the chaotic, dangerous surfeit of vegetation and people it often contained. Descriptions of wasteland are always lurid and sensational; they reel in the reader, and then they offer a reassuring promise: to take away this landscape that is frightening and yet preserve it too, because it is so fascinating. Wasteland was, truly, a dangerous geography:

> It is well known to all, what vast quantities, and what great circumferences of ground so at this day lay wast and desolate (in forrests, and fenny grounds, and other commons) almost in all the Countreys of this Nation, . . . yet either sluggishnesse or worse, drownes the sense of those discommodities, so that little or no consideration is had . . . for their improvement; which as it is a shame and reproach unto Irish, and other lazy People, so much more is it a shame to us English, because we bear the name and reputation of an ingenious and industrial people; but now our hopes are, that such as are now set in the throne of Authority, will not only be the repairers of some breaches but also will convert the desolate wasts into fruitful fields, and our wide howling wildernesse into comfort-

able habitations, that in this (as well as in other things) we may injoy at last some benefit by all our revolutions, transplantings and overturnings in Authorities. (1)

This passage is all about the emptiness of a geography that is in practice anything but empty, and it shows how the empty/full paradox of waste could get used for political purposes. The "vast quantities" and "desolate wasts" make use of the etymological connections between waste, vastness, and emptiness, and the "great circumference" and "wide howling wilderness" imply an evacuated territory through which winds whistle. In reality the land was inhabited by commoners, cultivated, and in some places densely wooded. But the language associated with wasteland manages to create the empty, uncultivated geography that the polemicist needs to make his case for improvement. Notice that the improvements promised here are of a rhetorical rather than a practical order: desolate wastes can be transformed magically into fruitful fields, wilderness to comfortable habitations, as the prevailing imagery of the passage switches from biblical wilderness to georgic plenty. It's a fiction, but it claims to be literal truth.

Crude as it is, polemic like this shows how waste comes to occupy such a powerful place in people's imaginations, extending what Rachel Crawford calls "the symbolic power of cultivated landscapes"[16] to uncultivated ground as well. In seventeenth-century enclosure debates, the proponents of containment promised that it would control and efface unwanted remnants, create a new Eden of excess that would be undermined by no countervailing, deflating waste. But such idealizations were doomed to failure. The creation of value, Milton would argue in *Paradise Lost*, could never be achieved through ideological coercion or political manipulation. The fantasy of luxuriance without waste could only be fulfilled through moral means, through divine agency, never through human maneuvering. Only God can value rightly:

> So little knows
> Any, but God alone, to value right
> The good before him, but perverts best things
> To worst abuse, or to their meanest use.   (4.201–4)

The first time we see Eden in *Paradise Lost*, the reader is positioned outside it, looking in. It feels as though we're in the middle of a wasteland, a desert landscape from which Paradise is cordoned off like a protected, walled enclosure. The reader, along with Satan remains outside the walls, in the wilderness, longingly viewing the forbidden enclosure within:

> So on he fares, and to the border comes
> Of Eden, where delicious Paradise,
> Now nearer, crowns with her enclosure green,
> As with a rural mound the champain head
> Of a steep wilderness, whose hairie sides
> With thicket overgrown, grottesque and wild,
> Access deni'd.   (4.131–36)

It seems at first that by making Eden an enclosed green, surrounded by a "steep wilderness" whose "hairie sides" deny access and by having the phrase "grottesque and wild" resonate with the "dismal situation waste and wild" encountered by Satan in Hell, Milton is distinguishing between the degraded wastes outside Eden and the fruitful abundance within. But this is not the case. Although Paradise is bounded and protected in Milton's poem, its enclosure does not make it safe. The seeming juxtaposition between wilderness outside and Paradise within is not straightforward, and Eden's walls are not enough to forestall invasion.[17] Satan does overleap them. And when he gets inside, Eden turns out to be composed not solely of "fruitful fields," the topography idealized in enclosure polemic. Instead, its terrain oddly resembles the "vast, wide, wild forrests" of English wasteland. Sure enough, Satan's journey through Eden is "through wood, through waste, o'er hill, o'er dale" (4.538). As Karen Edwards affirms, "[waste] is an unexpected terrain to encounter in the garden of Eden. Waste suggests that which is excessive, redundant, and extraneous to the fulfilled relations between place and inhabitant ordained by the Creator."[18] The proximity of waste wilderness and verdant cultivation, which England's enclosers set out to efface, is preserved in Milton's Paradise—affirming that the distinction between waste and value must be achieved by means other than the creation of physical boundaries. In Eden there is excessive verdure, "wanton growth . . . tending to wild," and, according to the angel Raphael, Eden is a "Wilderness of sweets . . . Wild above Rule or Art"—delightful, to be sure, but certainly not controlled or contained. Although Paradise is enclosed, it can still be invaded by Satan, and though private, it is a site of common labor. Though it is fruitful and luxuriant, Eden is yet a wilderness, wide, vast, and wild. Thus, the brooks run with "mazie error" (4.239), watering "Flowers worthy of Paradise which not nice Art / In Beds and curious knots, but Nature boon / Powrd forth profuse on Hill and Dale and Plain" (4.241–43). Raphael's first perceptions of Eden re-produce vocabulary associated with Satan's own first encounter ("wild," "wilderness," "wanton'd"), albeit crossed with the imagery of sensual delight:

> Into the blissful field, through Groves of Myrrh,
> And flowering Odours, Cassia, Nard, and Balm;
> A Wilderness of sweets; for Nature here
> Wanton'd as in her prime, and plaid at will
> Her Virgin Fancies, pouring forth more sweet,
> Wild above Rule or Art; enormous bliss.   (5.292–97)

In Eden, wilderness is desirable.[19] While Eden's luxurious surpluses are not surprising to readers of Milton (of course Paradise can contain benign wilderness), they do nonetheless signal Milton's refusal to accept existing solutions to the problem of keeping waste and abundance segregated. They reflect, moreover, explicit engagement with the seventeenth-century politics of waste: "it is shocking to find waste among the hills, dales and woods of the garden of Eden not because it implies matter un-assimilated to paradise but because, directly though fleetingly, it marks the presence in paradise of seventeenth century social relations."[20] In seventeenth-century England it was common for cultivated gardens to contain "wilderness," but Milton is telling his readers that, morally and politically speaking, the ideal landscape of "a wilderness of sweets" can-not be achieved by force, any more than a paradise can be achieved by physically separating cultivated land from waste. Untroubled excess can be created by God alone. (It cannot even be imagined by the chaste Lady in A Masque, who resolves the problem of luxury by imagining even dis-tribution.) Only divine creation can construct the impossible landscape of Eden. Yet its very impossibility remains a matter of curiosity to Eve, even in her unfallen state. She cannot believe her eyes, nor her ears, that excess is something she and Adam don't have to worry about.

II

When Eve begins to contemplate the issue of oversupply in Paradise, she perceives that luxuriance is both abundant and yet seemingly worthless—confusing for a dweller in Eden. Eve separates from Adam because she wants to trim wild growth; she finds herself unable to accept that unused plenitude is as gloriously benign as she's been told it is. She wants to control waste, and of course this is the move that gives Satan his "in." Eve, in her prelapsarian state, does not experience an ambivalence to excess divided between attraction and repulsion, because Edenic waste does not yet tend toward putrefaction, the "apprehension of death." Waste, like everything else in Eden, is only "life-intended" before the fall. But she does experience confusion, or at least curiosity. She asks Adam many questions about the status of the material world in Paradise, and while these questions are occasions for Milton to explicate his material philosophy, they are also moments in which Eve has intimations of material ambiguity—intimations that when excess is at stake, desire and disgust are very closely linked.

Ambiguity, the condition of being two things at once, is fundamental to the problem of abjection, partly because the disgusting object is also, always appealing. But as Kristeva has shown, abjection is the site of ambivalence ultimately because it is the borderline at which subject and object are confused, where the "I" confronts the fact that it is separated from, and yet tended toward, the putrefying world of remainders. The abject is an object that is not an object; it is a border. The sight of the abject signals in part the spectacle of one's own death, and so it is both unwanted and infinitely desirable. It is significant, then, that Eve is the character to notice the possible ambiguity of luxuriant growth in Eden. Eve is herself materially ambiguous, forged as she is from a leftover piece of Adam. And, ambiguous being that she is, "manlike, but different sex" (8.471), she is quick to apprehend possible material ambiguities in the world around her. Adam, by contrast, cannot bear to be separated from Eve: "I waked to find her, or for ever to deplore / Her loss, and other pleasures all abjure" (8.478–80). Eve is waste matter out of Adam; no wonder that he longs to hold on to her, even as he strives to reject her:

> Should God create another Eve, and I
> Another rib afford, yet loss of thee
> Would never from my heart: no, no! I feel
> The link of nature draw me; flesh of flesh,
> Bone of my bone thou art, and from thy state
> Mine never shall be parted, bliss or woe. (9.911–16)

Loss is the condition in which Adam and Eve's love is created, and it is the kind of loss deriving from the apprehension of waste.

Eve is outspoken about her concern with wild growth, observing that it quickly takes over the places they have tended. She is unsure whether the couple should try to displace wilderness with ordered cultivation. Thus, she says:

> But till more hands
> Aid us, the work under our labour grows,
> Luxurious by restraint; what we by day
> Lop overgrown, or prune, or prop, or bind,
> One night or two with wanton growth derides
> Tending to wild. (9.207–12)

To establish the opposition of excessive growth and adequate restraint, Eve's language, bizarrely, starts sounding like the agitated tones of a pamphleteer. "Lop," "prune," and "bind" promise the safety of restraint; "luxurious,""wanton," "wild" suggest the dangers of transgression.[21] Eve's mistake, of course, is to assume that wasteful growth is valueless. In Milton's theology, value is based on virtuous worth, not seeming status. Waste and wilderness do not contaminate the geography of Eden, though Eve seems to intimate that such contamination might be possible— which is to say that she intimates the ambiguous relationship of waste to value. The landscape of Eden is constructed precisely upon the principle of miraculous abundance; it is an impossible terrain in which lavish growth can be kept from turning into waste.

Oversupply in Eden is the subject of grateful prayer, not lament, as Adam and Eve's daily thanksgiving reveals:

> This delicious place
> For us too large, where thy abundance wants
> Partakers, and uncropt falls to the ground.   (4.729–31)

The vastness, the uncultivated terrain of Eden, leads to a sense of delicious fullness, not fruitless emptiness. Unworked ground, which in political treatises amounts to wasteland, in Paradise supplies the dynamic, active landscape that animates the "happy garden state." Eve's language in the discussion about divided labor encourages the distinction between the rhetorical function of wilderness in enclosure polemic and its descriptive resonance in Eden, where it is benign, luxuriant, pleasing. If Eve's language does push her argument toward the claim that abundance might amount to a kind of degraded surplus, Adam quickly amends it. He "corrects" the association between wilderness and waste by breaking the link between excessive growth and wilderness, between expansiveness and waste:

> These paths and Bowers doubt not but our joynt hands
> Will keep from Wilderness with ease, as wide
> As we need walk, till younger hands ere long
> Assist us   (9.244–47)

Adam's defense of common labor, expressed in the phrase "joynt hands" and the image of paths exactly enough for two, "as wide / As we need walk," has the effect of eliminating wastefulness from the terms of argument and of allaying the anxiety, or fear of loss, which attends the image of waste.

Abundance on Earth is always, potentially, a source of waste, though in prelapsarian Eden, waste is always benign, never threatening. When Milton describes Eve's fertility, he does so through the metaphor of fruitfulness, a figurative choice that reminds the reader that fecund growth, like procreation, has within it the capacity for oversupply and degeneracy. This salutation is expressed through a hybrid imagery connected not only to Heaven and Paradise but also Sin and Death and to the dangerous fruit of knowledge:

> Hail mother of mankind, whose fruitful womb
> Shall fill the world more numerous with thy sons
> Than with these various fruits the trees of God
> Have heaped this table. (5.388–91)

Thus the passage binds corruption and decay into abundance and plenitude. The mother's "fruitful womb" takes the reader back to Sin's womb "excessive grown" and filled with "prodigious motion" in book 2. "Fruitful womb" not only alludes to the bounteous meal given Raphael in Eden but ties this, unexpectedly, to the fruit that Eve eats in book 9, contaminating the metaphor of fruitful abundance with Satanic excess—which is always associated with waste. The images here also gesture to the fruit trees in Eden, which

> overwoodie reach'd too farr
> Thir pamperd boughs, and needed hands to check
> Fruitless imbraces (5.213–15)

reminding the reader that excess in Eden is potentially threatening; the language of containment is framed in terms of physical restraint ("needed hands to check"). In Heaven, by contrast, containment is part of excess itself. "Bounds" is echoed in "bounteous" although they are not etymologically related; Milton implies that the nature of God's plenitude is such that control becomes linked to abundance, even though such a link isn't found elsewhere in the poem. Moreover, the language of supply and abundance in Heaven is not metaphorical—which is to say that descriptions of Heavenly excess move away from the domain of figurative language that might fold the possibility of decay into divine abundance.

Milton's descriptions of wasteland are made up of self-conscious paradoxes: excess that is not waste, labor that does not entirely reform wilderness, improvement that does not eliminate wasteland. In other words, he rejects the idea that waste is the proper term for matter that is without use or without commercial value. So what does make waste abject for Milton? When is wasteland not precious?

In the opening books of *Paradise Lost*, the representation of Satan as an imperial commander is complicated by the implication that he is, also, an occupier, and potentially also an improver, of a wild terrain of waste. When Satan is "hurl'd headlong flaming from th'Ethereal Skie," Milton characterizes the terrain of Hell as wasteland:

> At once as far as Angels kenn he views
> The dismal situation waste and wild   (1.59–60)

Milton describes a topography that we recognize from the descriptions of wasteland in enclosure polemic. Hell is the "dreary Plain, forlorn and wild," a "vast recess," a "desart soil," a "frozen Continent." When the fallen angels disband to explore Hell, the landscapes they find all around are indeed desolate wastes:

> Dark and wild, beat with perpetual storms
> Of Whirlwind and dire Hail, which on firm land
> Thaws not, but gathers heap, and ruin seems
> Of ancient pile   (2.588–91)

Like "vacant" common lands, or the empty wastes of Ireland, Hell seems empty although, paradoxically, it is filled with debris—an obstacle course of unwanted matter over which the despairing angels clamber. Satan aggressively occupies Hell in a rhetorically flamboyant rejection of the georgic and pastoral landscapes he knows in Heaven:

> Farewel happy Fields
> Where Joy forever dwells: Hail horrours, hail
> Infernal world, and thou profoundest Hell
> Receive thy new Possessor   (1.249–52)

The "happy fields" to which Satan bids farewell recall the fruitful fields and comfortable habitations promised in *Wasteland's Improvement*. Positioned thus, Milton raises at least the possibility, though it will never be fulfilled, that Satan might actually succeed in reforming the waste-land of Hell, turning it to a place of plenty. And indeed, Satan occupies this wasteland with the bravado of a politician: the brassily alliterative quality of his "farewell happy fields" and "hail horrors" sounds like the victorious chant of imperial triumph. But, as so often with Satanic utter-ance, declaration of success or triumph is uttered in the language of pro-found failure, indicating that Satan's rhetoric cannot improve the waste-land he has been consigned to. His resolution to occupy Hell is linked to his recognition of his own wasted intellect, his moral failure. In the four lines following Satan's declared possession of Hell, he half perceives that he is not an improver or cultivator, that he can create waste, but not recover it, for he views the landscape with

> A mind not to be chang'd by Place or Time.
> The mind is its own place, and in it self
> Can make a Heav'n of Hell, a Hell of Heav'n.
> What matter where, if I be still the same   (1.253–56)

And indeed, it turns out that the wasteland that Satan perceives is already (en)closed. He is in a prison without boundaries, for as far as he can see, he views

> A Dungeon horrible, on all sides round
> As one great Furnace flam'd yet from those flames
> No light, but rather darkness visible   (1.61–63)

When Milton describes the irrecuperable waste in Pandemonium, he an-ticipates the rib from which Eve is created. Pandemonium is built from the "ribs of gold" ransacked from the earth, but these ribs, waste from Hell, are incapable of being redeemed:

> soon had his crew
> Opened into the hill a spacious wound
> And digged out ribs of gold. Let none admire
> That riches grow in Hell; that soil may best
> Deserve the precious bane.   (1.688–92)

Satan tries to be like God, to make a wound and create life from waste,
but like the ransacker of a grave, he can only exhume death. The contrast Milton draws between Eve, created from Adam's rib, and Pandemonium, forged from infernal golden ribs, is based on the capacity of each to
change. Satan, disobedient to God, is unable to participate in the hierarchy of upward-tending motion toward God. As John Rumrich explains,
"the horror of Satan's lot . . . lies in the fact that those in hell cannot be
otherwise. . . . Despite his many changes, he remains fixed in his opposition to God's creation, its variety determining his ceaseless oscillations.
From an ironic perspective, it is therefore Satan who suffers the weight
of unalterable being, though mere contradiction defines his inescapable
fate. . . . All his changes, far from providing refuge from his burden, simply track his unending opposition to God's metamorphic creation."[22]

The binaries of wilderness and cultivation, chaos and order, plenty and
wasteland, upon which the enclosure pamphlets rely, do not work as such
for Milton, in spite of Satan's best efforts to prove the contrary. Although
Satan can occupy this wasteland, he cannot project its transformation
into "fruitful fields" or a happy garden. The topographic wilderness of
Hell cannot be cultivated; it is a waste that cannot be improved. When
Satan does "improve" the wasteland by building the city of Pandemonium, it serves further to emphasize the failure of his project.

Not only is Pandemonium built from a lavish abundance of stone
and precious metal, but the devils are themselves represented in terms
of abundance, a diabolical analogue to the massed angels in Heaven—or
the generations to whom Eve will give birth. The devils "pour forth . . .
In clusters" (1.770–71); "thick swarmed," they "throng numberless"
through the halls of Pandemonium, in direct parallel to the language of
plenitude characterizing Heaven. Raphael sets out toward Earth from
"among / Thousand celestial ardours" (5.548–49), heavenly fires that
are a counterpart to the infinite flaming furnaces in Hell. Abundance in
heaven is benign and glorious; its plenitude does not become threatening or dangerous, nor does it proliferate uncontrollably. In a wonderful
description, we learn that the angels

> Quaff immortality and joy, secure
> Of surfeit where full measure only bounds

Excess, before the all bounteous king, who showered
With copious hand, rejoicing in their joy   (5.639–41)

The metrical emphases in this passage equally balance abundance with
control. "Surfeit," "Excess," and "copious" have the opening stresses in
three consecutive lines, but it is the language of restraint, "secure" and
"bounds," that brings lines 639–40 to a close. "Measure" has the central
stress in line 640, but in the following line, "bounteous" occupies the
parallel metrical position. In line 641, "joy" is neatly contained by "rejoicing," tying the final line of the quatrain back to the first "immortality
and joy." Milton's poetic point makes his philosophical point, also: excess
in Heaven need not be forcibly restrained and does not dangerously proliferate. The careful balancing of security and plenitude in this passage reflects the angels' obedience to God. In the landscape of heaven, obedience
is recognized by the Father in his "shower[ing] with copious hand."

But even Heaven can become a wasteland. As Barbara Lewalski observes, "heaven is also a place of testing, and its paradisal landscape is also
vulnerable, requiring care."[23] Obedience, not force, prevents excess from
becoming unwanted. The rebel Angels confront the spectacle of "Mountains upward turn'd" (6.649), of "Promontories flung, which in the Air /
Came shadowing" (6.654–55), hills "Hurl'd to and fro with jaculation
dire" (6.665). Like the "regions dolorous" that the Angels dismally explore in Hell, Heaven seems disordered and chaotic, and at the same time
seems to constrain and imprison them. Thus, when the Angels attempt
to escape from under the fallen mountains:

Long struggling underneath, ere they could wind
Out of such prison, though Spirits of purest light,
Purest at first, now gross by sinning grown.   (6.659–61)

The description recalls Satan's first glimpse of Hell, a "Dungeon horrible," with "Adamantine Chains and penal Fire" (1.61; 48). The images
of Heaven during the war echo the imagery through which Satan perceives the wasteland of Hell—"dismal shade," "Infernal noise," "wrack,"
"ruin," "tumult"—as well as the descriptive terms of the pamphlets on
wasteland. Moreover, Milton fuses the language of infernal wasteland
with the imagery of Chaos: Heaven is in "uproar," "horrid confusion

heapt / Upon confusion" (6.668–69). The echoes imply that the Angels'
upturning of this landscape is of sufficient force to return even the heavenly kingdom to its uncreated state—to render it, once more, wasted
substance.

Milton's descriptions of Eden make it clear that a benevolent abundance of goods is conditional upon obedience; supply in Eden is figured
as a divine gift. Adam tells Eve to prepare for Raphael:

> And what thy stores contain, bring forth and pour
> Abundance, fit to honour and receive
> Our Heav'nly stranger; well we may afford
> Our givers their own gifts, and large bestow
> From large bestowed, where nature multiplies
> Her fertile growth, and by disburd'ning grows
> More fruitful, which instructs us not to spare.   (5.314–20)

The way Milton treats waste in *Paradise Lost* reminds us why it is precious in theological terms, why waste need not be different from glorious
surplus. Profusion, overgrowth, abundance that has no use—none of this
is degraded unless it is part of a disobedient landscape. And the con-
verse is true, too: glorious abundance is only as valuable as it is obedient.
In *Paradise Lost* we see that both waste and value are produced in acts
of creation, and that wasteful excess is as crucial a marker of a creative
presence as glorious abundance. Waste and value are distinguished from
one another by God; the Creator gives matter its status in the cosmic
hierarchy. However distasteful or strange the idea of obedient matter
might now seem as the mechanism by which value is distinguished from
abjection, the implications for literature are important. Abject matter is
as important as precious substance. Waste is a sign of creation.

III

Toward the end of *Wasteland's Improvement*, its author stumbles upon
what will be Milton's paradigmatic wasteland: Chaos. The polemicist
writes:

That which we have to offer to serious deliberation is, that those many and wild vacant wast-lands scatter'd up and down this Nation, be not suffered to lye longer (like a deformed Chaos) to our discredit and disprofit, but that some way be effectually thought upon for their best imployment and improvement.

Like the substance of Milton's Chaos, English wasteland in this passage is represented as unemployed and unimproved; the very phrase "wild vacant wast-lands" anticipates Milton's description of Satan's flight through the "wild expanse" of Chaos, with its "shock / Of fighting Elements" (2.1014–15). But Milton repudiates the kind of argument that the author of *Wasteland's Improvement* attempts to make; in the moral scheme of *Paradise Lost*, the "imployment" of Chaotic matter does not necessarily constitute its "improvement." It is vital to the significance of Milton's Chaos that it can be used both to create the beneficent plenitude of God's universe and for Satan's malevolent construction of a bridge between Earth and Hell. That is, unused, or wasted, substance can generate created matter that is either degraded or magnificent; use does not in itself constitute improvement, as the author of *Wasteland's Improvement* attempts to suggest.

When Belial describes God's absolute authority, he uses words more appropriate to Satan. Belial attempts to persuade the rebel angels that rebellion against the Father is futile, describing him perversely as their "Enemy":

> Yet our great Enemy
> All incorruptible would on his Throne
> Sit unpolluted, and th'Ethereal mould
> Incapable of stain would soon expel
> Her mischief, and purge off the baser fire
> Victorious.   (2.137–42)

From his morally degraded perspective in Hell, Belial can only perceive divine bounteousness as an inversion of contaminated surplus. God's difference from Satan is articulated by Belial as a negative contamination; rather than describing God as pure, Belial sees him as not impure. While Milton certainly admits the existence of waste matter in the universe, therefore, its relationship to valuable abundance is very carefully delineated. He is fascinated, nonetheless, with problems of similitude: the proximity of waste to wilderness, as well as parallels between Satanic and divine creation or between infernal excess and divine bounty. And as we have seen, he reproduces imagery from polemics on waste, alluding to secular arguments from the period in which the excess associated with waste was made exchangeable with the plenitude of value. But it is exactly this secular account of matter, with its assumption that language itself has a transforming effect on the nature of surplus, which Milton rejects.[24] The status of waste matter in *Paradise Lost* underscores two of the most important aspects of Milton's theology. The first is that while the material and the spiritual worlds of his poem may appear distinct or separable, they are related: "spirit and matter become for Milton two modes of the same substance: spirit is rarified matter, and matter is dense spirit."[25] The animation of the physical world is not, as Hobbes would have it, a merely mechanistic phenomenon (both deterministic and, potentially, atheistic) but rather an effect of animation, included in Milton's platonic model of a "metabolic" ascension from base matter to pure substance.

Seemingly an eccentric byway in Milton's philosophy, the idea of metabolism turns out to show us a great deal about why waste is so resonant in literary texts. Milton's theology figures material change as graduated movement, a metabolic shift from substance to spirit. Matter cannot change instantly from one to the other. Milton's distinctions between kinds of matter are based in moral discriminations that belong to the world of people and angels: "the ascent of good creatures is modeled on metabolic sublimation, and the descent of the evil on excretion and expulsion."[26] In his treatment of bodily waste, therefore, Milton's language emphasizes the alliance of the moral and the material. Raphael's speech on the digestive system of Angels sets out Milton's position:

> To whom the Angel. Therefore what he gives
> (Whose praise be ever sung) to man in part
> Spiritual, may of purest Spirits be found
> No ingrateful food: and food alike those pure
> Intelligential substances require
> As doth your Rational; and both contain
> Within them every lower facultie

Of sense, whereby they hear, see, smell, touch, taste,
Tasting concoct, digest, assimilate,
And corporeal to incorporeal turn.   (5.404–13)

The uninterrupted procession from base matter (food) to incorporeal substance in this passage depends on a set of syntactical devices that render
the physical transitions virtually invisible. The echo of "spirit" in "spiritual" and of "corporeal" in "incorporeal" and the repetition of "food"
give the impression of a transition from gross to pure substance that is
graduated like a musical scale. Change is represented incrementally and
almost imperceptibly, so that the transition from "taste" to "assimilate"
occurs through a sequence of words that seem almost synonymous. The
sophistication of Milton's poetics reveals the immense sophistication of
the process he describes, the affinity between the Angels' literal capacity
for digestion and their moral commitment to obedience. Digestion here
seems marvelous, like alchemy, and yet each metabolic stage is specifically
detailed—there is no magical transformation involved. In *Paradise Lost*,
therefore, the expulsion of waste is always ethical in character: "Milton
finds the process of digestion to exemplify the principles of material
transformation that animate his hierarchical yet meritocratic and monist
universe."[27]

Although I have said that Milton rejects the idea of sudden, miraculous transformations from waste to value, or, conversely, from benign
plenitude to wasteful excess, there are of course some critical moments
in the poem when metamorphoses of this kind do take place, such as
in God's creation of the world from Chaos ("more swift / Than time
or motion" [7.176–77]), or the war in Heaven. Crucially, on the three
occasions in the poem when radical transformation does take place, it
involves God's direct agency or intervention; God alone is capable of
converting wasteful excess to divine abundance. Milton's metaphors for
radical change are the metaphors of waste matter, created and eliminated. When Adam is expelled from Paradise, losing the two great gifts of
happiness and immortality, he is "purged" by the laws of nature, guided
by the Father:

But longer in that Paradise to dwell,
The Law I gave to Nature him forbids:

Those pure immortal Elements that know
No gross, no unharmonious mixture foul,
Eject him tainted now, and purge him off
As a distemper, gross to air as gross,
And mortal food, as may dispose him best
For Dissolution wrought by Sin, that first
Distempered all things, and of incorrupt
Corrupted.   (11.48–57)

The language of moral judgment is fused with the vocabulary of mechanical separation: Nature "forbids" Adam and Eve to remain in Paradise and "ejects" them as "tainted." Dissolution and Distemper, alchemical processes, are wrought by sin. The chiastic phrase "of incorrupt corrupted" manages a shifting between the symbolic notion of moral corruption and the physical notion of corrupted, of wasted, substance, rendering these two phenomena equivalent.

Alexander Pope, a professional writer living in the new environment of London's fledgling publishing trade, continued to be vexed by the same issues of the relationship between waste and value that plagued Milton. He lived among the dross and detritus of London's hack presses, and yet he watched as that same intellectual effluvia became the bestselling literature of his day. What he regarded as degraded leftovers, everybody else seemed to be hailing as precious spoil. In response to this—in response to the same perplexity that troubled Eve in prelapsarian Eden—Pope created the chaotic, degraded landscapes of the *Dunciad*, diabolically reworking the wastelands of *Paradise Lost* as a way of understanding the secular setting of the eighteenth-century book trade.

3

Milton's Chaos in Pope's London

MATERIAL PHILOSOPHY AND

THE BOOK TRADE

THIS chapter is about an instance of literary and philosophical nostalgia. Pope, writing in the secular, commercial environment of eighteenth-century London (the final *Dunciad* was published in 1743), looks back to the landscapes of *Paradise Lost*, the great theological epic of the previous century. He chooses as the setting of his mock epic one of the most complex locations in Milton's poem: Chaos, the landscape through which Satan struggles in his ascent to earth, and the matter from which Milton's God makes the world. Milton's Chaos is a material surfeit that can be turned into an abundance of life, seeming waste that God can transform into miraculous plenitude. Chaos is characterized both by surplus and void; it is where proliferating matter feels hollow and empty. It is perhaps the landscape in *Paradise Lost* most crucial to our understanding of Milton's material philosophy, his unorthodox concept of the nature of substance introduced in the last chapter. In modeling the *Dunciad* on the Miltonic antecedent in Chaos, Pope turns firmly back toward a set of seventeenth-century questions about the origins of the material world and the status of originary matter. He does so to attack his rivals in the seemingly indomitable world of the commercial book trade; Pope's reworking of Milton's Chaos explores the secular phenomenon of the making of books through a theological account of the making of the universe.

But recognizing the Miltonic influence in Pope begs a new question: why should Milton's material philosophy be more valuable to Pope than the prevailing ideas of his own day: post-Newtonian explanations of matter, motion, and waste?

Pope is explicit about the place of Milton's poem in his own. Pope's Grub Street, the habitat of London's hack writers and printers, is a place of confusion and decay, from which the Dunces' scribblings will emerge. It is "a Chaos dark and deep, / Where nameless somethings in their causes sleep" (1.55–56). At the end of Pope's poem Dulness presides over the rising of "Chaos, and of Night, / To blot out order, and extinguish light" (4.13–14), and in the final ringing quatrain, Pope's speaking persona cries triumphantly, "Lo! Thy dread empire, Chaos! is restored" (4.653). The "cave of poetry" from which Dulness views the Chaos surrounding her is waste and vacant: "Keen, hollow winds howl through the bleak recess, / Emblem of music caused by emptiness" (1.35–36). The Chaos of *Paradise Lost* is a "wasteful Deep" of "warring winds," filled with the noise of "endless warrs" and confusion (2.891ff.). Like Milton's Chaos, Pope's is guarded by four "fierce Champions" (for Milton, hot, cold, moist, and dry; for Pope, fortitude, temperance, prudence, and poetic justice). And, like Milton's, Pope's Chaos is the original site of creation. In *Paradise Lost* the Holy Spirit calms the wilds of Chaos so that they generate the created world; in the *Dunciad*, Dulness presides over Chaos until it spawns the clumsily written poems, pamphlets, and plays that fill Pope's version of Grub Street.

Pope's story is of the Goddess Dulness's imperial triumph over London's intellectual culture. Ostensibly, he offers a counterhistory to Milton's creation narrative; Pope's London is "uncreated" through the restoration of Chaos.[1] Pope's Dunce-King, Colley Cibber, is described as the "antichrist of Wit" (2.16), reminding us that he is to be compared with Milton's Satan, who travels through the wilds of Chaos in his treacherous passage toward Eden. The Dunces' attempt to invade and occupy London's literary environment plays out as a struggle for territory, similar to Satan's attempt on Heaven, his eventual occupation of Hell, and his conquest of Eden in *Paradise Lost*. Dulness turns the conquered London into a Miltonic Chaos, rendered by Pope as the site of wasted texts and failed imaginative exertions.[2] The *Dunciad*, confused, filthy, excremental, and excessive, is one of the most famous secular icons of eighteenth-century writing. Yet paradoxically, the only poem from its period to deal in full with the powerful commercial phenomenon of the publishing industry declares an unlikely interest in theological arguments about the nature of remaindered matter.

Milton's philosophy of matter is unorthodox, reflecting a radical departure from arguments about the nature of creation and the relationship of mind to matter that prevailed in English philosophy and theology during the period in which he was writing.[3] Milton adopts a radical monist account of substance, arguing that the matter of Chaos is dispersed from God and propagated and extended infinitely to form the originary matter of Creation.[4] As John Rumrich explains, "Anarch Chaos and his Consort Night represent the material dimension of God's own being."[5] He rejects the notion that matter is dead, or inanimate, and instead attributes the property of being or essence to substance: he gives it life.[6] Stephen Fallon has observed that "in Milton's universe, everything is both material and alive: angels are not incorporeal, and what we think of as inanimate matter is animate."[7] Milton's "animist materialism" (as it is known in the scholarship) aligns him with the vitalist movement in the seventeenth century, which held "in its tamest manifestation the inseparability of body and soul and, in its boldest, the infusion of all material substance with the power of reason and self-motion."[8]

All of this seems a far cry from the drama of the fall in *Paradise Lost* and even further from the drama of literary and cultural fallenness in the *Dunciad*. Why was material philosophy of such pressing political significance for Milton? Like other well-known figures of the vitalist movement, such as Harvey (who established that blood circulated through the heart), Margaret Cavendish, Gerard Winstanley, and Andrew Marvell, Milton was attracted to a monist philosophy of animate matter because it meant he could refuse the mechanist arguments adopted by Descartes and followed by Hobbes, who declared that "there can be no cause of motion, except by a body contiguous and moved."[9] The problem with Hobbes's position was its assertion that action was initiated by an external, determining force, and this in turn justified the authoritarian, monarchical model of government described in *Leviathan*.[10] Milton's reasons for resisting Hobbesian mechanism are not hard to fathom; the vitalist position that action was initiated by the individual, and the monist belief that the individual was an indivisible entity or being enabled Milton to assert the individual's capacity for free will and doctrinal obligation to exercise freedom of choice. It justified his rejection of authoritarian government, since, unlike Hobbes, he believed that action was willed rather than determined. It is in relation to Milton's antimechanistic philosophy that Stephen Fallon comments, "Milton's insistence on freedom also helps to account for what many have seen as an anomaly in *Paradise Lost*: the idiosyncratic, animist materialist universe in which the epic action is set." [11] Vitalist metaphors of the individual and a model of action free from determining authority were adopted by seventeenth-century advocates of individual free will: Harrington in his *Commonwealth of Oceana* (1656), the Cambridge Platonists Ralph Cudworth and Henry More, and the Leveller Richard Overton.[12] The largest significance of animate matter in Milton is that it offers an account of what change means. Milton's universe is capable of limitless dynamism and animation, and it is a model of animation that cannot be manipulated arbitrarily. In John Rumrich's eloquent account:

> Where Platonists tend to see reality as perfectly constant, and change as belonging to the shadowy world of appearance, Milton, like Aristotle, saw change as the mode of reality's progress from chaos to perfection. Milton stressed potency and act, not appearance and reality. The nature of creation is such that creatures *must* change in order to become what God wants. Consequently, in order to attain the final glory of apocalyptic communion, creatures must recognize God and his will; they must desire what he desires, as fully as possible.[13]

In the long theological treatise that forms the basis of our understanding of Milton's philosophy and theology, *De Doctrina Christiana*, Milton argues that matter we would conventionally think of as being devoid of life is animated by the same divine force as that which animates mankind.[14] In the section of *De Doctrina Christiana* that deals with creation, he suggests that matter and being are "mixed" inextricably: life, which is characterized by animation and movement, is suffused into substance, endowing matter with the capacity for self-generated movement that mechanists would refuse: "God breathed the breath of life into other living things besides man, and when he had breathed it, he mixed it with matter in a very fundamental way, so that the human form, like all other forms, should be propagated and produced as a result of that power which God had implanted in matter."[15] Milton's claim that matter can be self-generative, that Chaos can ferment Creation, reminds us that in the seventeenth century his philosophy was regarded as unorthodox, and that he subscribed to some of the most incendiary positions of the period.[16] These are the ideas that Pope decides to reconstruct in his secular poem dealing with the commercial activities of the publishing industry. Yet Pope's Catholicism, Toryism, and support for the Stuart succession represented an inversion of Milton's radical politics and religion. So what significance would a controversy that had raged nearly a century earlier over the nature of matter have for a mock-epic about tiresome writing and the "dunces" who produced it? As far as Milton was concerned, moral degradation rendered matter waste. The value of a substance, in the Miltonic theology, depends on its moral nature, not the uses to which it can be put. Rumrich explains Milton's account of material change in this way: "through a moral and natural process of refinement, creatures can voluntarily reunite with God. Recognition and desire—proceeding from reason and will—are the dynamic agents of creaturely glory in *Paradise Lost*. They bring about the substantial metamorphoses that are at once morally just and naturally fitting."[17] Milton gave Pope a political philosophy that he could turn mockingly against the books that Whig rivals produced.

By the time he published *Paradise Lost* the monarchy had been restored, and in that context Milton's animist materialism was essentially a covert confession of his unquenched republicanism and radical religion.[18] As Barbara Lewalski writes, Milton encourages readers of *Paradise Lost* "to think again, and think rightly, about the ideological and polemic controversies of the recent war and its aftermath—about monarchy and tyranny, religious and civil liberty, and revolution."[19] It is the heretical resonance of Milton's philosophy that attracts Pope. He is not (of course) confessing to latent republicanism but asserting a parallel with Milton in his own commitment to unfashionable, even dangerous politics and his rejection of the political culture that dominated London's literary market-place under the sway of the Whigs. Here is Pope's limitless capacity for provocation: he adopts a material philosophy radically at odds with his own political sympathies—that of a writer whom the Whigs would claim as one of "their own."[20] And he reproduces this politically progessive, anti-authoritarian doctrine precisely in order to explain the terms on which he rejects the progressive, antiauthoritarian culture of the eighteenth-century book trade.

But Pope is not merely casting about for another clever device to bolster his attack on Grub Street. He also deliberately turns away from writings on matter and motion that dominated early eighteenth-century science (accounts that he shows himself elsewhere to be familiar with, and in many ways captivated by) to take up an account of substance that is of primarily theological rather than scientific interest. The shift flags the fact that there was something about the post-Newtonian view of substance that disquieted Pope when he was creating an intellectual framework for the *Dunciad*. What had eighteenth-century science done to matter that Pope didn't like?

The answer is summed up in an account given by Alexandre Koyre in the mid-twentieth century. Koyre claims that the birth of modern science (rung in by the publication of Newton's *Principia*) is signaled by a fundamental shift in outlook, which he characterizes as the "death of the cosmos." He writes:

> The . . . world of science, the real world, is no more seen, or conceived, as a finite and hierarchically ordered, therefore qualitatively and ontologically differentiated whole, but as an open, indefinite, and even infinite universe, united not by its immanent structure but only by the identity of its fundamental contents and laws; a universe in which, in contradistinction to the traditional conception with its separation and opposition of the two worlds of becoming and being, that is, of the heavens and the earth, all its components appear as placed on the same ontological level. . . .
>
> This, in turn, implies the disappearance—or the violent expulsion—from scientific thought of all considerations based on value, perfection, harmony, meaning, and aim, because these concepts,

from now on *merely subjective*, cannot have a place in the new ontology. Or, to put it in different words: all formal and final causes as modes of explanation disappear from—or are rejected by—the new science and are replaced by efficient and even material ones.[21]

The key idea in this powerful and evocative description is that the real world is no longer to be seen as "qualitatively and ontologically differentiated." The problem with the new science for Pope is that it seeks to make all matter ontologically equal, or at least equivalent; it deprives the material world of the value-based hierarchy Milton had given it. As post-Newtonian science sought to explain the weird phenomenon of attraction that draws matter, motion, and space into a unified whole, the idea that substances are characterized by their worth or value drops away, as does the notion that value itself renders substances ontologically distinct. This is not to suggest that religion is absent from eighteenth-century science. It is well known that the opposite is the case; Newtonian science is "based on a dynamic conception of physical causality and was linked together with theistic or deistic metaphysics."[22] But the vital difference between science and theology in the eighteenth century was that final causation is not "a constitutive or integrating part of the Newtonian science; it does not penetrate into its formal structure."[23] And yet qualitative distinctions between seemingly identical material entities, excluded from scientific inquiry, were exactly what most interested Pope when he wrote the *Dunciad*. So he turned back to Milton's material philosophy, with its explicit attention to the inherent value of substance.

The *Dunciad* is a satire on London's publishing industry. The action of the poem follows the Dunces' progress through a day of mock-ceremonial games in honor of the Goddess Dulness, who presides over Grub Street and its hack writers. At the end of the poem, Dulness triumphs over the world of literary and intellectual enlightenment, vanquishing learning, taste, and good writing. The poem is filled with tedious writers and their second-rate manuscripts, with the literal filth of London's streets and the intellectual and cultural dross of its literary world. Commentators on the *Dunciad* often remark on Pope's genius for animating the inanimate; for imbuing an apparently lifeless world of objects with energy. One of the most famous sequences in the poem is Pope's description of the emergence of "creation" from Chaos, in which metaphor and meter spring to life under the Dunces' inept guidance. Pope's experiments in animation are in fact exquisitely derivative, for his devices in this passage are taken directly from Milton:

> Here [Dulness] beholds the chaos dark and deep,
> Where nameless somethings in their causes sleep,
> Till genial Jacob, or a warm third day,
> Call forth each mass, a poem or a play:
> How hints, like spawn, scarce quick in embryo lie,
> How new-born nonsense first is taught to cry,
> Maggots half-formed in rhyme exactly meet,
> And learn to crawl upon poetic feet.
> Here one poor word an hundred clenches makes,
> And ductile dulness new meanders takes.   (1.55–64)

This section of the *Dunciad* might not immediately bring to mind Milton's description in *Paradise Lost* of the moment at which the animate substance forms itself into created matter, infused with "vital warmth" (7.236) and "satiate with genial moisture" (7.282) from the Spirit of God. But Pope's apparently inconsequential jokes about the bookseller Jacob Tonson and the conventions of the London playhouse—"Genial Jacob, or a warm third day"—in fact meticulously adopt the terms of Milton's Creation account, implying that even in the mock-landscape of the *Dunciad*, matter is animate and self-active as it is in *Paradise Lost*. The line "Here one poor word an hundred clenches makes," the "embrace" between tragedy and comedy, the procreation of farce and epic, at once pay homage to, and burlesque, the active, self-moving substance of *Paradise Lost*.[24] Think of the creation sequences of book 3 (708–13) and book 7 (232ff.), with the active shifting of matter into its formed state; the vivid animation communicated in Raphael's description to Adam of the "feeding habits" of matter in book 5 (414ff.); the active energies of Eden's landscapes, moving in a self-willed orisons (5.153ff.). And Pope's "madness of the mazy dance," the "jumbled race" begotten of farce and epic, and, later on, the "wild creation" and "momentary monsters" (1.82–83) resemble the aggressively clashing elements of Chaos in book 2 of *Paradise Lost*: "neither Sea, nor Shore, nor Air, nor Fire, / But all these in thir pregnant causes mixt / Confus'dly" (2.912–14).

When Pope satirizes the ludicrously improbable imagery and metaphorical language that emerges from Dulness's Chaotic empire, he knowingly reproduces the self-moving, self-forming matter of Milton's creation:

> How Time himself stands still at [Dulness's] command,
> Realms shift their place, and ocean turns to land.
> Here gay Description Egypt glads with show'rs,
> Or gives to Zembla fruits, to Barca flow'rs   (1.72–74)

Pope's shifting realms remind us of the radical geographic formations of book 7 of *Paradise Lost* ("over all the face of Earth / Main Ocean flow'd, not idle, but with warm / Prolific humour soft'ning all her Globe" [7.279–81]; "immediately the Mountains huge appear / Emergent and thir broad bare backs upheave / Into the Clouds" [7.285–87]). The personification of Description invites comparison with scenes such as the prayer sequence in book 5: "wave your tops, ye Pines, / With every Plant, in sign of Worship wave" (5.193–94). And we think again of one of Milton's most seductive descriptions in book 7:

> the bare Earth, till then
> Desert and bare, unsightly, unadorned,
> Brought forth the tender Grass, whose verdure clad
> Her Universal Face with pleasant green,
> Then Herbs of every leaf, that sudden flow'r'd
> Op'ning thir various colours   (7.313–18)

The Dunces' shoddy literary efforts spring spontaneously at Dulness's bidding with an extravagant inappropriateness that (Pope implies) is beyond the Dunces' control. But this lighthearted joke about the Dunces' inability to contain their imaginative confusion turns out to be a careful homage to Milton's argument that matter, endowed with the capacity for self-generation, moves from formlessness to form through its own animation:[25]

at [the Holy Spirit's] second bidding darkness fled,
Light shon, and order from disorder sprung:
Swift to thir several Quarters hasted then
The cumbrous Elements, Earth, Flood, Air, Fire,
And this Ethereal quintessence of Heav'n
Flew upward, spirited with various forms   (3.712–17)

Of more immediate relevance to the world of Pope's Grub Street than Milton's "ethereal quintessence of Heav'n" is Milton's waste matter, the base, unwanted substance to which Pope implicitly compares his colleagues' writing. In *De Doctrina Christiana*, Milton explains that it is possible for substance to be corrupted by the sway of a wrong-headed or evil consciousness that propels it away from its originally "good" state. The explanation is complex:

[T]o argue that there could have been no imperfection in a substance which God produced out of himself, is only to transfer the imperfection to God's efficiency. For why did he not, starting from nothing, make everything absolutely perfect straight away? But in fact matter was not, by nature, imperfect. . . . But really it is not the matter nor the form which sins. When matter or form has gone out from God and become the property of another, what is there to prevent its being infected and polluted, since it is now in a mutable state, by the calculations of the devil or of man, calculations which proceed from these creatures themselves?" (*CPW*, 6.308–9)

Milton's description of imperfect substance relies on his account of disobedient beings: substance, being animate and self-willed, can become corrupted of its own volition, even though the will to be disobedient is not conscious as it is in beings such as humans and angels.[26] It's an eccentric account of good and evil, but the critical point is that matter itself, active, animate, autonomous, is not merely acted upon by an external, determining force or consciousness. For Milton, the hierarchy of matter participates in the hierarchy of animate beings (such as people and angels), and substance, simultaneously corporeal and spiritual, ascends and descends a material hierarchy according to its merit. We think not only of the wild confusion of tragedy and epic in the *Dunciad* but of the Dunces themselves, who fling themselves gleefully into the Fleet Ditch in a burlesque of Milton's rebel angels and "tartareous dregs." Through the imagery of *Paradise Lost*, the *Dunciad* calls attention to its own interest in unwanted surplus and to its preoccupation with the distinction between waste and profitable abundance in the print market of Grub Street. The warring elements of Chaos and tartareous dregs of *Paradise Lost* become the glut of published material that circulated among London's private booksellers and in private collections. It is overproduced and excessive, a plague of surplus objects: "show'rs of sermons, characters, essays / In circling fleeces whiten all the ways: / So clouds, replenished from some bog below, / Mount in dark volumes, and descend in snow" (2.359–61).

In *Paradise Lost* Chaos is the site not only of desolate confusion but of ordering; the imagery of Chaos is in vital exchange with the vocabulary of Creation, as Milton's description of the first days suggests:

I saw when at his Word the formless Mass,
This worlds material mould, came to a heap:
Confusion heard his voice, and wild uproar
Stood rul'd, stood vast infinitude confin'd.   (3.708–11)

Milton is describing the theological paradox of wasted, confused matter that can be converted into created life. The matter of Chaos *is* the matter of Creation; it is extruded from God, but it is transformed by divine agency from wasteful surplus to benign plenitude. The paradox of matter in Milton's poem is that the waste in Chaos forms the vast abundance of Paradise. Milton expresses this seeming contradiction through the word "vast," which has been recuperated and transformed from its etymological counterpart in "waste." So Milton's phrase "vast infinitude confin'd" conveys the miraculous achievement of Creation, for the language of wasteland is literally reconfigured to make the language of abundance. When "formless Mass," "Confusion," "wild uproar" are confined by God, overproduced matter comes to signify miraculous "infinitude," and the void of waste is changed by the exhilarating possibilities of "vastness." Whenever Milton uses the word "vast" in *Paradise Lost*, he is negotiating exactly the problem that vexes Pope: the sense that it is difficult to distinguish the void of waste from the plenitude of "vastness," since both seem unbounded and characterized by superfluity. Thus when Satan describes the toil with which he has "Voyag'd th'unreal, vast, unbounded deep / Of horrible confusion" (10.471–72), "vast" is a surrogate word for "waste." But when the Spirit of God broods on the "vast Abyss," or creates Earth "vast and round, a place of bliss" (2.832), "vast" recuperates and effaces the implied void or debasement of surplus matter. The same oscillation between the meaninglessness of waste and the imaginative possibilities of vastness shapes the *Dunciad* through Pope's reworking of Milton's Chaos.[27]

In *Paradise Lost*, Chaos is the place where a surfeit of uncreated matter comes into contact with God's creative bounty and Satan's rebellious excesses. But Milton draws clear distinctions between these encounters. God is able to create from Chaotic matter:

> But on the watrie calm
> His brooding wings the Spirit of God outspread,
> And vital vertue infus'd, and vital warmth
> Throughout the fluid Mass   (7.234–37)

The essential act of Creation is to render base substance animated, to invest in it those qualities of action, animation, and freedom peculiar to Milton's account of matter. The Spirit's "brooding wings . . . outspread" reveal that creation is simultaneously a physical and an intellectual phenomenon—in other words, there is an invited parallel with the mechanical and mental processes of secular creative work. Satan is able only to struggle through Chaos, sinking and clambering up toward earth. In Satan's encounters, the terrain is almost unrecognizable as the substance "infus'd" with "vital virtue" by the Son:

>   So eagerly the fiend
> O'er bog or steep, through strait, rough, dense, or rare,
> With head, hands, wings, or feet pursues his way,
> And swims or sinks, or wades or creeps, or flies:
> At length a universal hubbub wild

Of stunning sounds and voices all confus'd
Borne through the hollow dark assaults his ear   (2.947–53)

Here, the calm brooding of God's spirit is reconfigured in the eager-
ness with which Satan attempts to extricate himself from Chaotic matter. Unable to infuse the "fluid Mass" of uncreated substance with "vital
warmth," Satan is indeed confused about the nature of Chaotic substance
itself; he cannot tell whether he is in a fluid, in air, or on land. Thus he
"swims or sinks, or wades or creeps, or flies." These radically different
encounters with Chaos show how Milton makes use of the essentially
negotiable status of waste: at the moment of Creation, Chaos turns into
the abundant, copious plenitude of life, but Satan perceives a Chaos that
weighs on him with the dense pressure of unsupported matter. He is
hardly able to keep moving through the weight of Chaotic matter; the
Son is able to balance and control it exquisitely.

Only once Satan is at the very outskirts of Chaos can he feel the calm
of air that is not weighed down by the pressure of too-abundant matter:

Satan with less toil, and now with ease
Wafts on the calmer wave by dubious light
And like a weather-beaten Vessel holds
Gladly the Port, though Shrouds and Tackle torn;
Or, in the emptier waste, resembling Air,
Weighs his spread wings.   (2.1041–44)

Only now that he is beyond Chaos can Satan resemble God, who earlier:
"on the watrie calm / His brooding wings . . . outspread."

Milton's account of divine creation and the transformation from surfeit into plenitude gives Pope a set of terms for describing the work of
writing in a commercial print culture. Pope recognizes that the commercial value of a text does not necessarily correspond to the aesthetic
value that he would want to assign it—hence his nervous acknowledg-
ment that sometimes texts written by Dunces will turn into best-sellers.
It is this recognition that gives Milton's monist philosophy a compelling
significance in the *Dunciad*, for by refusing the distinction between the
substantial and the essential qualities of an object, Pope (with Milton)

insists that matter is arranged in a hierarchy that cannot be manipulated arbitrarily by the determining authority of an external force.

The final lines of the *Dunciad* repeat but reverse the Creation scene from *Paradise Lost*:

> Lo! thy dread empire, Chaos! is restored;
> Light dies before thy uncreating word;
> Thy hand, great Anarch! lets the curtain fall,
> And universal darkness buries all.   (4.653–56)

The "restoring" of Chaos takes us back to the "ruling" of "vast infinitude" in *Paradise Lost*; Dulness's "dread empire" is both a vast and a bounded space. We learn, also, that like the created universe in *Paradise Lost*, the empire of Chaos is infinite, since universal darkness buries *all*. The triumph of un-creation, then, like creation itself, is marked by the proliferation of excess. But in the figure of a falling curtain—"Thy hand, great Anarch! lets the curtain fall"—we recognize the nature of this new "empire" that is engulfed by Chaos even as it contains it. We are in the empire of the theater: the setting of Pope's apocalypse is the proscenium arch under which the Dunces produce their turgid dramas.[28] We realize, suddenly, that the "restoration" alluded to at line 653 is the Restoration of the Stuarts, and the licensing of unbounded, excessive, trivial literary production associated with the Restoration stage. The "dying light" of line 654 is the light of the theater, snuffed at the end of a performance; the "uncreating word" secularizes the Word of God in *Paradise Lost*, turning a Christian creation narrative into a commercialized narrative about a failed literary production.

In the *Dunciad*, Cibber's attempts at poetic composition are figured as a version of Satan's flight through Chaos. But Pope intricately merges the language of Satan's flight with images of God creating, emphasizing the proximity of divine creation to infernal waste in Milton's Chaos:

> Then [Cibber] gnawed his pen, then dashed it on the ground,
> Sinking from thought to thought, a vast profound!
> Plunged for his sense, but found no bottom there,
> Yet wrote and floundered on, in mere despair.
> Round him much embryo, much abortion lay,

Much future ode, and abdicated play;
Nonsense precipitate, like running lead,
That slipped though cracks and zigzags of the head   (1.118–24)

The language of this passage is almost all taken from *Paradise Lost*: Cibber's "sinking," "plunging," and "floundering" reminds us both of Satan's flight from Hell through Chaos and his expulsion into the Abyss from Heaven. The episode in fact correlates very closely with Satan's launch into Chaos, when, after an initial rise on the currents of matter, Satan "meets / A vast vacuity: all unawares / Flutt'ring his pennons vain plumb-down he drops / Ten thousand fathom deep" (2.931–34). As the implied oscillation between "vast" and "waste" reveals, the essential feature of Chaos is its composition from negotiable, or unfixed, matter. The phrase "vast profound" echoes Milton's "vast infinitude" (referring to the Spirit's brooding over Creation), but because it is blanketed by sinking and plunging, the word "vast" reads in Pope's text as a substitute for "waste." The phrase alludes explicitly to the moment in *Paradise Lost* when the Son as God's agent creates the "just circumference" of the World: "One foot he center'd, and the other turn'd / Round through the vast profunditie obscure" (7.228–29). Profundity has a positive valence in Milton's passage precisely because it is being bounded (and therefore seems profound in its intensity, rather than for its empty depth), whereas Cibber sinks without hope of recovery ("found no bottom there"); the profundity of Cibber's thought is merely a void. In its history of the word "dunce," the *OED* cites Thomas Fuller, who in 1642 described the dunce as "void of learning, but full of books"—precisely the oscillation between emptiness and surplus that characterizes descriptions of Milton's Chaos.

Cibber's inability to transform base matter into created life is revealed in the discovery that "round him much embryo, much abortion lay" (1.21). The image is linked very directly to Milton's triangulation of surplus, Chaos, and Creation, since it inverts the description from the opening invocation to the Father in *Paradise Lost*:

> Thou from the first
> Wast present, and with mighty wings outspread
> Dove-like sat'st brooding on the vast Abyss
> And Mad'st it pregnant   (1.20–22)

In Milton's proem, "brooding" takes us forward to the "brooding wings" of the creation scene in book 7, but also reminds us that embedded in the grand opening lines of *Paradise Lost* is Milton's confession that he, too, broods over his own imaginative work. The echo reveals Pope's connection between creation and imagination in the *Dunciad*: as Cibber produces embryo and abortion, Pope himself spreads his brooding wings over the Chaos of London, in emulation of Milton. But Milton's words "brooding" and "pregnant" open up the precise terms of the relationship of creation to matter in these poems.

The Godhead in Milton's poem does not merely form confused matter into Earth, Heaven, and Hell in a mechanical reconfiguration; he actively endows substance with autonomous life. In making the Abyss pregnant, God renders matter "animate, self-active and free." Moreover, God's creation of the earth is described in explicitly procreative terms: "The Earth was form'd, but in the Womb as yet / Of waters, Embryon immature involv'd, / Appear'd not" (7.276–77). Unlike Cibber's productions, the embryo Earth is destined to grow to its full term, nourished with "genial moisture" by the primordial Ocean (7.281–82). Cibber's creative pregnancies either miscarry in "embryo" or are terminated in "abortion" (and the "genial moisture" of Milton's creation is ironically rendered in the *Dunciad* in the figure of "genial Jacob," as we saw). By contrast, the matter Cibber produces is base and inanimate, "nonsense precipitate, like running lead / That slipped through cracks and zigzags of the head" (1.123–24).

Cibber's creative work is teeming and copious, but capable only of generating waste and formlessness, never plenitude or pleasurable abundance.[29]

As we have seen, the eighteenth-century scientific context appeared to resist the kind of argument that Pope wanted to make in the *Dunciad* by reference to Milton. In the years after Newton's death, waste itself, known variously in scientific literature as decomposition or putrefaction, was regarded merely as a necessary stage in the reconstitution and revitalization of all matter. In 1674, Newton had written that "nothing can be changed from what it is without putrefaction"; that "nothing can be generated or nourished (but of putrefied matter)," and that "[Nature's] first action is to blind and confound mixtures into a putrefied chaos. Then they are fitted for new generation or nourishment."[30] For the generation of scientists who came after Newton, decay was a scientific event; it no longer raised the theologically troubling specter of valueless or "bad" matter. Betty Jo Teeter Dobbs, a scholar of Newton's alchemical writings, observes that, for Newton, "it is putrefaction that reduces matter to its ultimate state of disorganization, where the particles of matter are all alike and hence can be remodeled in any form whatsoever."[31] The link that Dobbs is making in this remark is that the decomposition of matter into like particles makes possible not only the Newtonian universe itself but also Newton's seemingly unscientific belief in alchemy. Radical, quasi-miraculous transformation of the kind that alchemy imagines possible is enabled, paradoxically, by the scientific discovery that putrefaction is necessary to maintain generative momentum in a clockwork universe. Pope turns so decisively away from contemporary scientific knowledge to Milton's vitalist materialism because he is resistant to this lingering image of miraculous, alchemical change.

In what sense did the idea of radical material alteration or transformation pervade the early eighteenth-century imagination? By the time Pope was writing the *Dunciad*, the English Revolution, the cultural paradigm that had shaped Milton's intellectual and imaginative work, had been displaced by a different historical paradigm through which to ponder the nature of matter. The new obsession was just as powerful; it divided the country politically and appeared to threaten the economic future of Britain. The English Revolution had been supplanted by the disaster of the South Sea Bubble.

The Bubble burst in 1720, causing a massive downturn in England's economy. It created the greatest public sensation of the century, and its lessons were never to be forgotten. As is well known, the South Sea Bubble was a Whig venture in public finance, in which stocks in the South Sea Trading Company were sold to the public, enormously overvalued. The Company proposed in 1720 to take over the national debt, and the proposal, backed by Walpole's ministers, attracted a mania of speculative investment as the South Sea stocks became increasingly inflated. The English public watched the venture collapse and their investment

disappear, leaving a devastated stock market in London. Endless satires
on the disaster were printed, pointing out that the Whiggish directors
of the South Sea Company had fraudulently claimed to be able to turn
nothing into something, tricking the public with delusional schemes of
impossible economic growth.

The image common to all South Sea satires was that of a magical (and
fraudulent) metamorphosis from an object that was worthless into something of immense value. Pope described it through the image of a greedy
company director who idiotically "thinks a loaf will rise to fifty pound."[32]
Swift opened his poem on the South Sea affair with a bitter attack on the
trickery of the stock market, with its false promise to turn one sum magically into a much larger one:

> Ye wise Philosophers explain
> What Magick makes our Money rise
> When dropt into the Southern Main,
> Or do these Juglers cheat our Eyes?
> Put in Your Money fairly told;
> Presto be gone—Tis here ag'en,
> Ladyes, and Gentlemen, behold,
> Here's ev'ry Piece as big as ten.[33]

The political struggle of the seventeenth century that compelled Milton's
interest in animist materialism had been replaced by the more pressing
preoccupation of the stock market. The Whig economy of the first half
of the eighteenth century depended upon the financial systems that had
been created by the advent of national debt and pubic credit. Catherine
Ingrassia writes: "with new financial institutions, the types of negotiable
paper available proliferated: lottery tickets, stocks, bills of exchange, and
letters of credit were among the numerous forms of 'credit'-able paper
in circulation."[34] At the center of political debate in the early eighteenth
century was the question of whether the system of credit on which the
English economy depended was viable. As a result of the new economy, the nature of value was newly understood as volatile, exchangeable, and negotiable. By implication, so was its relationship to material
objects.

Credit presented a new way of imagining substance: exchangeable and subject to the fluctuations of the marketplace. Could things, and in particular money, be inflated or deflated, multiplied or effaced through the "virtual" manipulations of a finance economy? Credit was explained by its advocates and detractors alike as a system of finance that could turn sums written on pieces of paper into heaps of real gold. In Pope's words:

A leaf, like Sibyl's, scatter to and fro
Our fates and fortunes, as the winds shall blow:
Pregnant with thousands flits the scrap unseen,
And silent sells a king, or buys a queen.[35]

Credit offered a strange new account of physical substance as something that could be changed, suddenly and seemingly effortlessly. But skeptics like Swift and Pope (we shall see what Swift had to say about this in the next chapter) would point out that credit relied upon a quasi-alchemical claim that it could turn ordinary guineas into far more valuable units of currency:

So cast it in the Southern Seas,
And view it through a Jobber's Bill,
Put on what Spectacles You please,
Your Guinnea's but a Guinnea still.[36]

Pope and Swift found the image of Credit threatening because it could seemingly make surplus out of waste, convert scraps of paper from trash to treasure.[37] Credit, frequently represented as a goddess, was an arbitrary deity—precisely the kind of remote, determining force for change that Milton's animist materialism was constructed to resist. It is against this background that Pope describes the book market of the *Dunciad*, a market that derived much of its force from the creation of a credit economy. Catherine Ingrassia points out, in her study of the overlap between Grub Street and Exchange Alley, that "the social fluidity, transgressive behavior, and speculative economic activity that marked Exchange Alley were, in a sense, replicated in the literary environment of Grub Street. . . .

Just as stock-jobbers and diverse investors, including women, competed
for economic gains and enhanced (if fleeting) status, so, too did a host of
professional writers, speculators of another sort, compete for cultural or
literary space and its potential profits, both symbolic and material. . . .
making the hack writer equally dependent on the goddesses of disorder,
Fortuna and Credit, as well as the deity that completes the triumvirate,
Dulness."[38]

The fluctuating values of the print market made Pope's own writing
simultaneously like, and radically unlike, that of the Dunces whom he
disparaged. To put it crudely, a poem by Pope and one by Smedley could
have identical material attributes and yet have absolutely different values
assigned to them. Think, for example, of a ludicrous pamphlet about the
varieties of human turd, which became a bestseller after it was attributed
to Swift in a second printing.[39] Milton's philosophy of matter gives Pope
the conceptual framework he needs to represent the paradoxes of radical
unlikeness between texts that have apparent similitude. In *Paradise Lost*,
God's creation from Chaos is a creation from waste, revealing the transformation of confused substance into miraculous plenitude. But the lin-
guistic affinities between waste and vastness mean that substances which
are radically unlike in the moral hierarchy separating dregs from cornucopia can be drawn into a relationship of similitude through the imagery
of abundance. Through a systematic reconstruction of Miltonic imagery,
Pope imposes his own stability on Grub Street; he creates a hierarchy of
texts independent of the magical conversions of the competitive marketplace. Milton's animist materialism gives Pope a doctrine that accords
a value to matter determined by its degree of obedience to the creative
force "brooding" over it.

At one of the climactic moments in the first two books of the *Dunciad*, Pope parodies the Miltonic prayer scene, a freely performed confir-
mation of obedience to the Father. The reassurances of Miltonic prayer,
which affirms the hierarchically ordered, animate universe described
above, is displaced in the *Dunciad* by a random plea on the part of the
Dunces that their literary efforts be favored with commercial success. As
Lintot races toward the effigy of the poet Moore, he attempts to outstrip
Curll, and prays to Jove for victory:

Then first (if poets aught of truth declare)
The caitiff vaticide conceived a prayer.
"Hear Jove! Whose name my bards and I adore,
As much at least as any god's, or more;
And him and his, if more devotion warms,
Down with the Bible, up with the Pope's Arms."   (2.77–82)

Through the device of his written "prayer" to Jove, Lintot generates a
document that is itself subject to the vagaries of a kind of marketplace—
which is to say that his supplication is delivered to Jove on the chance
that he will read it and favor its producer. But Lintot makes it clear that
his allegiance to Jove is quite random; in "adoring" Jove's name only "as
much at least as any god's," it is evident that Jove is an exchangeable deity,
whom Lintot would be happy to swap for another if he thought his work
would be better favored. The fixed authority of the Father in *Paradise
Lost* is transformed here to an unfixed one that is tied to a constantly fluctuating marketplace. In the final line of his prayer, it appears, bizarrely,
that Lintot makes a plea for a counterreformation—for a different set of
doctrinal attitudes through which the text is to be interpreted. But in fact
he is asking that his printing house be more successful than Curll's, by
publishing more volumes. The material world—in this case the material
text—attempts to renounce the morality of doctrine and instead to embrace the kind of preeminence conferred by competitive success.

In book 3 of the *Dunciad*, Milton's account of the distinctions created
between abundance and waste (Creation and Chaotic dregs) is juxtaposed
starkly with the claim that all forms of literary surplus can be converted
to financial gain in a competitive market. Pope's satirical vehicle for this
is the elaborate stage machinery used for the production of plays by Cibber, Theobald, Addison, and others in London's theaters. Pope describes
scenes in which the managers attempt to stage "mock-apocalypses" in
the theater: they create overproduced, tumultuous effects, too filled with
clashing and contradictory devices to have any real dramatic impact. In
their hands, apocalypse is reduced to a confused excess of gimmicks and
inconsistent images. John Rich, the master of the Theater Royal in Cov-
ent Garden, comes in for Pope's particular scorn:

Immortal Rich! How calm he sits at ease
'Mid snows of paper, and fierce hail of pease;
And proud his mistress' orders to perform,
Rides in the whirlwind, and directs the storm.   (3.261–64)

"Immortal Rich!" suggests a comparison between the manager and God—in which Rich of course comes off looking rather inadequate. The apocalypse he generates is, like God's, tumultuous and excessive—a massive physical display of wrath—but unlike God's, his is mere artifice, evacuated of its violent, destructive force. Apocalyptic excess, which expresses the power of the Almighty, the frailty of man, the sovereignty of God's will, becomes, in Rich's rendition, merely ornamental excess: confused and noisy, and finally inadequate.

The scenes staged by the Dunces remind the reader of the war in Heaven in *Paradise Lost*, that conflict is of such force that mountains are uprooted and the landscape literally turned upside down. Cibber's theatrical efforts attempt, likewise, to create havoc, but in his case, the inverted, confused landscape that he creates implies his idiocy—as though he did not realize that sea and land are distinct:

Hell rises, Heaven descends, and dance on earth:
Gods, imps, and monsters, music, rage and mirth,
A fire, a jig, a battle, and a ball,
Till one wide conflagration swallows all.
Thence a new world to nature's laws unknown,
Breaks out refulgent, with a heaven its own:
. . . .
The forests dance, the rivers upward rise,
Whales sport in woods, and dolphins in the skies;
And last, to give the whole creation grace,
Lo! One vast egg produces human race.   (3.237–48)

The scene reads like a clumsily staged version of the creation scenes that are so meticulously described in Milton's poem. Excesses that are theologically resonant in *Paradise Lost*—the stupendous force of war in Heaven, the bountiful, vital warmth that God infuses through Chaos at the Creation—are converted in the *Dunciad* into mere tricks to lure an audience into London's theaters. In other words, surpluses depicted in Milton's theological epic (and in other religious texts) supply a set of theatrical novelties for a competitive marketplace. The biblical trope of apocalyptic wasting is converted by Rich and Cibber quite literally into mechanical devices intended to produce fiscal gain. Milton adopted the doctrinal position that all substance, corporeal or incorporeal, is most free at the moment when it exercises the greatest obedience to God's will. In *Paradise Lost* he finds ways to make this counterintuitive claim persuasive, by showing that it is in the landscape of Eden that obedient matter reveals its true autonomy (it is at once wild and exquisitely tame, "a wilderness of sweets"). Pope transfers this tension between obedience and autonomy to a setting so unmistakably commercial in character that its resemblance to the Miltonic original is distorted.

Pope's rewriting of Milton's Chaos allows him to play a double game. By reproducing the terms of Milton's animate materialism, Pope distances himself philosophically from the need to submit to the fluctuations in literary and commercial value that characterize the marketplace. The speaker of the *Dunciad*, who pays homage to Dr. Swift in its opening lines, unashamedly confesses to his fear, his sense of threat, his disgust, at the success of "lesser" writers in the literary marketplace. And in representing his poem as Miltonic in character, Pope reminds us of Milton's unworldly retirement at the time of his great, late poems, and his resistance, earlier on, to the culture of professional writing. Pope can use Milton to tell the story of his own retirement to Twickenham, even as he engages wholeheartedly in the animosities and political struggles of Grub Street. Pope never impersonates Miltonic poetics without reserve—in truth he resists the notion of actual retirement, and his status as a poet elevated above the mean skirmishes of Grub Street is entirely dependent on his having profited mightily from them. This was no secret at the time: Pope must have known that he laid himself open to ridicule by attacking the very world on which he depended. And, sure enough, the ridicule came his way: attacks on Pope in Curll's *Compleat Key to the Dunciad* and *The Female Dunciad* make the point that Pope is as much a part of the commercialized, competitive world of Grub Street as the Dunces that he attacks.[40] So Pope cheekily reminds us that he is the poetic and intellectual equal of his gigantic predecessor, Milton, while simultaneously pointing out that Milton's political and poetic ideologies have been displaced by a new literary environment in which Pope nonetheless thrives.

Pope pays meticulous attention to the terms of Milton's materialism, and yet he simultaneously parodies the Miltonic convention of explaining complicated philosophical and doctrinal claims in poetic meter. Pope's poem is, then, at once a homage to Milton and a joke about him; it draws together a tissue of Miltonic allusions and half-rewritings of passages from *Paradise Lost*, only to take the wind out of Milton's sails by having the apocalyptic sequences of that epic performed, masquelike, in London's theaters. Pope imports the language of a political and theological debate about matter into the secular world of commercial writing. Milton's animist materialism remains just visible enough in the *Dunciad* to suggest that a seventeenth-century conception of waste found its place in a profoundly eighteenth-century debate.

4

The Man on the Dump

SWIFT, IRELAND, AND

THE PROBLEM OF WASTE

NOBODY relished leftovers like Jonathan Swift. His writings are filled with waste matter: excrement, snot, sweat, nail clippings, garbage, dead dogs. With a meticulous attention that often looks like neurotic obsession,[1] Swift rehabilitates matter that has been discarded by the polite worlds of eighteenth-century London and Dublin, playing endlessly with the fact that filth and abundance can be made to look the same. In political terms the similarity meant that English Whigs—in Swift's view, opportunists looking to defraud the Irish economy—could pass off debased coinage, devalued exports, and worthless imports as precious surpluses. In cultural terms, Swift prized waste not because it could be converted into glorious spoils but because, in its abjection, it told a story of Englishness that he particularly wanted to have told.

Swift's landscapes are wastelands, at once full and empty, alienating but eerily familiar. The piles of filth and heaps of excrement that fill the terrain of his writing invert the luxurious goods, the costly commodities, the piles of money crammed into the writings of his political and literary enemies. Swift refuses outright to clean up the landscapes of his poetry and prose, and even when he writes in celebration, it is in the language of filth, not of splendor. In "A Description of a City Shower" (1710), excrement and filth flush through the city in a deluge, eclipsing the signs of value and commerce. Waste supplants prosperity as the source of plenitude. The closing triplet is a case in point (the triplet itself is a sign of formal overabundance):

> Sweepings from butchers' stalls, dung, guts and blood,
> Drowned puppies, stinking sprats, all drenched in mud,
> Dead cats and turnip tops come tumbling down the flood.[2]

This torrent of garbage has the energy of a dynamic urban crowd; it accumulates speed and force as it cycles through the city and through the poem, connecting parishes that are far apart, accruing a perverse symbolic value in its variety and abundance. The poem rewrites the biblical Flood narrative, itself a type for apocalypse. But instead of apocalypse ending in resurrection and glory, it ends, like the *Dunciad*, in undifferentiated chaos, this time of urban garbage. Swift takes the same pleasure in residues that his Whig adversaries do in plenitude. His tone here reminds us of Comus's relish in nature "pour[ing] her bounties forth," but in this case, instead of excessive luxuriance generating the repulsion associated with decay, repulsive matter reminds us of an "augmentation of life: a heightened announcement of the fact that life *is there*."[3]

I

Swift depicts an Ireland that is literally covered in burdensome residues dispatched from England—manufactured goods, coins, imported cloth—dumped on Irish soil and made to seem as though they have value. In essays such as "A Proposal for the Universal Use of Irish Manufacture" (1720), the *Drapier's Letters* (1724–25), and "A Short View of the State of Ireland" (1727), Swift attacks the English government for turning Ireland into a wasteland even as it professes to supply the Irish with the means of prosperity and growth.[4] Paradoxically, abundance in Ireland marks it as a waste—a dump for English goods, stripped bare by successive English landholders.[5]

The most notorious instance of Swift's satirical substitution of plenitude for waste in his Irish writing occurs in "A Modest Proposal" (1729).
The Projector, Swift's speaking voice, infamously recommends that "a
prodigious number of Children" be turned to commercial account as
joints of meat. In one of the most notorious moments in the essay, he
announces: "a young healthy Child, well nursed, is, at a Year old, a most
delicious, nourishing, and wholesome Food; whether *Stewed, Roasted,
Baked*, or *Boiled*; and, I make no doubt, that it will equally serve in a
Fricasie, or *Ragout*."[6] At the essay's outset, we get a glimpse of reality (or
something like it): "It is a melancholy object to those, who walk through
this great town, or travel in the country, when they see the streets, the
roads and cabbin-doors crowded with beggars of the female sex, followed
by three, four, or six children, all in rags, and importuning every pas-
senger for an alms." But the Projector sets out to turn this real wasteland
into a possible paradise of abundance: "whoever could find out a fair,
cheap and easy method of making these children sound and useful members of the commonwealth, would deserve so well of the publick, as to
have his statue set up for a preserver of the nation." He relies upon what
Lynn Festa has called the "abstraction of value," in which "value does not
inhere in the object proper, but outside of it, in its differential relation to
other commodities."[7] He is able to turn wasted human "stock" into commercial gain, but only by ignoring the qualitative differences that exist
between them, conjoining "human and thing." Children are simultaneously worthless and limitlessly valuable.[8]

Swift describes the poor, ill, wasted infants of the Irish poor with
Rabelaisian relish, turning paucity into plenty. As Bakhtin would later
say, "the material bodily principle is a triumphant, festive principle, it is
a 'banquet for all the world.' "[9] Swift's carnal prose transforms the bodies
of the poor, transferring onto Irish children the corpulence of the bour-
geois bodies that will consume them:

A child will make two dishes at an entertainment for friends, and
when the family dines alone, the fore or hind quarter will make a
reasonable dish, and seasoned with a little pepper or salt, will be
very good boiled on the fourth day, especially in winter. I have

reckoned upon a medium, that a child just born will weigh 12 pounds, and in a solar year, if tolerably nursed, encreaseth to 28 pounds. I grant this food will be somewhat dear, and therefore very proper for landlords, who, as they have already devoured most of the parents, seem to have the best title to the children.[10]

Swift's speaker makes children into goods, waste into value, putrefaction into life.

But there's a further twist, not immediately apparent. The Projector isn't the only person in "A Modest Proposal" to convert human waste into commercial value. The "victims" do it too, the Irish of whom the Projector plans to make use. "The mindless brute with his base family life, and the soundly calculating Whig planner, unite in their commercial priorities, with Swift wishing a plague on both their houses," Claude Rawson writes.[11] This is the complication that throws Swift's own position in the essay into doubt. If the victims as well as the perpetrators can't, or don't want to distinguish humans from commercial goods, then why should Swift, whose life in Dublin seemed doomed by his unsatisfactory dealings with both? We begin to suspect that Swift secretly longs for the very outcome he condemns: the elimination of Ireland's impoverished multitude.[12] Rawson puts it well: "[Swift's] belongs to an extermination rhetoric which is assumed not to be quite literal, but flirts actively with its literal potential."[13] But the satire doesn't stop with the allegation that English and Irish alike are greedy, self-interested wretches. In the spectacle of parents who would sell their children off to be eaten, Swift is also satirizing the Catholic sacrament and the doctrine of real presence: the belief that Christ's body is literally present in the host. "A Modest Proposal" flirts provocatively with the idea that, for some people, it's not insane to think of eating children's flesh. Roman Catholics do it every Sunday, Swift mischievously implies, and the child they eat is not just with any old child but God's Son. The claim that abject matter is precious constitutes, after all, the essence of the Catholic sacrament.

Swift's claim in his political pamphlets is that he undoes the making of false value. The *Drapier's Letters*, written in response to a policy known as Wood's halfpence scheme, controversial between 1722 and 1725, deal with the volatile matter of England's coinage, a unit of exchange more inherently ambiguous than the children of "A Modest Proposal."[14] Here Swift's manipulations of waste and value achieve new complexities. Wood's scheme involved an attempt to infuse the Irish economy with newly minted coins that were imported from England, although their real value was less than English halfpennies of the same name. Swift criticized the scheme by arguing that the 100,000 pounds brought into Ireland in Wood's coins was degraded currency: "trash that will not be worth Eight or Nine thousand pounds real value."[15] The policy is designed to create a surplus of coinage in Ireland, but Swift argues that it is merely an abundance of almost worthless metal.[16] Swift spins out his argument in a voice of satirical hysteria, explaining the mad delusions one would seemingly need to be under to accept that Wood's brass halfpence were actually worth something. He imagines a corrupt Irish landowner struggling under the weight of junk money as he fleeces his tenants for a year's worth of base coinage:

> They say Squire Conolly has Sixteen Thousand Pounds a Year; now if he sends for his Rent to Town, as it is likely he does, he must have Two Hundred and Fifty Horses to bring up his Half Year's Rent, and two or three great Cellars in his House for Stowage. But what the Bankers will do I cannot tell. For I am assured that some great Bankers keep by them forty thousand pounds in ready Cash, to answer all Payments, which Sum in Mr. Wood's Money, would require Twelve Hundred Horses to carry it.[17]

In Swift's satire, people are literally incapacitated by the sheer volume of Wood's coins: eight thousand pounds requires 250 horses and three cellars. What most people think is a sign of wealth is turned into a spectacle of collective lunacy: calculations about teams of horses and vast rooms take the place of the issue that, in Swift's view, is really at stake: the fact that absentee landowners and city bankers prosper while the Irish people collapse. Swift's comic vision turns plenty into false plenitude; the plenitude of Wood's coin is intended to remind readers that the impoverishment of the Irish has come about even though Ireland is rich

in resources. The vision, moreover, impugns the moral carelessness of
bankers and landowners whose greed permits them to accept as foolish
a scheme as Wood's. By showing what Wood's coins mean in terms of
sheer physical volume—material surplus—Swift discredits the pretense
that they have the plenitude of financial value.[18] The joke relies on the
context of the coinage debates, because the vision of nominal value represented by Wood's re-coinage had the effect of making value anonymous and seemingly exchangeable.[19] Lynn Festa calls it "the promise of
exchangeability." For Swift, this promise would mean that value could
stand, fraudulently for waste.[20]

In his *Spectator* essay on public credit (March 1711), Joseph Addison,
Swift's famous literary and political adversary, had announced triumphantly that seeming nothingness, stuff of no value, could be converted
magically into splendid abundance.[21] Addison explains the concept of
paper credit by picturing piles of dross and heaps of paper transformed,
by the Midas-like touch of Lady Credit, into mountains of shining gold.
Unlike Swift, Addison was committed politically to the position that
such proliferation is desirable—encouraged by the advent of public
credit, with its promise of limitless growth. Hence Lady Credit is figured
as "a beautiful Virgin, seated on a throne of Gold,"[22] fostering the expansion of the English economy and the increase of private wealth. Under
a Whig-led Bank of England (which Addison champions), Lady Credit
conjures massive material wealth: "behind the Throne was a prodigious
Heap of Bags of Mony, which were piled upon one another so high that
they touched the Ceiling" (16). Lady Credit is an alchemist: "she had
the same Virtue in her Touch, which the Poets tell us a *Lydian King*
was formerly possess'd of; and she could convert whatever she pleas'd
into that precious Metal" (16). In Addison's fanciful allegory, the mystery of alchemy, which had eluded scientists and mystics for hundreds
of years, had finally been unlocked by the advent of the stock market,
which seemed to generate real wealth from a pile of paper bills: "At their
first Entrance the Lady [Credit] reviv'd, the Bags swell'd to their former
Bulk, the Piles of Faggots and Heaps of Paper changed into Pyramids
of Guineas" (17). Through Addison's optimistic eyes (nearly ten years
before the South Sea Bubble) abject matter could be converted magically
into value.

But Addison's essay takes a distinctly Swiftian turn when the piles of gold shrink suddenly into nothing. In Addison's view, the change would be caused by a Tory-led administration that refused public credit:

> There was as great a Change in the Hill of Mony Bags, and the Heaps of Mony, the former shrinking, and falling into so many empty Bags, that I now found not above a tenth Part of them had been filled with Mony. The rest that took up the same Space, and made the same Figure as the Bags that were really filled with Mony, had been blown up with Air, and called into my Memory the Bags full of Wind, which *Homer* tells us his Hero receiv'd as a Present from *Aeolus*. The great Heaps of Gold on either side the Throne, now appeared to be only Heaps of Paper, or little Piles of notched Sticks, bound up together in Bundles, like Bath-Faggots. (17)

Ideological opponents though they were, Swift and Addison reached the same conclusion. Hills, heaps, bags, piles that seem so gloriously abundant can be woefully empty an instant later. Being writers, not financiers, Swift and Addison's shared insight is that writing itself performs this miraculous alchemy, which Swift ridiculed and Addison celebrated. On opposite sides of the political and literary spectrum, they were brought together by the discovery that, on the page, waste could be made to look like plenitude.

The duplicities at large in "A Modest Proposal" and the *Drapier's Letters*—the attempt to pass waste off as plenitude, to reframe human value as commercial waste; the mistaking of base matter for glorious spoils—finally enable the full-blown delirium of Swift's pamphlet *An Examination of Certain Abuses, Corruptions and Enormities, in the City of Dublin* (1732). Published anonymously, Swift writes in the assumed voice of a paranoid Whig pamphleteer. He warns that Dublin's street dwellers, vendors, muckrakers, and street criers are Tory and Jacobite propagandists, seeking to overthrow the Whigs and to incite Catholic rebellion. Swift's speaker describes the piles of excrement in Dublin's streets, which he interprets as evidence of a Tory plot:

> Every Person who walks the streets, must needs observe an immense number of human Excrements at the Doors and Steps of

waste Houses, and at the sides of every dead Wall; for which the
disaffected Party hath assigned a very false and malicious cause.
They would have it that these Heaps were laid there privately by
British Fundaments, to make the World believe, that our *Irish* vul-
gar do daily eat and drink; and, consequently, that the Clamour
of Poverty among us, must be false; proceeding only from *Jacobites*
and *Papists*. They would confirm this, by pretending to observe,
that a *British Anus* being more narrowly perforated than one of our
own Country; and many of these Excrements, upon a strict View
appearing Copple-crowned, with a Point like a Cone or Pyramid,
are easily distinguished from the *Hibernian*, which lie much flatter,
and with less Continuity. I communicated this Conjecture to an
eminent physician, who is well versed in such profound Specula-
tions; and at my Request was pleased to make Trial with each of his
fingers, by thrusting them into the Anus of several Persons of both
Nations; and professed he could find no such Difference between
them as those ill-disposed People allege.[23]

It's a complicated argument, best summarized as follows: the speaker is
a Whig, accusing the Tories of spreading antigovernment slander. Alleg-
edly, the Tories have put it about that the human excrement in the streets
of Dublin has been put there by the Whigs, to make it look as though
the Irish people have plenty to eat and drink. But the Whig speaker hotly
retorts that his party would never do that. The streets just happen to be
full of excrement. The Tories are paranoid madmen. And lo and behold,
this is exactly Swift's polemical point. The streets are full of filth. The
British government has let Dublin deteriorate into filthy wasteland. The
argument in the end is that the Whigs would rather fall into a lunatic
political skirmish with the Tories than do anything about the problem
of Irish poverty.

The scene is an allegory of the state of Ireland under Walpole's government: the country is saturated with surplus manufactures, stripped of
resources by the Whig administration, and yet the Whigs will go to any
lengths to make it look as though Ireland is flourishing. Swift's satirical
game affords him a damning description of English political leadership,
culminating in the spectacle of Whigs and Tories arguing about the com-

parative size of English and Irish rectums. The allegory is so confusing and elaborate that by the end of the passage it is impossible to keep track of the competing symbolic meanings of English and Irish waste matter. The English physician who does his bit for the Whig cause by shoving his finger into various anuses is the figure who tips the scene into real insanity—and, as always with Swift, we suspect that the insanity is his as much as theirs whom he lampoons. We are surrounded by a crowd of madmen rubbing their hands and fingers in human excrement. The truth was that nobody wanted to clean up Dublin's streets: not the Whigs, not the Tories, not Swift himself. Swift collaborates in keeping Ireland filthy—in making sure that waste doesn't disappear.

The sheer difficulty of explaining how Swift's satires work dramatizes the way they trick us into experiencing the madness he represents—the confused insanity of not being able to tell the difference between waste and value. On the one hand, Swift inhabits the same ontological universe as Milton and Pope, in the sense that he holds waste and plenitude to be categories assigned by differences in intrinsic, not extrinsic, worth. He considers them discreet, not exchangeable. Like Milton and Pope, he notes that ontologically distinct categories share the property of excess that makes them superficially interchangeable. On the other hand, Swift's writing feels radically different because he allows the shared property of excess to look as though it is a shared ontology; he allows the distinct attributes of waste and value to collapse into each other. This sets the experience of reading Swift apart from the experience of reading either Milton, or Pope, who relieve us from confusion and fear (despite the confusing and sometimes frightening implications of some of their ideas) by a continual formal assurance of the writer's own control and clear-headedness. As we watch the collapse take place, we, like Swift's speakers, experience the quicksand tug of madness.

II

Swift's satirical vision is Protestant in its nature. It rejects the Roman Catholic doctrine that base matter can be made divine, and it adheres to the logic that where glorious meaning arises, it leaves a leftover, a kernel of material reality. Ironically, Addison's Whiggish optimism led him into a logic of metaphor far more popish in character than Swift's Tory skepticism. For Swift, the transports of Addison's view of credit are impossible, because waste can never, literally, turn into splendid abundance. It is no more than the vehicle from which glorious meaning is created. In his earliest successful satire, *A Tale of a Tub* (1709), Swift lampoons the Catholic sacrament. Peter, the allegorical figure of the Catholic Church, dines with his brothers, insisting that the Roman Catholic sacrament has handy practical implications for domestic frugality:

> When Peter came home, he would needs take the Fancy of cooking up this Doctrine into Use, and apply the Precept in default of a Surloyn, to his brown Loaf: *Bread*, says he, *Dear Brothers, is the Staff of Life; in which Bread is contained*, inclusive, *the Quintessence of Beef, Mutton, Veal, Venison, Partridge, Plum-Pudding and Custard: And to render all compleat, there is intermingled a due quantity of Water.* . . . Upon the strength of these Conclusions, next Day at Dinner was the brown Loaf served up in all the Formality of a City Feast. *Come Brothers*, said Peter, *fall to, and spare not; here is excellent good mutton; or hold, now my Hand is in, I'll help you.* At which word, in much Ceremony, with Fork and Knife, he carves out two good slices of the Loaf, and presents each on a Plate to his Brothers.[24]

The joke here is that Peter is a madman, "tak[ing] the Fancy of cooking up this Doctrine into Use" and insisting that a loaf of bread is really a joint of meat that will sufficiently feed the family of three brothers.[25] Swift's parody depends upon the Protestant position that even after the consecration of the Mass, the sacrament retains the sensible accidents of bread and wine.[26] The Anglican sacrament draws a distinction between the profane and the sacred; in Anglican doctrine there is no real presence. When we look at this passage from the *Tale*, we start to see why Swift was so particularly horrified by Catholic doctrine. The same logic that led Peter to say that a loaf of bread actually was a haunch of meat enabled Wood to say that a pile of brass was worth 100,000 pounds and enabled the Projector to assert that the wasted lives of impoverished Irish babies would be redeemed by selling them as food.

For his contemporaries, Swift's preoccupation with excrement, discarded matter, and bodily waste seemed to disqualify him from serious consideration as a cleric or theologian. But Swift's Anglican theology was sound. The intellectual background for his views on the place of abject matter in doctrine is the theology of the early eighteenth-century rationalist school, which argued that doctrine could, and should, be understood through the new methodology of natural philosophy. Following on from Locke, Stillingfleet, and Tillotson, the Anglican rationalist position was that doctrine is within the reach of human reason and that its truth should be determined, where possible, by recourse to the evidence of the senses. This school of theology provided a means to refute the doctrinal claims of Catholics and nonconformists.[27] (Not all mystery was rejected, however: the rationalists rejected Roman Catholic transubstantiation, but retained the orthodox mystery of Trinitarianism.) But the confusing terms "natural religion" and "rationalism," and the intellectual allegiances that existed between the Anglican Rationalist position and the experimental philosophy of the Royal Society, gave rise to the belief that the Rationalists were attempting to establish theology as a natural science.[28]

In 1730 Swift wrote a poem called "A Panegyric on the Dean in the Person of a Lady in the North," ostensibly defending his identity as a clergyman and respected spokesman for Ireland. But the most memorable part of the poem is a long fantasy sequence in which Swift takes to building public latrines in the Irish countryside. The "Panegyric" is spoken in the voice of Swift's patron, Lady Acheson, giving an imaginary description of Swift's daily routine while he is in the country, revolving around the endlessly time-consuming tasks of living in a country house. Formally it parodies poems about intellectual retirement such as Marvell's "The Garden," and Pope's "Epistle to Dr. Arbuthnot." The problem with retirement, Swift finds, is that it leaves him with too much thinking time. His mind is overactive; his creative inventions are too abundant to conform to the constraint and confinement of a retired setting.

Halfway through, the "Panegyric" swerves wildly off course, when we hear that Swift has spent a large part of his time in the country building latrines and writing a history of the Goddess Cloacine, the deity of excrement, who receives the daily offerings of human waste, delivered to her shrine by way of a privy. Swift claims that toilets offer privacy to Irish youths who come to worship:

> Here, gentle Goddess Cloacine
> Receives all offerings at her shrine.
> In separate cells the he's and she's
> Here pay their vows on bended knees:
> (For, 'tis profane when sexes mingle;
> And every nymph must enter single;
> And when she feels an *inward motion*,
> Comes filled with *reverence* and devotion.)
> The bashful maid, to hide her blush,
> Shall creep no more behind a bush;
> Here unobserved, she boldly goes,
> As who should say, *to pluck a rose.*   (213–16)

In this typically Swiftian verse, crude but playful in its linking of devotion and excretion, Swift figures defecation as prayer. His joke is to treat excreting as though it has liturgical significance, referring to separate cells, vows, bended knees, inward motions. Like praying, defecating here has a quasi-sexual quality, reminiscent of perfect piety in high Anglican or Catholic devotional lyric. (The boys and girls "enter single," forbidden to mingle; they "com[e] filled with reverence.")

In the last part of the poem Swift makes this explicit, by way of an invented history of the cult of Cloacine. In the Golden Age, Swift claims, everyone knew that defecating was the orthodox means of practicing devotion:

> Ten thousand altars smoking round
> Were built to thee, with offerings crowned:
> And here thy daily votaries placed
> Their sacrifice with zeal and haste:
> The margin of a purling stream,
> Sent up to thee a grateful steam.
> (Though sometimes thou wert pleased to wink,
> If Naiads swept them from the brink.)   (237–44)

Swift imagines a time when devotional enthusiasm was synonymous with a constant and unconstrained discharge of excrement, unlike his own day, when both crapping and praying have become regimented, shameful acts:

> Ah! Who in our degenerate days
> As nature prompts, his offering pays?
> Here, nature never difference made
> Between the sceptre and the spade. (287–90)

Swift purports to save the Irish people by reforming Irish religion and Irish hygiene simultaneously. In other words, he gives them somewhere to shit. The "Panegyric" winds down with a Miltonic interjection to the Muse:

> But stop, ambitious Muse, in time;
> Nor dwell on Subjects too sublime.
> In vain on lofty heels I tread,
> Aspiring to exalt my head:
> With hoop expanded wide and light,
> In vain I tempt too high a flight. (319–24)

Swift's allusion plays off Milton's proems to books 3 and 7 of *Paradise Lost*, where he asks his muse first to allow him to ascend from the description of Hell to Heaven and, later, to descend again from heavenly speculation to earthly poetics.[29] But in implying that he is a latter-day Milton, as much interested in base matter as glorious abundance, Swift also makes it clear that his writing inverts the work Milton did. Instead of asking for expanded wings so that he can justify the ways of God to men, Swift's speaker asks the muse to clip her wings, to take herself down from the heights of philosophical speculation. Swift's is a worldly, temporal vocation, not heavenly and philosophically dense as Milton's is. For Swift, after all, his real power as a clergyman derived from the extent to which it enabled him to intervene in the world of politics and satire; his life as a theologian and churchman inflected much that he wrote, but was not the part of his life he cared most about.

III

Swift's ecclesiastical parodies in turn caused other eighteenth-century satirists to pay attention to the role waste played in rationalist theology. A series of satirical pamphlets from the 1730s lampooned theologians for their excessive concern with temporal matter, a concern that, after the Restoration, signaled the Anglican rejection of Catholic and nonconformist interest in mystery. Swift's "Panegyric" forms part of a group of such satires, now rarely read. One such lampoon, *Human Ordure, Botanically Considered; or, The Benefit of Farting Explained*, was actually attributed in its 1733 printing to Dr. S——t, though it had previously been published anonymously.[30] The pamphlet satirizes both botanical classification and learned publications by Anglican churchmen:

> There is no Man that ever was so humble as to observe Human Or-
> dure, but must confess there is a wonderful variety in all produc-
> tions of this nature. . . . For my part, I have found such a variety,
> that I have Trib'd and Clas'd them, with as much pleasure and care
> as Botanists do Plants.[31]

The satire burlesques the vocabulary of empirical inquiry and observation, implying that its commitment to observing visible phenomena is a cover for the theologian's neuroses and obsession with different kinds of human excrement. The joke works because phrases common in scientific writing—"observ[ing]," "wonderful variety," "pleasure and care"—are the same words that an excremental fetishist would use. Yet in the act of satirizing English rationalists for their scatological obsession, the writer affirms the crucial connection in Protestant theology between profane leftovers and sacred meaning—the former have value because they are signs of the latter.

Human Ordure was by no means a one-off: the previous year an anonymous satirist had achieved considerable notoriety for his tract entitled *Reason against Coition . . . To Which Is Added A Proposal for Making Religion and the Clergy Useful* (1732), written in the voice of an idle clergyman obsessed with human excrement and superfluous bodies in Ireland. Like *Human Ordure*, this pamphlet was attributed to Swift at various times, though it is unclear whether the printer was using Swift's name to attract an audience or the pamphleteer was a Whig satirist seeking to smear Swift's reputation.[32] The argument is that by giving rational, "natural" interpretations of scripture, Anglican clerics are doing their bit to save Ireland from poverty and degradation.

The pamphlet is a mock sermon, *A Discourse Deliver'd to a Private Congregation, By The Reverend Stephen M——*. Its argument, which is a crude parody of religious philosophizing, is that poverty and overpopulation in Ireland can be solved by the "cessation of Procreation, and the Efficacy and Power of Resolution."[33] This pamphlet starts at the same place that "A Modest Proposal" did, pointing out that Ireland's biggest problem is population control—there are just too many people. In the voice of a mock-clergyman, the satirist exhorts the Irish to "let all Calamity end in [them]selves, by refraining from propagating Children, that inevitably must feel it" (29). People shouldn't procreate, he claims, because human beings are repulsive. He argues that copulation breeds rank nastiness, citing the filthy, compulsively breeding Yahoos of *Gulliver's Travels*. But the Reverend M—— doesn't find breeding distasteful merely because of his Gulliver-like aversion to children. Like *Human Ordure*, the pamphlet affirms the critical role played by material leftovers in Protestant theology. The satirist justifies his claims with a pseudotheological argument: since flesh is base, the terrestrial frame is abject—humans ought not to make yet more abject matter:

> [S]ays that wise Traveller Mr Gulliver, "when I began to consider, that by copulating with one of the *Yahoo* Species, I became a parent of more, it struck me with the utmost Shame, Confusion and Horror." By the breath we enjoy, we know the Unhappiness of it in others: We know how true it is, That, *Man that is born of a Woman, hath but a short Time to live, and is full of Misery: He cometh up, and is cut down like a Flower; he fleeth as it were a Shadow, and never continueth in one Stay.* (35)

The logic here, as in *Gulliver's Travels* and as in "A Modest Proposal," is that breeding makes waste. Gulliver knows it, and so does Christian doctrine. The temporal body is always, already waste, since it will be discarded at the Resurrection, and considered from the point of view of Christian resurrection, human flesh is abject. But emotionally and psychologically the opposite is the case, which is why this speaker, like Swift's Hounhymns, seems so callous: the human flesh is all that we can possess of a person, the vessel containing the soul. Theologically fated to be a leftover, and yet infinitely precious, the human body is the most valuable waste there is.

These ideas get played out more fully in the appendix to the 1732 edition of *Reason against Coition*, a second treatise named *A Scheme for Making Religion and the Clergy Useful*. This rewrite of Swift's "Panegyric on the Dean," in which the speaker claims that it would be better for the people of Ireland to build a big open-air privy to which they could repair on Sundays than to sit in airless churches, unable to relieve their bodily needs. The idea, here as in Swift's poem, is that praying and defecating are more or less the same: "For my own Part, I always looked upon Religion as a very good Thing; and am now about to consider it, not as a Politician, but as a Christian; in Hopes I may set it in a proper Light, by making it useful to Mankind, (as it was at first design'd), by stripping it of the Superstition, with which it is at present miserably incumbered" (51). His point is that rational Protestantism amounts to little more than the attempted glorification of waste. The satirist is probably a Catholic sympathizer, or at least a conservative Anglican, since he suggests that reformed Anglican worship has become merely a means to deal with human surpluses, both fleshly and spiritual: thoughts, feelings, beliefs, and of course human bodies.

This position is reflected in a lampoon on the pious prayers made in damp, uncomfortable Irish churches on Sunday mornings:

> I can, indeed, by no means allow, that the present Practice of it is of any Use (except to the Physicians and Apothecaries,) as confined to a Set of Prayers, and a Sermon in a damp House, close shut all the Week, and consequently full of noisome and unwholesome Vapours, exhaled or transpired through the Earth, from the numberless dead and putrifying Carcases lodg'd within, and close about the Walls of the several Churches in this Kingdom; which Practice, as it was introduced by Popish Superstition, might have been

very wholesomely abolished by that religious Prince Henry VIII of
pious Memory, at the same Time that he suppressed the Abbeys
and Monasteries. (52)

The satirist's somewhat obscure point is that reformed Protestants pay
attention only to the literal "noisome and unwholesome Vapours" in
churches, and are insensitive to the spiritual resonance of smells and bells.
The bodies of saints and martyrs, similarly, have become mere carcasses,
"dead and putrefying," stripped of their status as relics. Without superstition, rational religion does nothing more than exalt waste.

These satires on piety and human excretion make a crucial argument
about the effect of Protestant belief on literary culture: that it causes waste
matter and abject leftovers to be valued as symptoms of meaning, even
as they are devalued as degraded. In the closing paragraph of *A Scheme
for Making Religion and the Clergy Useful*, as his final sally against the literature of rational religion, the satirist recommends building a great big
privy in lieu of a church:

> I would have certain Eminencies, within three Miles of this City,
> mark'd out for Groves; in the Midst of which there may be a
> Temple built in the Form of a ———, or any other Shape the People
> shall judge proper, supported by Pillars, and open on all Sides, to
> keep the Air clear and healthful. To these Groves and Temples the
> People may repair on *Sundays* or Holidays, which will contribute
> much to their Health, and the Clergy may officiate, I think, in the
> present Manner. (56)

Reformed Protestantism turns human remainders into precious matter.
It's a joke, but, as we will see in the next chapter, it's a joke that turns
out to be serious.

This chapter has argued that leftovers are valuable and important for
their own sake, not because they can be reclaimed or rehabilitated. Swift
insists on the reality of waste in order to rebuke his political adversaries—to stop them from pretending that debased coins, impoverished
children, filthy, polluted streetscapes, heaps of paper, loaves of bread

(and all the other things Swift's enemies try to rehabilitate) are anything other than dross. But Swift's refusal to conflate waste and plenitude, his determination not to assign value to abjection, his obsessive insistence on pointing out the difference between base and precious matter, cannot be explained away as the skeptic's insistence on truth. Swift finds waste everywhere—because he only goes looking in the places where he knows he will find it. London, Dublin, the imaginary lands of *Gulliver's Travels*, the private dressing rooms of fashionable ladies. Swift doesn't just document the presence of waste matter when it crosses his path; he actively seeks it out. Swift's desire to write is a desire to write about waste.

This book began by pointing out that waste is animated by paradoxes. It is empty but full. Abject but life-intended. It putrefies, and it proliferates. Perhaps most importantly, we want to dispose of it, and we long to hold on to it. Waste is a sign that our lives are beset by loss. Since the spectacle of loss is intolerable, since it reminds us of the inevitability of death, our instinct is to banish waste from sight, but our deeper desire is to memorialize it, to forestall loss. Literature lets us honor that desire, since abject matter does not putrefy on the page. Waste, a site of decay, disaffection, disgust, dismay, refusal, is a physical manifestation of the human experience of loss, the closest we get to death on a daily basis.

In Swift's greatest writing, the oscillation between disgust at and desire for loss initiates, sustains, and consummates the text, and nowhere so painfully as in the anthology piece "The Lady's Dressing Room." Probably the most notorious of all Swift's poems, this is the one in which his hero Strephon cries out, "Celia, Celia, Celia shits." The sight of his beloved's excrement stimulates Strephon's horrified recoil from Celia— even though he is also compulsively attracted to her brimming chamber pot. For Strephon, and Swift, erotic desire is virtually indistinguishable from disgust, a connection Swift confesses to by using the language of courtly love-lyric to describe Celia's putrefying waste matter. "The Lady's Dressing Room" parodies and pays homage to the central claim of courtly lyric, that a work of art can preserve the beloved from decay. Swift fills his poem up with literal waste, burlesquing the lyric speaker's generic anxiety about the effects of time and decay upon physical beauty. The conventional lyric lament that beauty is doomed to decline—the regret "that thou amongst the wastes of time must go"—is absurdly literalized in

"The Lady's Dressing Room." A glut of discarded matter surrounds the speaker and his beloved, who languish among waste of all descriptions. In substituting a catalogue of the beloved's effluence for a catalogue of her beauties, Swift reveals that the language of lyric invention readily permits the substitution of decay for perfection and repulsion for attraction, much as it appears to insist on their opposition.

Swift embeds phrases into "The Lady's Dressing Room" that evoke the expressive register of a courtly sonnet and thus emphasize its likeness to the mode it seems to parody. He appropriates Shakespearean imagery to describe the by-products of Celia's toilette:

> The basin takes whatever comes
> The scrapings of her teeth and gums,
> A nasty compound of all hues,
> For here she spits and here she spews.
> . . . .
> No object Strephon's eye escapes,
> Here, petticoats in frowzy heaps;
> Nor be the handkerchiefs forgot,
> All varnished o'er with snuff and snot.
> The stockings why should I expose,
> Stained with the moisture of her toes.   (43–48)

Strephon sees Celia's bodily discharge through an artist's eyes, observantly attuned to its arrangement, texture, and appearance. The words "compound," "counterfeit," "varnished," "stained," and later "disguise" reveal that Strephon's catalogue of filth has been carefully composed for artistic effect. His gaze actively preserves what has been discarded ("nor be the handkerchiefs forgot"), collecting and framing the picture into an aesthetic whole ("no object Strephon's eye escapes"). Thus, the "paste of composition rare" that clogs her combs, the "nasty compound of all hues" in her basin, the handkerchiefs "all varnished o'er with snuff and snot," and (later in the poem) the "rings and hinges counterfeit" on the chamber pot explicitly invoke the imagery of Shakespeare's sonnets, memorializing effluence as though it formed part of the beloved's charms.

The poem's most famous lines substitute Strephon's discovery of Celia's excrement for the anticipated lyric climax of rapturous praise at the sight of the beloved's body. Strephon displays his disgust at the climax moment at which the lyric speaker should confess his desire. As Strephon peers excitedly into Celia's chamber pot, Swift's parody makes it clear that disgust can be all too readily substituted for desire.

> Thus finishing his grand survey,
> The swain disgusted slunk away,
> Repeating in his amorous fits,
> "Oh! Celia, Celia, Celia shits!"   (115–18)

"Amorous fits" meshes perfectly with "Celia shits"—*amor* is as much at ease with the discovery of excrement as it would be with the unveiling of Celia's physical charms. His rapture trips along just as metrically whether it is filthy refuse or sensual delight under the speaker's gaze. And ghastly as the conclusion of Strephon's survey is, it hardly comes as a surprise, either to us or to the hero himself. After all, what else would follow from the word "fits" than the rhyme "shits"? Strephon's surprise here is affected. He already knew what was within Celia's pot:

> Resolved to go through thick and thin;
> He lifts the lid: there need no more,
> He smelt it all the time before.   (80–82)

The fact that Strephon already knows what he will find in Celia's chamber pot suggests that his desire is not diminished by the knowledge that she defecates, but rather is actively enabled. Effluent is, after all, evidence of a functioning female body, which is the locus of desire in erotic poetry. In other words, Strephon's discovery of Celia's excretions does not threaten to block or forestall the idealizations of courtly lyric but can be incorporated very comfortably into the mode.

Crucially, Swift's brutal parody of an amorous lyric retains the style and structure of the original. The famous final couplet stabilizes his dark poem through a resolution that glibly exchanges desirable and degraded matter:

Such order from confusion sprung,
Such gaudy tulips raised from dung.

The substitution of disgust for enchantment, of bodily discharge for bodily perfection, implies their exchangeable character. Swift's poem is disturbing because the language of admiration collaborates too readily with the imagery of human filth. He aligns desire and disgust with such ease that we recoil. The implication of so ready an affinity is that desire and disgust are usually directed toward the same object, and that the things we most love threaten to decay into the putrefaction of which we are most afraid.

5

Holding On to the Corpse

FLESHLY REMAINS IN

A JOURNAL OF THE PLAGUE YEAR

In 1665 the plague took hold of London, killing more than forty thousand people.[1] It was the first of the calamities to fall on England's capital in the 1660s—to be followed by the fire of 1666 and the invasion of the Medway by the Dutch fleet in June 1667. Nearly sixty years later, in 1722, Daniel Defoe published his quasi-historical account of the epidemic, *A Journal of the Plague Year*. The *Journal* describes London as a city bereft: emptied of healthy, prosperous citizens and filled instead with the corpses of plague victims. As many commentators have observed, Defoe's city is a dystopian version of eighteenth-century London: populated by disease-wracked bodies instead of able-bodied men and women, it is a city in which contagion spreads like conversation, where "exchange" does not signal healthy trade among prosperous citizens but rather the threat of infection, the unwitting transfer of deadly germs.[2] The London of Defoe's *Journal* is a place of surplus and excess, and in this respect it has something in common with the thriving capital city of the *Tatler* and the *Spectator*. But unlike these eighteenth-century idealizations, abundance in the *Journal* is figured not in prosperity and fiscal plenitude but in the corpses of plague victims that litter the streets, fill up the newly dug plague pits, and lie around putrefying in houses, often for weeks on end.

In Defoe's account of the plague, the corpse becomes waste, stuff that has to be disposed of as quickly and cleanly as possible, and it also remains the glorious body of a loved one. This is the paradox of feeling in the *Journal*; it is, moreover, the paradox of the terrestrial body in Protestant theology, as Defoe's text will remind us. Lying in the deserted streets of plague-ridden London, human bodies are unwieldy surpluses, the contagious remnants, or debris, of the city's work force. The uncanny thing about plague corpses is that they no longer permit abjection to be separated from selfhood: real people, friends, relations, become waste. Recently-alive, recognizable people become the leftovers that begin to decay in London's streets and houses. In Defoe's *Journal*, the narrator, H.F., describes how piles of corpses are collected en masse each night, thrown into the plague pits, and covered roughly with earth. There are bodies scattered through the city streets, untouched and even unnoticed, people left dead and dying in houses, ignored for many days until they begin to putrefy and smell. Bodies pile up across London, which itself grows emptier and more desolate as the year wears on. Defoe's narrative tells two stories at once: the tragic, human drama of death and the fear of decay, and a prosaic, quotidian narrative about the problem of dealing with urban waste.

The London of the *Journal* is a wasteland, littered with the bodies of plague victims as it was soon to be littered with the rubble and debris from the Great Fire.[3] By telling a story in which putrefying corpses become the waste matter polluting the city's thoroughfares, Defoe makes explicit the fear that haunts all the writings explored in this study: that ordinary refuse and human decay are metonymically linked. As Caroline Bynum writes, "the body that dies is also the body that remains; whether, and how, we handle it makes a difference. Those who have experienced the loss of loved ones in the violent disappearances of spacecraft explosions, air crashes, drownings, or war can understand how Jewish and Christian resurrection belief arose in the context of persecutions that threatened to make it impossible to reassemble the shattered bodies of the martyrs for burial."[4] At last we get to the heart of the matter. In the gruesome, tragic spectacle of disposable bodies, we see why people long to hold on to waste. We are reminded again of Kolnai's suggestion that waste matter reminds us of our own mortality by way of "physiological reminiscences": waste is "simply the presence, the non-obliteration, of traces of life."[5]

I

In 1665, the problem posed by the presence of so many corpses was relatively straightforward: how could, and where could, so many bodies be buried quickly? The solution was to dig vast plague pits around the periphery of the city, the largest of which was in Finsbury Fields. The bodies were buried there by night and covered with lime, and then the mass graves were left open for the next group of victims. When H.F. goes to see the pits, he describes the burials in fascinated detail and returns to look again, unable to turn away. Defoe's interest in reconstructing the spectacle of the plague pits is itself worth noting. He must have realized that even in 1722 the remnants of these bodies were only just out of sight beneath the rebuilt city of London. The city had spread out over the plague pits; trade and commerce had resumed above the decaying bodies of the previous generation. The pits haunted Defoe's eighteenth century, as the ghosts of traitors haunted Dryden's Restoration. These literary works are in part made from remnants, not only the literal remnants I have been describing but the remains of earlier texts. The competing desires to preserve and discard, so central to material waste, are an essential part of the psychology of literary history too. Defoe intimates this in the historical retrospective of the *Journal*, reminding us that even this most modern of eighteenth-century writers was drawn, like the others in this book, to the remnants of his literary and cultural past.

The pits served on the one hand to make the fleshly decay seem like any other kind of disintegration; they stripped the corpse of its mystique, reminding eighteenth-century Londoners that the dust of the corpse, like the ashes of the Fire, was supposed to be built upon. But on the other hand, by making putrefaction more visible, the unceremonious plague burials caused people to realize how disturbing, how uncanny, is the spectacle of fleshly decay. If remnants and residue were perversely precious in eighteenth-century culture, surely it was because of their metonymic connection with the residues that no one can bear to acknowledge as waste: the bodies of the dead. In Bynum's words again, "the sort of presence we usually mean by body and the sort of tug we usually mean by desire are radically related to each other in both the medieval and the modern periods. We do not usually speak of desire for a ghost or a memory, or think of our desire as in our minds."[6] Desire and grief are felt for the body itself.

The idea that we're supposed to make connections between victims' corpses and other, more prosaic forms of urban waste is suggested by Defoe's descriptions of the way plague victims were buried. The unceremonious disposal of the bodies into pits "40 foot in length, 15 or 16 Foot broad" and eventually "near 20 foot deep" make these troughs seem more like cavities made for a city dump.[7] H.F. encourages the comparison when he tell us that the city magistrates "ordered [a] dreadful Gulph to be dug; for such it was rather than a Pit" (59). Into this pit, we're told, "bodies are shot promiscuously" (63), from carts that rumble through London's streets "very full of dead bodies" (63). With its talk of bodies being heaped into carts by night as though they were dung and ferried to vast troughs at the periphery of the city, H.F.'s narrative recalls much more routine acts of waste disposal that were so often discussed and debated in the city records. Garbage disposal, as Swift reminds us, was by no means a problem of the past. Emily Cockayne reports on the issue: a hundred cartloads of rubbish were dumped near Lincoln's Inn in 1679; butchers dumped rotting viscera, "the soyle and filth of their Slaughter houses and hogstyes," in a Westminster churchyard. Six men were indicted for nuisance in 1721 after throwing animal blood and excrement into the streets. The contents of chamber pots were dumped onto dunghills, across open streets, or tipped over private walls.[8] By 1762 the problem was still nowhere near resolved; extensive legislation attempted to bring about the removal of garbage, filth, and nuisance from London's streets.[9] The confusion of interment with garbage disposal is what gives Defoe's burial narrative its horrifying impact; corpses that proliferate like urban garbage need to be swept away like the "dead dogs and turnip tops, tumbling down the flood" of Swift's "City Shower."

In one of the most lurid passages of the *Journal*, H.F. tells us that the plague victims race to the pits, not for a final glimpse of their loved ones, but in order to bury themselves. The victims inter their own bodies, and the officers cover them over, clearing the city of its corpses before they can start to rot. The system, dreadful as it is, amounts to a diabolically efficient means of waste disposal:

> People that were Infected, and near their End, and delirious also, would run to those Pits wrapt in Blankets, or Rugs, and throw themselves in, and as they said, bury themselves: I cannot say, that the Officers suffered any willingly to lie there; but I have heard, that in a great Pit in Finsbury, in the Parish of Cripplegate, it lying open then to the Fields; for it was not then wall'd about, came and threw themselves in, and expired there, before they threw any Earth upon them; and that when they came to bury others, and found them there, they were quite dead, tho' not cold. (60)

What we see here is a desire for putrefaction on the part of the victims—a wish to become a rotting corpse, just like their friends and companions. The last act of will manifest in these terrestrial bodies reflects their desire to putrefy. Indeed, as H.F. adds the gruesome detail that the victims' bodies still give off warmth, we sense almost that decomposition begins while the victim is still alive. H.F.'s technique is to make the transition from living flesh to material waste instantaneous, because the fictionally "slowed" shift from life to death performed by the funeral ceremony has been suspended. These people will wait for nothing in their desire to be in the ground. The scene is defined by repeated running and throwing—"run to those pits," "throw themselves in" (a repeated motif), "quite dead, tho' not cold"—such is the violence with which they hurl themselves into death. (Even the syntax of the passage is distorted; it becomes increasingly difficult to separate the living and the dead, as pronouns referring to the officers collapse into those referring to the dying.) The description emphasizes, again, the proximity of vitality to waste. The animate, vigorous body that propels itself into the ground is the very body that will begin to putrefy only moments later. The ideal body in a time of pestilence is one that embraces its status as a residue.

H.F. insists on the literal sense in which the flesh becomes refuse during the plague: "whole families, and indeed, whole Streets of Families, were swept away together; insomuch, that it was frequent for Neighbours to call to the Bellman, to go to such and such Houses, and fetch out the People, for that they were all Dead" (102). The metaphor "swept away" exposes the way in which the language of waste disposal is applicable to the treatment of plague corpses. We are being presented with a diabolical vision of the Enlightenment shift to a secularized corpse, where bodies become matter that has not been adequately disposed of; waste too over-whelming to be shifted efficiently: "and indeed, the Work of removing the dead Bodies by Carts, was now grown so very odious and dangerous that it was complain'd of, that the Bearers did not take Care to clear such Houses, where all the Inhabitants were dead; but that sometimes the Bodies lay several days unburied, till the neighbouring Families were offended with the Stench" (102). The problem of dead bodies involves the pragmatic threat of bad hygiene and contagion; the fear of the corpse is rendered as a secular dread of its unsavory properties, not, as we might expect of someone writing in the Puritan tradition, a sign of anxiety about the individual's fate at the Last Judgment. In the spectacle of the pits we are reminded of the living conditions even in a healthy city: Lincoln's Inn Fields, for example, was described as having "for some years past lain waste and in great Disorder, whereby the same has become a Receptacle for Rubbish, Dirt and Nastiness of all Sorts."[10]

When Giambattista Vico published the *New Science* in 1725, he chose the burial of the dead as one of three paradigmatic social practices that are the signs of civilized culture. Vico explained that all civilized cultures bury their dead because not to do so would be barbaric:

> [L]et us imagine a brutish state in which human corpses are left unburied as carrion for crows and dogs. Such bestial behavior clearly belongs to the world of uncultivated fields and uninhabited cities, in which people wandered like swine, eating acorns gathered amid the rotting corpses of their dead kin. This is why burials were rightly defined in a lofty Latin phrase as "the covenants of the human race."[11]

Vico's description of burial encounters the same paradox underwriting Defoe's burial narrative: the idea that the corpse has an ineradicable cultural value, even though it is a material remnant. This is what makes

Defoe's description of the plague pits so shocking: the corpse is no longer treated as though its value is elevated above that of other residues. But when Vico says that sophisticated societies refuse to regard the corpse as a mere leftover, he is not arguing that the attitude would be wrong as such. On the contrary, it would be exactly correct; the corpse is a form of waste, considered dispassionately. Both Vico's and Defoe's accounts acknowledge that it is their very tendency to decompose that gives corpses a special significance. They would merely be filthy remainders, "carrion for crows and dogs"—except that they are also the surviving parts of one's family and friends. Each writer is responding to the problem inherent in corpse disposal—that even though corpses putrefy, they retain a special status. Vico's account of burial helps to explain why Defoe's *Journal* articulates a tension between the desire to retain and the desire to dispose of the corpse. As we have seen, it is a tension inherent to narratives of surplus, of which the corpse is the paradigmatic instance.

Descriptions of abundance evoke both the desirability of cornucopia and the undesirability of surfeit, akin to decay. On the one hand, burial does not eradicate decay; it merely makes it invisible. On the other hand, the burial ceremony recognizes that the corpse is not merely waste; "rotting corpses" are, simultaneously, "dead kin"—corpses are precious remnants, or echoes, of the living person. So the interment of the dead turns surplus to loss: the remainder of a person is converted ceremonially into a residue that putrefies. Joseph Roach eloquently points out that "this paradox of immortality amid physical decay . . . discovers the profoundly ambivalent emotions human beings harbor for the dead, who once belonged among the living but who now inhabit some alien country whose citizens putrefy yet somehow endure."[12]

A Journal of the Plague Year charts an alteration that takes place among Londoners in their attitudes to the victims' corpses. H.F. reports that the streets came to be filled with bodies, who at first attract a good deal of attention but which eventually cease even to be noticed by passersby:

> These objects were so frequent in the Streets, that when the Plague came to be very raging, on one Side, there was scarce any passing by the Streets, but that several dead Bodies would be lying here and there upon the Ground; on the other hand it is observable, that tho' at first, the People would stop as they went along, and call to

the Neighbours to come out on such an Occasion; yet, afterward,
no Notice was taken of them. (79)

As H.F. explains, corpses have at first a special significance as the remnants of the living: "the People would stop as they went along." But
eventually, the recognition that they are to be distinguished from other
kinds of remnants passes. It is not that the bodies of the dead go away,
but London's citizens stop seeing them. Is this, in fact, the city of Vico's
description, in which "people wandered like swine, eating acorns gathered amid the rotting corpses of their dead kin"?

The passage above reads like a distorted version of a ghost story, in
which the spirits of the dead are replaced by the haunting presence of
their lingering corpses. Instead of describing the return of the ghosts or
spirits of the deceased, the passage suggests that their corporeal remains
threaten to obstruct the passage of secular, civic life in very practical
ways. In the place of a then familiar argument against the superstitious
practice of believing in ghosts, Defoe's fable warns us about the perils
of allowing the remnants of the dead to remain within sight of the living. Defoe's text seems to be saying that it is vital to separate the dead,
as waste matter, from the living, to prevent putrefaction from festering
amid the habits of modern commerce. But in fact the *Journal* is not calling for so straightforward a segregation of waste flesh from living beings.
As we read on, we realize that the bodies of plague victims are troubling
to London's citizens because in fact they want to retain the waste flesh of
the deceased as much as they need to dispose of it. "Whereas remember-
ing lets the spirits rest and be forgotten, relics . . . keep the person present."[13] The desire to hold on to the corpse as it putrefies shows us why
waste, paradoxically, has value. The flesh that decays is the flesh of the
same body that, in life, generated energy, vigor, and abundance.

II

For Defoe, the plague represented an episode in which an entire city began
to rot from within in which putrefaction took place amid—and progres-
sively took the place of trade and commerce. At one point Defoe describes the City after the outbreak of plague as an unnatural dreamscape,

where people walk in file up the center of the streets, desperate to avoid any contact with their fellow citizens: "I went up to Holbourn, and there the Street was full of People; but they walk'd in the middle of the great Street, neither on one Side or other, because, as I suppose, they would not mingle with any Body that came out of Houses, or meet with Smells and Scents from Houses that might be infected" (17). The street is "full," giving the impression of life continuing as normal, but no one speaks or goes in or out of the buildings. The habits of a prosperous city cannot be maintained: people will not "mingle with any Body," and Defoe's telling phrase "meet with Smells and Scents" reminds us that communication and exchange have been displaced by a *fear* of communication, of "meeting." The corpses lying in houses and on the street represent a bizarre version of an alienated urban crowd. "Occupants spilled out of their crowded homes and possessed the urban spaces. The streets rang with broadcasting of municipal news, canvassing, debate and conversation. Doorstep tittle-tattle blended with rowdy banter and marketplace barter."[14] But in Defoe's plague-stricken London, "mingling" does not take place among people; "anybody" becomes "any Body," as the circumstances of the epidemic force the living to mingle, silently, with the unburied dead. How would this description have sounded to readers in the London of the 1720s, when Defoe wrote the *Journal*? The "full streets" of plague London invoke the teeming city of the eighteenth century, reminding Defoe's readers of the effects of disease and putrefaction, of the importance of urban hygiene, both literal and figurative. When we mingle and meet in eighteenth-century London, Defoe's text seems to imply, is it to be with the prosperous and healthy, or with the diseased and dying? The tension in the passage between fullness and an impending sense of emptiness and desolation is crucial to Defoe's theme: are the city's surpluses to take the form of prosperity and abundance, or of a surfeit of bodies, and the saturating "scents and smells" of putrefaction?

But in spite, or perhaps because, of this uncanny affinity between the living person and the putrefying corpse there were a series of attempts at the end of the seventeenth century to draw more rigid distinctions between the living and dead: cemeteries were removed from the center of London, so that the bodies of the dead could be kept within more decorous boundaries. Joseph Roach describes how "in his 'proposals' of

1711 for constructing the churches, Sir John Vanbrugh, architect, dramatist and comptroller of works under Queen Anne, laid out the Enlightenment's case for reorganizing urban space to ghettoize the dead."[15] Vanbrugh proposed that cemeteries must be provided "at the skirts of towne."[16] As we know from texts written in the aftermath of the 1666 disaster, London's suburbs were regarded as threatening to trade and commerce in the city; lying outside the perimeters of commercial activity, they could represent only dissipated civic energy ("Tell us not of the Suburbs, Citizens know how inconvenient they are for their business," intoned Samuel Rolls in 1668).[17]

The removal of London's cemeteries indicated that there were to be newly demarcated *boundaries* between the living and dead. Paradoxically, however, the effect of such segregation is to obscure the point at which the flesh becomes a residue, at which the body turns into waste matter. In the self-burial scene from the *Journal*, by contrast, such a transition is made too visible. The proximity of material waste and material abundance becomes uncomfortably real when living people commit their own bodies into an open pit to putrefy. By the time Defoe wrote *A Journal of the Plague Year*, people were aware of how uncomfortable it made them to look too closely at the moment when material loss takes place, when matter turns into waste.

Implicit in Defoe's account of the plague victims being left to rot in the streets and houses of London is his sense that things have improved: that public life in the eighteenth century was more hygienic, more scrupulously attentive to the clean disposal of the corpse. Putrefaction was no longer taking place in the open. But although the phenomenon of bodily putrefaction had been made more decorous, the sweeping away of the dead bodies in order to dump them unceremoniously into the pits does resonate with a very commonplace sentiment in eighteenth-century London. There was a group of people who seemed to lie about in the streets, figuratively, if not actually, rotting in passageways. In the eyes of those who hurried about in pursuit of commercial gain, beggars and vagrants filled the streets like garbage, blocking the progress of passersby. The notion that London was full of "waste people" generated passages like this one, which describes the unregulated movement of anonymous bodies as a material impediment needing to be cleared away, as though they were so many gigantic waste heaps: "[T]wo persons cannot come together in the Streets but they are instantly encircled with a crew of Beggars and a Man that hath occasion to pass in haste had need to hire a lusty fellow to go before him with a truncheon to clear the way of those vast Bodies of them that obstruct the Passengers with Brooms, Brushes and crutches."[18]

When the word "vast" appears in this passage, it reads like a surrogate for the suppressed term "waste." The surplus of London's beggars makes them seem disposable, a mere glut of wasted matter. The imagery of clearing and cleaning quickly becomes confusing; the people employed to sweep London's streets and alleys become pollutants themselves, needing to be cleared away with the more forceful instrument of a "truncheon." The kind of low-level violence described in the passage seems much more benign when it is represented as a clean-up operation, a public work. Peter Linebaugh points out that London's beggars and vagrants were regarded as a contaminating presence in the eighteenth-century capital: the "'idle 'prentice' was a social figure every bit as threatening to the established order as the 'sturdy rogue' of the sixteenth century, or the 'sectary' of the seventeenth century, or the 'factory proletarian' of the nineteenth century."[19]

In the pamphlet quoted above, the problem of human flesh as waste matter moves back into the realm of the living. In place of the claim that the *corpse* is a residue or leftover, without utility, needing to be removed, is the claim that certain *living people* are residual, surplus to the demands of consumer society, and even threatening to its operation. This shift from the dead to the living reorients what is essentially an epistemological claim about the status of the body to a sociological argument about the marginal status of particular groups. By situating their argument among the living rather than the dead, texts dealing with the body can resist the image of the corpse itself as remaindered matter.

In a pamphlet entitled *An Enquiry into the Frequent Causes of Executions at Tyburn* (1725), roughly contemporaneous with Defoe's *Journal,* Bernard Mandeville would make his argument for dissecting the bodies of criminals in these terms:

Where then shall we find a readier Supply; and what Degree of People are fitter for it than those [criminals] I have named? When Persons of no Possessions of their own, that have slipp'd no opportunity of wronging whomever they could, die without Restitution, indebted to the Publick, ought not the injur'd Publick to have a Title to, and the Disposal of, what the others have left? And is anything more reasonable, than that they should enjoy that Right, especially when they only make use of it for commendable Purposes?[20]

Mandeville's characteristically cynical attitude here is that the corpse is without utility, and therefore the dissection of criminals is fair game. He represents the flesh as a leftover, "what the others have left," a residue subject to disposal. But the left-over corpse is converted in the language of Mandeville's passage from the body of the criminal into a *debt*, owed to the "injur'd Publick." The flesh is explicitly figured as unclaimed property, to which the public has a "title" and "right." By invoking the rights of property, Mandeville reproduces the logic of those enclosure pamphlets discussed earlier, which pressed for the "improvement" of wasteland. As we saw in the discussion of wasteland's improvement, it is the potential utility of waste, combined with its degraded condition, which constructs a seemingly irrefutable argument for possession. Mandeville reproduces this argument here with the phrases "ready supply," "make use," and "commendable Purposes," which remind the reader that the unclaimed bodies of criminals, in abundant oversupply, are waste. Mandeville takes up arguments familiar from tracts on the use of uncultivated land to generate his case for reusing the corpse.

There is something in the tone of Mandeville's argument that sounds defensive. He shifts into social arguments about the body of the criminal precisely *because* he is conscious that his support for the dissection of corpses is hard to justify. He is not, after all, talking about land use or other kinds of secular residue but about the remains of the living, watched over at the Tyburn gallows by friends and relatives—and by a heaving crowd of London's poor, spoiling for a fight. The attempt to figure the corpse as a material leftover is deeply unsettling. By pointing out that certain kinds of citizens are leftovers, Mandeville implies that not *all* bodies should be regarded as waste—only the corpses of those who "owe" their flesh to the public. A little later in the pamphlet, he reassures the reader that he or she need not fear dissection themselves, since "the Dishonour [of dissection] would seldom reach beyond the Scum of the People." Instead of relying on the claim that the corpse itself is waste matter, Mandeville makes the paradoxically *less* controversial argument that there exists a stratum of social scum, the effluvia of society. Social waste, for Mandeville, is constituted by London's criminals, who take from society without repaying their debt. He suggests, therefore, that there is a kind of living waste, a body of leftover or remaindered people needing to be "disposed of." He obviously expects that such a supposition will be more readily accepted than the idea that when a person, any person, makes the transition from life to death, their body becomes waste. As evidence of a similar instance of the attempt to produce a class of "waste people," Foucault describes a prisoner in France, who is carried to the scaffold in a cart generally used for carrying garbage: "even as late in the eighteenth century as 1772, one finds sentences like the following: a servant girl at Cambrai, having killed her mistress, was condemned to be taken to the place of her execution in a cart 'used to collect rubbish at the crossroads.'"[21]

Implicit in Mandeville's argument is his sense that there is something intolerable about the notion of human flesh as waste. Even though at face value he adopts a secular, enlightened attitude toward the body, even though he argues strongly for the recycling of the body after death and against a superstitious attitude to the corpse—something in him shies away from adopting completely neutral, scientific terms. Mandeville's text on the Tyburn gallows reveals that the notion of a class of "waste people" is, paradoxically, a more acceptable position than the idea that the corpse is a form of secular waste matter. Peter Linebaugh implies a similar point when he shows that the move to regard the bodies of the dead as mere matter, subject to the fluctuations of a market economy, was a far more controversial claim than that which represented criminals as the refuse or waste matter of society: "by the end of the [eighteenth] century some writers combined arguments of scientific utility with the language of political economy and wrote of the 'supply and demand' of dead bodies. Such arguments of scientific utility were still rare in the early eighteenth century and typically were mixed with the frank expression of class hatred."[22] The association of London's "hanged" with the notion of the residual or waste body enables most people to retain the idea that the corpse is always an "other." The frightening sense that one's own self might be treated, literally, as waste is mollified in texts such as Mandeville's by his assurance that only the bodies of metaphorically "waste people" will become involved in a secular economy of the corpse. Jonathan Sawday makes a similar point: "some Europeans looked into the marginal members of their own societies—the criminal, the poor, the insane, suicides, orphans, even, simply, 'strangers'—as potential 'material' upon which they could legitimately practice their own researches and investigations into the human form."[23]

A Journal of the Plague Year responds to these contemporary debates by investigating what it means for a culture to retain its residues. Defoe's treatment not only of the body but of historical narrative itself enables him to suggest that the collective desire to relinquish the past always competes with the desire to retain it. Through his narrator, Defoe revives an episode from the Restoration and describes it as though it constituted the immediate present. He also turns back to providential, millennial narrative modes associated with the upheavals of the previous century, although the story he tells, and the culture he describes, are self-consciously outmoded by the 1720s. The text is filled with remnants and leftovers: the bodies lining the city streets, the spectacle of the plague pits, still lying beneath the thriving capital of Defoe's day; the Bills of Mortality and population statistics; the lists of parishes and drawings of astrological charts—remainders make up the fabric of Defoe's narrative. *A Journal of the Plague Year* reveals that an anthropology of London is located not only in the residues of everyday life but also in the historical remnant itself—the episode from the city's past that must, somehow, be made to constitute the present.

III

H.F.'s description of the plague pits figure a distorted account of a burial ceremony in which Defoe rewrites Christian interment as a narrative of self-disposal. But although the scene is stripped of all the ceremonial aspects of burial, it distills nonetheless two of the most critical strains in reformed Christian doctrine: the will to die and an acceptance of putrefaction. These are, indeed, the only desires that Defoe's citizens feel, as they rush frantically into the ground. Defoe has linked the theological paradoxes surrounding the terrestrial body's decay to the containment and eradication of urban waste matter, a crucial issue in the London of 1722. So what might look at first like feverish insanity on the part of Defoe's plague victims can also be read as a willing renunciation of the terrestrial body.

The corpse is waste matter both in secular and in theological terms. Its significance as secular residue was actively considered in a number of important texts from the Restoration that argued that the corpse was unsavory, and that it needed to be removed from the daily sight of civic society.[24] In 1665, for example, Robert Boyle published his *Occasional Reflections upon Several Subjects* (significantly enough the year of the plague). He argued here against prevailing superstitions about the dead body, calling for widespread acceptance of its dissection for anatomical study. In other words, Boyle is making a case for reusing bodies that will otherwise go to waste. Jonathan Sawday points out that "what Boyle's text offers us is an idealized view of the scientific conquest of the body. This is how one *should* feel, Boyle is saying, if the body is no more than a machine."[25] The status of the corpse was complicated, moreover, by the bodies of the diseased, who were regarded as actively malevolent, "not just offensive to human dignity, but as dangerous to human health, waging what Voltaire called 'the war of the dead against the living.'"[26] Mary Douglas's famous aphorism, "dirt is matter out of place," now applied to the human body: "uncleanness or dirt is that which must not be included if a pattern is to be maintained."[27] While these developments were taking place in the world of secular, or civic, considerations, a strikingly similar set of debates was taking place amongst the theologians of the period.

The division in Defoe's narrative between secular and theological habits of thought is revealed in H.F.'s grateful declaration that "in this terrible Judgment of God, many better than I was swept away, and carried to their grave: But . . . I was mercifully preserved by that great God" (65). As we've seen, the phrase "swept away" is literally true; the bodies of the victims were gathered up in the dead-cart and "carried to their grave" in the plague pits like refuse. In the interests of public health and hygiene, it was necessary to "sweep away" the bodies of the deceased. But the phrase also has theological implications, drawing attention to the apparently random distinction between those who are infected and those who are "preserved." H.F.'s remarks shift away from their secular register with the providential claim that he was "miraculously preserved by that great God." The disposal of bodies is on the one hand a sign of divine intervention and on the other a matter of pragmatic, secular convenience.

When Richard Baxter, a divine of enormous influence and renown among nonconformists at the Restoration, wrote *The Saints' Everlasting Rest* (1650), he devoted a significant part of his text to "Reproving Our Unwillingness to Die." Here he argued forcefully against feeling a strong attachment to the flesh, not only because death comes with the promise of eternal life for the Christian, but also because Christ willingly endured, and then renounced, his human frame: "The Lord Jesus was willing to come from heaven to earth for us, and shall we be unwilling to remove from earth to heaven for ourselves and Him? . . . Shall He come down to our hell, from the height of glory to the depth of misery, to bring us up to His eternal rest, and shall we be after this unwilling? Sure Christ had more cause to be unwilling."[28]

The unwillingness of these hypothetical sinners, who aren't yet ready to die, is reversed in the hyperwillingness of Defoe's plague victims, who cannot wait to forsake their flesh and begin to rot. In the terms of Baxter's argument, the "willingness to die" that Defoe's characters manifest so clearly is theologically important because death represents the moment at which the flesh can be discarded. According to Baxter, attachment to life is evidence of an overattachment to the body—a sign of the corruption in those who "value their flesh above their spirits, and their lusts above [the] Father's love." Baxter's interpretation of resurrection doctrine suggests that it is a perverse sign of piety to regard the body as disposable and the flesh as waste. When Defoe asks his readers to think about the significance of urban residues, or waste, he does so by connecting it to seemingly arcane debates surrounding the residue of the terrestrial body in resurrection theology. Jonathan Dollimore reminds us that the connection between desire and death is essential to the western imagination: "desire's impossibility derives from the fact that socialized desire is a lack which it is impossible to appease because it is the lack of death itself, with life merely an enforced substitute for death, a movement in the only direction available, which is forward, and one always undertaken against the more fundamental desire to regress, to die."[29]

In 1589, an anonymous pamphleteer, "Marphoreous," entered into the Marprelate debates with a boisterous satire announcing Martin's death: *Martin's Months Minde, That Is, A Certaine Report, and True Description of the Death, and Funeralls, of Olde Martin Marreprelate, the great makebate of England, and father of the Factious.*[30] The Marprelate satires mocked Puritan religious reform in the sixteenth century. Himself working within and coming out of the Puritan tradition, Defoe would not only have been familiar with the Marprelate satires but would have been struggling with Puritan attitudes toward the body—on the one hand eschewing its veneration, but on the other hand confronting the desire on the part of mourners to commemorate the body of the deceased. *Martin's Months Minde* includes a long passage in which the dying Martin orders his funeral, according to the Puritan dictate of a straightforward burial with an absence of ceremony. His proposal, however, amounts essentially to a demand that his body be left to rot like garbage—that it be treated, in other words, remarkably like the corpses of plague victims in Defoe's *Journal*:

> Next touching his bodie, (for it should seeme he had forgotten his soule, for the partie that heard it told me, he heard no word of it) he would, should not be buried in any *Church*, (especiallie *Cathedrall*, which ever he detested) *Chapell* nor *Churchyard*, for that they had been prophaned, with superstition: but in some barne, outhouse, or field (yea, rather than faile, dunghill) where their prime prophecyings had been used; without bell, pompe, or any solemnitie; save that his friends should mourne for him in gownes, and hoods, of a bright yellowe. . . . Minister he would have none to bury him, but his sonne, or some one of his lay bretheren, to tumble him into the pit.

This passage satirizes a supposed radical attitude toward the burial of the dead in the aftermath of the Reformation. Radical religious sects repudiated elaborate funeral rituals, regarding them as a reflection of the Catholic belief that the living could intervene on behalf of the dead.[31] Although the subject of salvation was contemplated with considerable uncertainty after the abolition of purgatory, English Puritans argued that there was no ongoing relationship with the deceased, and that the interment of the flesh should be as undemonstrative as possible.[32] *Martin's Month's Minde* parodies this position by figuring the body as a form of sacred waste matter. His list of possible alternative burial grounds places his earthly frame into closer and closer contact with the most profane of residues, human excrement. He imagines himself as a large disintegrating turd, lying, as such refuse does, in a barn, outhouse, or field. The passage secularizes the body by describing it in the imagery of garbage or refuse; the language of theology is evacuated and replaced with the imagery of temporal, physical residues. Which is to say that Martin makes the radical intellectual leap into imagining the corpse as a secular by-product—a move reflected in the descriptions of burial in the *Journal*.

In order to demand that the dead be relinquished without sentiment or residual attachment, nonsatirical tracts describing radical attitudes to the body use the argument that the corpse is a leftover, subject to decay. In other words, the connection between the living and the dead is articulated in theological as well as in secular writing by describing the body as physical waste matter, distasteful and, by implication, threatening to the living. A text from 1635, for example, *Mr Boltons Last and Learned Worke of the Foure Last Things*, argues for the disposal of the body in the following terms: "thy body, when the soul is gone, will be an horror to all that behold it; a most loathsome and abhorred spectacle. Those that loved it most, cannot now find it in their hearts to look on't, by reason of the griefly deformedness which death will put upon it. Down it must into a pit of carrions and confusion, covered with worms . . . and so moulder away into rottenness and dust."[33]

The logic that Bolton deploys is that the family should reject the corpses of their loved ones without ceremony since the body becomes mere remainder, debased and deformed, once the soul has departed from its fleshly frame. Bolton's urgent, overwrought prose emphasizes the dense materiality of the corpse, which makes the spectacle of its disintegration "most loathsome and abhorred." The passage suggests that the shift from life to death involves a ghastly shift in the material significance of the flesh itself: one's friends are changed into deformed bodies; they pass from animate selfhood into material residue, from individual identity to generic materiality. They must "moulder away into rottenness and dust." The strange phrase "griefly deformities" conveys the idea that grief is connected to imagining deformed flesh; we grieve by imagining that the body we once knew intimately is eroding gradually into nothingness.

Defoe's ghastly description of disposable bodies was not an isolated instance in the history of waste. Nor is it singular in the writing of the early eighteenth century (although it is certainly peculiar). Instead, one of the most contentious theological debates of Defoe's day revolved around the meaning of the putrefying corpse. John Locke, Edward Stillingfleet, and the other major divines and philosophers of the period argued at length about whether the resurrected body will be the *same* body. Their disputes revolved around the interpretation of chapter 15 of Paul's first letter to the Corinthians and the distinction drawn there between the terrestrial and the celestial body. As theologians of the resurrection were quick to point out, the passage from 1 Corinthians is as much concerned with the decay of the flesh as it is with the resurrection of the body; Paul's text is filled with references to waste, disintegration, the eating away of the flesh, and the rotting of the carcass. He insists upon the soul's rapid loss of its fleshly frame after death, explicitly declaring that we must, literally, leave our bodies behind: "we brought nothing into this world, and it is certain we can carry nothing out." The dead are not to be raised up in the frame of their earthly bodies, for "flesh and blood cannot inherit the kingdom of God; neither doth corruption inherit incorruption." The fleshly body is corrupt; it is always, already wasted. "It is sown in dishonour; it is raised in glory: It is sown in weakness; it is raised in power: It is sown a natural body; it is raised a spiritual body. There is a natural body, and there is a spiritual body." The strain of worldly imagery that runs throughout 1 Corinthians relies on a comparison between the body and other forms of material residue or leftover that we more readily accept as waste. The signs of human beauty are to be eaten like a piece of cloth that has been disfigured by decay: "thou makest his beauty to consume away, like as it were a moth fretting a garment." We are reminded that we are like cut grass: "in the morning it is green, and groweth up: but in the evening it is cut down, dried up, and withered," and that we bloom briefly, like flowers: "He cometh up, and is cut down."

The phenomenon of material decay described here generates a set of associations with the disintegration of worldly commodities, with perishable goods.[34] It draws the text of the burial service into a relationship with the familiar secular phenomenon of physical disintegration, implying an unexpected parallel between the body of the deceased and the much more prosaic waste matter of secular society. In its attempt to diminish the attachment felt by the living to the bodies of the dead, the ceremony breaks apart our instinctive resistance to the idea that the corpse resembles other leftovers. The burial service concludes with the phrase: "we therefore commit his body to the ground; earth to earth, ashes to ashes, dust to dust." The "therefore" is crucial here and reveals why the wasted body is central to the logic of the resurrection. It is *because* we believe in the resurrection that we leave the body to decay; the spectacle of wasted flesh, of material decay, is a counterintuitive testimony to faith in salvation. This position is manifest in a fascination with the imagery of bodily decay. The morbid description of worms chewing through human skin and flesh is, paradoxically, a sign of belief in the glorified body to come: "though after my skin worms destroy this body, yet in my flesh I shall see God." It might seem misleading to align the body with the other kinds of waste-matter discussed here—the dust heaps, the piles of ashes after the Fire, the mounds of dirt around the plague pits. But in each of these is an echo from the famous phrases "earth to earth, ashes to ashes, dust to dust"; the liturgy for burial of the dead echoes in the description of wasteland.

Defoe's descriptions of the dead and dying will take us back to Martin's corpse, for the victims "were driven to dreadful Exigencies and Extremities, and Perish'd in the Streets or Fields for mere Want, or drop'd down, by the raging violence of the Fever upon them; . . . they have perished by the Road Side, or gotten into Barns and dy'd there, none daring to come to them, or relieve them" (54). The terms of Nashe's parody had been literalized by the plague, as bodies were laid to rest on unconsecrated ground. Defoe's descriptions of the disposal of bodies are anticipated in a passage from Pepys, which is of course contemporary with the real plague: "I was much troubled this day to hear at Westminster how the officers so bury the dead in the open Tuttle-fields, pretending want of room elsewhere; whereas the New-Chapel church-yard was walled in at the public charge in the last plague-time merely for want of room, and

now none but such as are able to pay dear for it can be buried there."[35]
In this passage Pepys's is exploring the idea that two different kinds of
physical remnant exist simultaneously in the spectacle of the corpse: a
secular leftover, like rubbish, and the sacred residue of the physical body.
Pepys's anecdote shows that these competing accounts of the corpse are
in uneasy exchange, although he obviously also thinks that they should
remain scrupulously distinct. The circumstances of the plague bring
about a strange situation in which some people can buy their way out
of being treated like waste; certain families can "pay dear" for the fleshly
leftovers of their deceased to be dignified as sacred remainders, whereas
others cannot.

By representing the corpse as waste, one's own body as matter to be
discarded, the author of *Martin's Monthes Minde* registers intuitive anxieties that one implication of Reformed doctrine would be the cessation of
relations between the living and the dead. If the corpse is waste, doesn't
that mean that the dead must be abandoned like other remainders? And
if so, how are we to respond to the deaths of those whom we love? This
is the fear registered in H.F.'s horrified descriptions of bodies dumped
into the plague pits. In texts such as the *Journal*, the desire to remember
is reflected in a literal holding on to the body, a literal struggle against
its disposal. By way of descriptions that are divided between holding on
to and letting go of the dead, Defoe's *Journal* negotiates a narrative that
simultaneously reflects the work of mourning—the desire to hold on
to the deceased—and the work of burial, the necessary disposal of the
body. Ironically, given Defoe's nonconformist background, the *Journal*
responds to the same divided impulses that Stephen Greenblatt describes
in relation to the doctrine of purgatory: "it enabled the dead to be not
completely dead—not as utterly gone, finished, complete as those whose
souls resided forever in Hell or Heaven."[36]

The most moving scenes from the *Journal* describe the agonizing
decisions that people take to abandon their husbands, wives, and children in order to avoid infection by plague. H.F. describes an episode in
which two men hear a great shouting and screaming inside a house, followed abruptly by total silence. Eventually one of the men investigates,
by propping a ladder up against the wall of the house and looking into
a window:

[H]e saw a Woman lying dead upon the Floor, in a dismal Manner, having no Cloaths on her but her Shift. . . . No Body was found in the House, but that young Woman, who having been infected, and past Recovery, the rest had left her to die by herself, and were every one gone, having found some Way to delude the Watchman, and get open the Door. (49–50)

One of the most chilling details of the account is the sudden silence that follows on the relatives' violent and noisy grieving. The abrupt transition from the intense communion of grief to the literal abandonment of the girl's body reflects a wrenching shift in attitude: the family change suddenly from regarding their daughter as a living person, manifest in an active, animate body, to the enforced recognition that they must abandon a corpse that threatens their own survival. The silence that fills the house suggests an exaggerated resignation to Puritan attitudes toward the corpse, which can be "immediately interred, without any ceremony."³⁷ Even the moment of interment is preempted by the departure of the family, who are forced to recognize that in the most horribly literal terms the *Directory for the Publique Worship of God* is right: a ceremonial lingering with the body is "in no way beneficial to the dead, and [has] proved many ways hurtful to the living."

H.F.'s own interest in the corpses is concentrated particularly on the moment of their burial, the moment when the living sever their connection with the dead. With the zeal of a scholar, which seems occasionally as though it might slip across into a form of necrophilia, H.F. determines to visit the pits just as the bodies are being loaded off the carts. "I resolv'd to go in the Night and see some of them thrown in" (60). He is intrigued by the transition which the body makes from being the vessel of a living person to insensible flesh, left over after death:

[T]he Cart had in it sixteen or seventeen Bodies, some were wrapt up in Linen Sheets, some in Rugs, some little other than naked, or so loose, that what Covering they had, fell from them, in the shooting out of the Cart, and they fell quite naked among the rest; but the Matter was not much to them, or the Indecency much to any one else, seeing they were all dead, and were to be huddled together into the common Grave of Mankind, as we may call it, for here was no Difference made, but Poor and Rich went together; there was no other way of Burials, neither was it possible there should, for Coffins were not to be had for the prodigious Numbers that fell in such a Calamity as this. (63)

H.F.'s uncertainty as to how he should regard the burial of the dead in plague pits reflects a parallel uncertainty in Defoe's London about the status of the body in relation to other leftovers, regarded unproblematically as material waste. When bodies are tossed into vast pits that resemble city dumps, when certain kinds of people are regarded as though they were themselves a kind of effluvium, how could the special status of the corpse be acknowledged? How could the corpse be honored? Defoe's response is suggested in one of the most moving, and symbolically resonant, passages in the *Journal*. A man searches through London for a midwife to help his infected wife with the birth of their child. He is unsuccessful:

The poor Man with his Heart broke, went back, assisted his Wife what he cou'd, acted the part of the Midwife; brought the Child dead into the World; and his Wife in about an Hour dy'd in his Arms, where he held her dead Body fast till the Morning, when the Watchman came and brought the Nurse as he had promised; and coming up the Stairs, for he had left the Door open, or only latched: They found the Man sitting with his dead Wife in his Arms; and so overwhelmed with Grief, that he dy'd in a few Hours after, without any Sign of the Infection upon him, but meerly sunk under the Weight of his Grief. (119–20)

The desires on the part of the living to keep hold of their dead give the passage its terrible complexities: the husband and wife labor together in the most intimate commemoration of life—the birth of their child—knowing not only that the child will die but that the wife will die soon afterward. The husband watches his wife die and cradles her body (like a baby) until the morning. The nurse comes, intending to assist with the newborn child, but finds the woman dead, still "held fast" by her grief-stricken husband. The knowledge that the bodies of the dead are remainders, the terrible intimation that they are a kind of waste, makes a person cling to them more dearly. It is the very recognition that when the watchman comes he will take the bodies to a plague pit that provokes the man's physical resistance to separation: "he held her dead Body fast till the Morning." The passage crystallizes the idea running throughout the *Journal* that resistance to the idea that the flesh is waste will always outstrip the recognition that it is, in some sense, a leftover like any other. Although it will decay, though it is waste matter, we cannot bear to release the corpse; its disposal is always a source of grief.

A Journal of the Plague Year has a strange affinity with Defoe's celebration of British prosperity, *A Tour through the Whole Island of Great Britain*. Plague-stricken London, marked by impoverishment, devastation, and savage disease, is a dark antitype to the London that is the centerpiece of Defoe's *Tour*, prosperous, well-governed, healthy.[38] The *Tour* is about the accumulation of wealth and prosperity since the Restoration, about the culmination during the first half of the eighteenth century of English hopes for renewal, of social energy, of political promise, of increased stability and religious settlement. The *Journal*, likewise, is concerned with the imagery of accumulation—not of wealth but of corpses, tabulated like financial records in the calculations scattered through H.F.'s narrative. The bodies of the dead, which accumulated in heaps and piles throughout the story, both echo and invert a description early in the *Journal* of the surging crowds returning to the capital in 1660:

> The Numbers of People, which the Wars being over, the Armies disbanded, and the Royal Family and the Monarchy being restor'd, had flocked to *London*, to settle into Business . . . was such, that the Town was computed to have in it above an hundred thousand people more than ever it held before. . . . All people gay and luxurious; and the Joy of the Restoration had brought a vast many Families to London. (18)

There is a comparison implied between the bodies of the Restoration crowd and the bodies of the plague victims that reveals a new and unexpected set of meanings attaching to the corpse. The dread of the corpses that pile up around London is not only related to the fear of death and judgment. The fear of the corpse is also a fear of *life*—of life without the dead. The spectacle of so many dead bodies reveals that limitless accumulation and growth is not possible. A ghastly flight to the suburbs takes place among the dead themselves, who are carried to the pits, leaving the city empty. The disintegration of civic life is registered, literally, in the heaps of corpses that take the place of proliferating commerce and communication. Hence the desire to hold on to the corpse—to arrest the segregation of the living and dead, even though segregation is exactly the means by which the modern city announces its commitment to efficiency and order.

Mr. Spectator's Tears
and Sophia Western's Muff

In one of the most remarkable essays that he wrote for the *Spectator*, Joseph Addison describes the pleasures of the Royal Exchange at the busiest moment of the trading day. "There is no Place in the Town which I so much love to frequent as the *Royal Exchange*," he begins.[1] The 'Change is, for Addison, a secular Eden, paradise in modern London. He watches with satisfaction and pride "so rich an Assembly of Country-men and Foreigners consulting together upon the private business of Mankind, . . . making this Metropolis a kind of *Emporium* for the whole Earth." In Addison's version of urban paradise, the garden of Eden has become one enormous shop; like Harrod's, there's nothing the Exchange doesn't sell. And, as in Milton's Paradise, all excess at the Royal Exchange is luxurious and splendid, never waste: it is "an . . . Emporium for the whole Earth." In this figure, the world becomes both the Exchange's stockist and customer; in one concise phrase, Addison includes the entire globe in a life of mutually agreeable mercantile transaction.

Addison has a clear picture in his mind of the kind of place the world would be were the Royal Exchange really its microcosm. It would be a place in which trade and its spoils were evenly balanced and regulated, where all of mankind participated in the pleasures of exchange and each country, each region, contributed its fair share of produce and harvested its fair share of gain. Addison's descriptions of global trade are framed in easy pairings and equivalences:

The Food often grows in one Country, and the Sauce in another. The fruits of *Portugal* are corrected by the Products of *Barbadoes*: The Infusion of a *China* Plant sweetened with the Pith of an *Indian* Cane: The *Philippick* Islands give a flavour to our *European* bowls. The single Dress of a Woman of Quality is often the Product of an hundred Climates. The Muff and the Fan come together from the different Ends of the Earth. The Scarf is sent from the Torrid Zone, and the Tippet from beneath the Pole. The Brocade Petticoat rises out of the Mines of Peru, and the Diamond necklace out of the Bowels of *Indostan*.

This is a utopia that combines Dryden's closing vision of commerce in *Annus Mirabilis*—"a constant trade wind will securely blow / And gently lay us on the spicy shore"—with the gorgeous profusion of Milton's Paradise, with its "Groves whose rich trees wept odorous gums and balm, / Others whose fruit burnished with golden rind / Hung amiable" (4.248–50). Seventeenth-century secular and sacred utopias merge in this Augustan vision of waste abolished. In Addison's harmonious phrases, the blessing of commercial exchange is that it makes all things equal and interchangeable; he achieves the vision of equivalence that Milton, Pope, and Swift all refused. Merchants "correspond" "between those wealthy societies of men divided from one another by Seas and Oceans"; even Nature herself seems designed with exchange in mind, "disseminat[ing] her blessings among the different Regions of the World, with an Eye to this mutual Intercourse and Traffick among Mankind." The key to exchange is that it involves fair conversions; it permits—indeed it ensures—balanced and, above all, exchangeable correspondence between people and nations. As Lynn Festa observes of a similarly utopian vision in Raynal's *History of the Two Indies*, "no coercive structure, no inequity, mars Raynal's happy vision of collective reciprocity."[2]

These are glorious imaginings, indeed. Under the spell of Addison's pen, colonial trade produces magical spoils, the grim details of whose production Addison's polished phrases pass lightly over. In Festa's words once again, "on the one hand, exchange is said to foster mutuality, parity, equity; on the other, the engine that drives trade is the accumulation of surplus wrung from another's loss."[3] With a lightness of touch that belies the real conditions of production, Addison causes the Muff and the Fan to come miraculously together from the different ends of the earth. About halfway through the essay Mr. Spectator reaches the high-water mark of his enthusiasm:

> As I am a great Lover of Mankind, my Heart naturally overflows with Pleasure at the sight of a prosperous and happy Multitude, insomuch that at many publick Solemnities I cannot forbear expressing my Joy with Tears that have stolen down my Cheeks. For this reason I am wonderfully delighted to see such a Body of Men thriving in their own private Fortunes, and at the same time promoting the Publick Stock; or in other Words, raising Estates for their own Families, by bringing into their Country whatever is wanting, and carrying out of it whatever is superfluous.

The sight of such another Eden is so powerful that Addison weeps tears of joy. In weeping, his own body mimics the bounty, the spoils, that the essay is commemorating. Tears represent his body's best efforts to reproduce the paradise of plenty that is created by exchange. Tears are, moreoever, superfluities that do not seem abject, they do not relate to putrefaction, like excrement, or even menstrual blood, which, as Kristeva and others point out, carries the threat of sexual danger. Rather, tears are an excess signaling purification rather than defilement. As the world overflows with the plenitude of trade, so Addison's heart and eyes overflow with cleansing fluid. In the final sentence of his essay, Addison tells us that superfluity shows there is no want. By weeping as he does, Addison is doing his best for the production of luxury. And by weeping he doesn't just mimic the bounty of the Exchange; he makes the Exchange resemble still more completely the Eden of *Paradise Lost*, where both humans and angels emit bodily discharges that serve only to make Edenic bounty still more replete.

And yet the tears are the one overflow in Addison's essay that is out of place. They are superfluous, but their superfluity does not, in fact, correct any want or lack. They are unnecessary, even bizarre: if we imagine the essayist standing amid the crowds at the Exchange weeping, we see just how strange these tears really are. But they are out of place for other reasons, too. This essay, after all, insists upon equivalence—upon the idea that want is satisfied by supply and production by desire. In Addison's account of trade, excess is always absorbed and want recuperated in the symmetry of exchange. Addison's tears are a remainder, a leftover that cannot be exchanged for anything. Though they appear to mimic the superabundance of the economy he describes, in actual fact they disrupt it. While they are symbolically uncontaminated, they have no value; they are pure surplus—and this is what makes them conspicuous in an economy of equivalence.

So why *does* Addison weep? Because the story he tells has such power. Commerce is so remarkable and new, it strikes Addison so forcefully with its novelty and power, that, as if affected by a sublime vision, he sheds tears of joy. So the significance of Addison's tears is not that they are figurative representations of successful commerce but figures for the power of commerce, successfully narrated.

In the later eighteenth century, tears become signs of feeling. When the Addisonian vision of national and cultural community achieved through commercial exchange is shown to be flawed—most catastrophically in the humanitarian disaster of the slave trade—sentiment becomes the unit of currency available to create community and equality among all people: "the world that cannot be united by commerce can be drawn together in sentimental feeling."[4] In this sense, Addison's teary vision prefigures sentimental fiction, not least in its naivete. But tears are not only redemptive and purifying. They also play a crucial role in the story of waste. In the midcentury, weeping features prominently in *Tom Jones* (1749), a novel that retains a connection with late seventeenth-century England through its depiction of Jacobite rebellion and its nostalgia for Stuart monarchy, and which takes us forward to sentimental fiction in its representation of Jones's incontinent sensibility. Early in the novel, Tom Jones is cast out of Allworthy's house by his loathsome adversary, Blifil. Sophia, forbidden to marry the bastard Tom, is betrothed to the same Mr. Blifil; Tom has secretly written to Sophia, instructing his beloved to regard him as one who is beyond the grave. She retires to her chamber in mourning:

Where she indulged herself (if the phrase may be allowed me) in all the luxury of tender grief. She read over more than once the letter which she had received from Jones; her muff too was used on this occasion; and she bathed both these, as well as herself, with her tears.

More tears. What is their occasion this time? Loss of the beloved, fatherly cruelty, youthful despair. And yet, as we watch Sophia anoint her muff and letter in a flood of tears, Fielding is getting at something more complicated, too. With the amusingly ironic comment that "the muff too was used on this occasion," Fielding communicates the idea that Sophia doesn't just weep onto the muff; that furry article actually stimulates her tears. The letter and the muff are Sophia's props, prosaic, yet exquisitely precious to her as she uses them to produce the luxurious release of grief. There is pleasure in her tears, which "bathe" the objects in a way that is partly baptismal and partly erotic.

Why do these things that give such pleasure also cause such distress? The contents of the letter are by now familiar to Sophia; her tears are no longer the tears of surprise, nor of the acute pleasure and pain that the letter gave when she first read over it. The object itself produces her feelings, and yet its effect seems out of proportion to its ordinariness. And the muff is indeed ordinary, in fact rather battered by this point in the novel. But both the letter and the muff have become more than their quotidian selves. They have acquired symbolic meaning. Although they are very ordinary artifacts, they affect Sophia as though they were sublime.

As anyone who has read *Tom Jones* will remember, Sophia's muff has a special significance in the book. When Jones first sees it, he secretly presses it to his lips and Sophia afterward treasures it like a relic, at one point snatching it from flames that are threatening to engulf it. Later in the novel, the muff reappears as Tom and Sophia, in turn, leave it behind to be found by the other party—a trace or surrogate for the real presence of the beloved. The muff acquires a value that exceeds its status as an object; it serves to conduct the narrative of Tom and Sophia's romance, a narrative that otherwise would have no trace, no presence in the text (since they are never together and rarely in communication). In other words, the muff and the letter are metamorphosed into relics of the lovers with whom they are metonymically associated. When Sophia cries, she is not weeping over the objects as such but over the stories they carry with them—what the objects represent, in other words. Addison's tears are the same: the Muff and the Fan as such aren't what cause him to cry but rather the global exchanges that have occurred in order that these exotic articles may appear before his appreciative gaze.

The muffs, the fan, the letter—the objects per se—are, in a sense, remainders. They are precious remainders: real things that have become inhabited by their symbolic meanings. Sophia believes that her muff holds the spirit of a living, breathing human being. But Sophia's credulity is no more irrational than the reader's credulity as he or she eagerly churns through nearly a thousand pages to discover what will happen to a group of imaginary people. We are, after all, looking at instances of the uncanny power of fiction. Commonplace objects, quotidian events, carry complicated meanings that outstrip their ostensible significance. Sophia's muff is a reminder that even in a century that tried to reject the irrational, the superstitious, fiction still lures us into irrational but convincing belief.

The supernatural, the sublime, the uncanny, are registered in the literal, quotidian objects of early and mid-eighteenth-century writing. In the instances I've looked at, what affects the viewer with an overwhelming combination of fear, pain, and joy, what causes him to weep, is not an appreciation of the object itself but the fact that the object means more than it should. Narrative gives meaning and significance to quotidian objects. Resonant as the objects are—the fans, the muffs, Sophia's letter—they are also leftovers. Like sacred relics, they linger behind their symbolic value, all the more abject and prosaic in comparison. The tears, like the objects themselves, are leftovers. They are luxurious residues, lingering behind in texts that are interested in the way objects circulate and get exchanged.

The tears are leftovers at the center of these texts. They are residues, and yet they are precious, too. They play no real part in the narrative, yet they tell us so much about the characters who weep. They are, in short, the instance of precious waste with which this book ends, looking forward to the late eighteenth century and the rise of fictions of the sublime. Addison and Sophia weep because something meaningful has happened. Objects have been given symbolic value, and yet they linger on, stubbornly prosaic and themselves, remnants of the part they play in the text. Waste marks the spot where literary meaning has been made.

NOTES

INTRODUCTION

1. Pierre Jean Grosley, *A Tour to London; or, New Observations on England, and its Inhabitants . . . Translated from the French by Thomas Nugent* (Dublin, 1772), 36.

2. "If, I say, we mind all these, we shall find that every Moment must produce new Filth; and . . . it is impossible London should be more cleanly before it is less flourishing." Bernard Mandeville, *The Fable of the Bees; or, Private Vices, Publick Benefits (1724)*, ed. F. B. Kaye (Oxford: Clarendon Press, 1924), 1: 11–12.

3. Julia Kristeva, *Powers of Horror: An Essay on Abjection*, trans. Leon S. Roudiez (New York: Columbia University Press, 1982), 1.

4. Peter Stallybrass and Allon White's *The Politics and Poetics of Transgression* has been continued recently by studies that combine theoretical readings of space and public practice with a history of material conditions. These include Cynthia Wall's *The Literary and Cultural Spaces of Restoration London* (Cambridge and New York: Cambridge University Press, 1998) and *The Prose of Things: Transformations of Description in the Eighteenth Century* (Chicago: University of Chicago Press, 2006); L. Orlin, ed., *Material London* (Philadelphia: University of Pennsylvania Press, 2000); Paul Griffiths and Mark Jenner, eds., *Londinopolis: Essays in the Cultural and Social History of Early Modern London* (Manchester University Press, 2000); and Mark Blackwell, ed., *The Secret Life of Things: Animals, Objects and It-Narratives in Eighteenth-Century England* (Lewisburg: Bucknell University Press, 2007).

5. The key essay on this topic for me is Stephen Greenblatt's celebrated "Remnants of the Sacred in Early Modern England," in *Subject and Object in*

Renaissance Culture, ed. Peter Stallybrass, Margretta de Grazia, and Maureen Quilligan (Cambridge: Cambridge University Press, 1996).

6. While my main focus is the relation of object to meaning at a conceptual or theoretical level, the remark that all the texts in this study participate in a Protestant narrative tradition depends on my reading of classic studies of the Protestant origins of the English novel, including Ian Watt, *The Rise of the Novel* (Berkeley and Los Angeles: University of California Press, 1965); J. Paul Hunter, *Before Novels: The Cultural Contexts of Eighteenth-Century English Fiction* (New York: Norton, 1990); John Richetti, *The English Novel in History, 1700–1780* (London and New York: Routledge, 1999); Michael McKeon, *The Origins of the English Novel 1600–1740* (Baltimore: Johns Hopkins University Press, 1987); Nancy Armstrong and Leonard Tennenhouse, *The Imaginary Puritan: Literature, Intellectual Labor, and the Origins of Personal Life* (Berkeley and Los Angeles: University of California Press, 1992); and James Thompson, *Models of Value: Eighteenth-Century Political Economy and the Novel* (Durham: Duke University Press, 1996).

7. The most vivid description of the extent and variousness of English filth is given by Emily Cockayne in *Hubbub: Filth, Noise and Stench in England* (New Haven: Yale University Press, 2007). Cockayne divides her book into nine chapters, each devoted to a different aspect of waste. Peter Earle's *A City Full of People: Men and Women of London 1650–1750* (London: Methuen, 1994) describes the teeming, chaotic nature of London's public life, as does Tim Hitchcock's *Down and Out in Eighteenth-Century London* (London and New York: Hambledon & London, 2004) and "Literary Beggars and the Realities of Eighteenth-Century London," in *A Concise Companion to the Restoration and Eighteenth Century*, ed. Cynthia Wall (Oxford and Malden, MA: Blackwell, 2005), 80–100. Peter Linebaugh's *The London Hanged: Crime and Civil Society in the Eighteenth Century* (London and New York: Verso, 2003) conveys the visibility and pervasiveness of crime and violence in the eighteenth-century city.

8. Cited in Roy Porter, "Cleaning up the Great Wen: Public Health in Eighteenth-Century London," in *Living and Dying in London*, ed. W. F. Bynum and Roy Porter (London: Wellcome Institute, 1991), 61–75.

9. Cockayne, *Hubbub*, 231.

10. Cockayne, *Hubbub*, 232.

11. Thomas Short, *A Comparative History of the Increase and Decrease of Mankind in England and Several Countries Abroad* (London, 1767), cited in Porter, "Cleaning up the Great Wen," 63. All statistics here are taken from Porter's article, 62–63.

12. The classic description of the slow march to civilized behavior is still Norbert Elias's *The Civilizing Process: Sociogenetic and Psychogenetic Investigations*, trans. Edmund Jephcott, rev. ed. (Oxford: Blackwell, 2000). For sanitary conditions in London, see Roy Porter, *London: A Social History* (London: Hamish Hamilton, 1994); and Mark Jenner, "Luxury, Circulation and Disorder: London Streets and Hackney Coaches c. 1640–c. 1740," in *The Streets of London: From the Great Fire to the Great Stink*, ed. Tim Hitchcock and Heather Shore (London: Rivers Oram, 2003), and "'Nauceious and Abominable'? Pollution, Plague and Poetics in John Gay's Trivia," in *Walking the Streets of Eighteenth-Century London: John Gay's Trivia*, ed. C. Brant and S. Whyman (Oxford: Oxford University Press, 2007).

13. Vic Gattrell's *City of Laughter: Sex and Satire in Eighteenth-Century London* (New York: Walker & Co., 2007) and Jenny Uglow's *Hogarth: A Life and a World* (London: Faber & Faber, 1997) both use the example of satiric art to argue that eighteenth-century representations both of splendor and of degradation depend, always, on invoking the opposite term. Hence the proximity of one to the other in Hogarth's art, and his dependence on dramatic juxtaposition for the titles of his works.

14. Alain Corbin, *The Foul and the Fragrant: Odor and the French Social Imagination* (Cambridge, MA: Harvard University Press, 1986), 213.

15. Aurel Kolnai, *On Disgust*, ed. and intr. Barry Smith and Carolyn Korsmeyer (Chicago: Open Court, 2004), 53.

16. Kolnai, *On Disgust*, 71.

17. Kolnai, *On Disgust*, 65, 62.

18. Mary Douglas, *Purity and Danger: An Analysis of the Concepts of Pollution and Taboo* (London: Routledge & Kegan Paul, 1966), 35.

19. Douglas, *Purity and Danger*, 37.

20. Douglas, *Purity and Danger*, 41.

21. Suzanne Raitt, "Psychic Waste: Freud, Fechner and the Principle of Constancy," in *Culture and Waste: The Creation and Destruction of Value*, Guy Hawkins and Stephen Muecke (Oxford: Rowman & Littlefield, 2002), 73.

22. Douglas, *Purity and Danger*, 96.

23. Martha Nussbaum, "'Secret Sewers of Vice': Disgust, Bodies and the Law," in *The Passions of Law*, ed. Susan A. Bandes (New York: New York University Press, 1999), 19–63, 22.

24. Kolnai, *On Disgust*, 74.

25. Kolnai, *On Disgust*, 54.

26. Kristeva, *Powers of Horror*, 9, 3.

27. Kristeva, *Powers of Horror*, 1.

28. Sigmund Freud, *Civilization and Its Discontents*, trans. and ed. James Strachey (New York: W.W. Norton, 1961), 46.

29. For a full account of the history of the treatise, see Gail Kern Paster, "The Epistemology of the Water Closet: John Harrington's Metamorphosis of Ajax and Elizabethan Technologies of Shame," in *Material Culture and Cultural Materialism in the Middle Ages and the Renaissance*, ed. Curtis Perry (Turnhout: Brepols, 2001), 139–58. And for a complete description of the court politics and scandal involved in Harrington's publication, see Jason Scott-Warren, "The Privy Politics of Sir John Harington's *New Discourse of a Stale Subject, Called the Metamorphosis of Ajax*," *Studies in Philology* (Chapel Hill, NC) 93, no. 4 (Fall 1996): 412–42; and Rick Bowers, "Sir John Harrington and the Earl of Essex: the Joker as Spy," *Cahiers Élisabéthains* 69 (2006): 13–20.

30. Elizabeth Story Donno, ed., *Sir John Harington's* A New Discourse of a Stale Subject, Called The Metamorphosis of Ajax (New York: Columbia University Press, 1962).

31. Precisely why this was the case is a matter of uncertainty. Scott-Warren writes: "Beyond the obvious facts that it is richly learned, laden with many now-indecipherable satirical references, moralistic, and remarkably earnest about the invention which spawns it, this work is not easily described. Those who mention it tend to agree on one point at least: that it was Harington's biggest mistake. In the fullest modern account of his life and writings, D. H. Craig states that 'in his own time, and since, it was notoriety rather than advancement or admiration that he achieved' through the New Discourse (4). Simon Cauchi calls it Harington's "most notorious literary indiscretion before 1603," contrasting it with lesser indiscretions from the courtier's Elizabethan career (5). "Sir John Harington made one mistake in life: he published a plan for a flushing lavatory in his treatise on courtly corruptions, punningly entitled The Metamorphosis of A-Jax. This has enabled critics ever since to sneer at him" (6).

32. Scholars have explained that such institutions were much more complex and hard to read than eighteenth-century readers might have hoped—politeness is now understood as a much more nuanced social model. Recent important expositions and modifications of the cult of politeness are found in Scott Black, *Of Essays and Reading in Early Modern Britain* (Basingstoke and New York: Palgrave Macmillan, 2006); Jenny Davidson, *Hypocrisy and the Politics of Politeness: Manners and Morals from Locke to Austen* (Cambridge and New York: Cambridge University Press, 2004); Lawrence E. Klein, "Politeness and the Interpretation of the British Eighteenth Century," *Historical Journal* 45, no. 4

(2002): 869–98; Paul Langford, "The Uses of Eighteenth-Century Politeness," *Transactions of the Royal Historical Society*, 6th ser., 12 (2002): 311–31; and Erin Mackie, *Market à la Mode: Fashion, Commodity, and Gender in the* Tatler *and the* Spectator (Baltimore: Johns Hopkins University Press, 1997).

33. Edward Ward, *The Second Part of the History of the London Clubs, Particularly, the Farting Club, the No-Nos'd Club, the Misers Club, the Atheistical Club; With A Comical Relation of the Devil in a Bear Skin* (London, 1709), 2.

34. Jonathan Swift, *The Works of Dr. Jonathan Swift, Dean of St. Patrick's Dublin*, vol. 7 (Dublin, 1758), 399.

CHAPTER 1

1. Mark Kishlansky summarizes the damage: "13,000 buildings, 87 churches, 44 company halls, 4 bridges. . . . One hundred thousand people were homeless, and the cost of rebuilding was reckoned at 10 million pounds, or eight times the annual revenue of the monarch." *A Monarchy Transformed: Britain 1603–1714* (Middlesex: Penguin, 1996), 214–15.

2. John Evelyn, *Diary*, ed. E. S de Beer (Oxford: Clarendon Press, 1955) September 7, 1666, emphasis mine. All quotations are from this edition.

3. Nathaniel Hardy, *Lamentation, Mourning and Woe, Sighed forth in a Sermon Preached in the Parish Church of St. Martin in the Fields, on the 9th Day of September Being the next Lord's Day after the Dismal Fire in the City of London* (London, 1666). William Sancroft, *Lex Ignea; Or, The school of righteousness, a sermon preached before the King* (London, 1666). Thomas Jacomb, D.D., *A Treatise of Holy Dedication, both Personal and Domestick* (London, 1768).

4. Samuel Rolls, *London's Resurrection; or, The Rebuilding of London Encouraged, Directed and Improved, in Fifty Discourses together with a Preface, giving some account both of the Author and Works* (London, 1668).

5. The competing claims made for each of these are discussed at length in Michael McKeon, *Politics and Poetry in the Restoration: The Case of Dryden's* Annus Mirabilis (Cambridge, MA: Harvard University Press, 1975), 130ff.; and E. Hooker, "The Meanings of Dryden's *Annus Mirabilis*," in *Essential Articles for the Study of John Dryden*, ed. Hugh Thomas Swedenberg (Hamden, CT: Archon Books, 1966).

6. Nigel Smith, " 'Making Fire': Conflagration and Religious Controversy in Seventeenth-Century London," in *Imagining Early Modern London: Perceptions and Portrayals of the City from Stow to Strype, 1598–1720*, ed. J. F. Merritt (New York: Cambridge University Press, 2001), 279.

7. See Smith, "Making Fire," 274–75 for a full list of biblical sources for fiery apocalypse.

8. Michael McKeon, *The Origins of the English Novel 1600–1740* (Baltimore: Johns Hopkins University Press, 1987), and J. Paul Hunter, *Before Novels: The Cultural Contexts of Eighteenth-Century English Fiction* (New York: Norton, 1990).

9. Smith, "Making Fire," 278.

10. Smith, "Making Fire," 275.

11. See Kristin Poole's study *Radical Religion from Shakespeare to Milton* (Cambridge: Cambridge University Press, 2000) for details of the range of imagery connected to natural disaster in pamphlet literature. Christopher Hill and Michael McKeon, among others, argue that although millenarian imagery was associated with dissent, it was connected to no single sect. Hill, "Heresy and Radical Politics," in *The Collected Essays of Christopher Hill: Religion and Politics in Seventeenth Century England* (Sussex: Harvester Press, 1986), and McKeon, *Politics and Poetry in the Restoration.*

12. Sancroft, *Lex Ignea.*

13. Stillingfleet, an important influence on the Anglican rationalist clerics of the early eighteenth century became archdeacon of London in 1677, dean of St Paul's in 1678, and bishop of Worcester in 1689. In 1697 he wrote *The Bishop of Worcester's Answer to Mr. Locke's Letter* and is now best known for his part in the "Locke-Stillingfleet Debates."

14. Edward Stillingfleet, *A Sermon Preached before the Honourable House of Commons at St. Margarets Westminster* (London,1666).

15. Stillingfleet, *Sermon.*

16. Robert Elborough, *London's Calamity by Fire bewailed and improved in a Sermon preached at St. James Dukes-Place wherein the judgments of God are asserted* (London, 1666), 23.

17. Sancroft, *Lex Ignea.*

18. Evelyn, *Diary,* September 3, 1666.

19. Wall, *Literary and Cultural Spaces,* 17.

20. Hunter, *Before Novels,* 197, 198.

21. Watt, *The Rise of the Novel,* 12.

22. Stillingfleet, *Sermon.*

23. Evelyn, *Diary,* September 7, 1666.

24. Samuel Pepys, *The Diary of Samuel Pepys,* ed. Robert Latham and William Matthews (Berkeley: University of California Press, 2000), September 7, 1666. All quotations are from this edition.

25. Blair Hoxby, *Mammon's Music: Literature and Economics in the Age of Milton* (New Haven: Yale University Press, 2002), 204.

26. In *A City Full of People: Men and Women of London 1650–1750* (London: Methuen, 1994), Peter Earle analyzes the breakdown of London's population to reveal the influx of "mobile" social groups such as these during the seventeenth century. Tim Harris argues that the London crowd was characterized by diversity and multiplicity of political interests. Political culture drew upper, middle, and lower classes into civic life through public displays of judicial power, civilian law-enforcing, local government, and popular unrest stemming from hostility to Catholicism, antipathy to foreigners, and an attachment to independent City government. *London Crowds in the Reign of Charles II: Propaganda and Policies from the Restoration until the Exclusion Crisis* (Cambridge: Cambridge University Press, 1987).

27. John Dryden, *Annus Mirabilis: The Year of Wonders 1666*, in *The Works of John Dryden*, ed. Edward N. Hooker and H. T. Swedenberg, vol. 1 (Berkeley: University of California Press, 1956). All quotations are from this edition.

28. Waller's panegyric was followed by four "Instructions to a Painter" satires, attributed at the time to John Denham but subsequently attributed in part to Marvell. The most famous satire in the genre is Marvell's celebrated contribution, "Last Instructions to a Painter" (1667).

29. Hoxby, *Mammon's Music*, 4.

30. Hoxby, *Mammon's Music*, 131.

31. See note 9 above for studies dealing with apocalyptic literature of the civil war period. See also Nigel Smith's *Literature and Revolution in England: 1640–1660* (New Haven: Yale University Press, 1994).

32. For a full description of these images, see "Eating Disorders: Feasting, Fasting, and the Puritan Bellygod at Bartholomew Fair," in Poole, *Radical Religion*.

33. The full debate surrounding these tracts and a history of the pamphlets written in skeptical response are laid out in McKeon, *Politics and Poetry* and in Hooker, "The Meanings of Dryden's *Annus Mirabilis*."

34. *MacFlecknoe* was printed in a pirated version in 1682 and then in an authorized form in *Miscellany Poems* in 1684. It had been in limited circulation in manuscript since 1676. *John Dryden*, Oxford Authors series, ed. Keith Walker (Oxford: Oxford University Press, 1987), 878.

35. Critics have often noted that waste is inherent to any production, perceiving it as an inescapable metaphor of urban life. Janette Dillon, discussing Thorstein Veblen's work on the leisure class, writes: "Veblen laments the unavoidably deprecatory overtones of the term 'waste,' which he claims to be using neutrally for analytical purposes, yet points out in passing that the very fact that the word 'waste' in everyday usage implies deprecation is significant in itself." *Theatre, Court and City 1595–1610: Drama and Social Space in London* (Cambridge: Cambridge University Press, 2000), 13.

36. Georges Bataille, "The Notion of Expenditure," in *Visions of Excess: Selected Writings, 1927–1939*, ed. Allan Stoekl (Minneapolis: University of Minnesota Press, 1985), 122.

37. Christopher Wren, "Proposals for the Rebuilding of the City of London, after the Great Fire," in *Parentalia; or, Memoirs of the Family of the Wrens* (1750) (Farnborough, Hants.: Gregg Press, 1965), part 2, section 2 (emphasis mine).

38. Milward, *Diary*, September 27, 1666.

39. Rolls, *London's Resurrection*, 40.

40. Porter, "Cleaning Up the Great Wen," 63.

41. Corbain, *The Foul and the Fragrant*, 57.

42. Porter, "Cleaning Up the Great Wen," 61–62.

43. Tim Hitchcock, "The Publicity of Poverty in Early Modern London," in *Imagining Early Modern London: Perceptions and Portrayals of the City from Stow to Strype, 1598–1720*, ed. J. F. Merritt (Cambridge: Cambridge University Press, 2001), 182–83.

44. Rosemary Weinstein, "New Urban Demands in Early Modern London," in *Living and Dying in London*, ed. W. F. Bynum and Roy Porter (London: Wellcome Institute, 1991), 29–40, 39.

45. Porter, "Cleaning Up the Great Wen," 75.

46. Cockayne, *Hubbub*, 181.

47. Cockayne, *Hubbub*, 183–85, 186.

48. Cockayne, *Hubbub*, 187.

49. Bataille, "The Notion of Expenditure," 119.

CHAPTER 2

1. Hoxby, *Mammon's Music*, 128.

2. Kolnai, *On Disgust*, 75.

3. Hoxby, *Mammon's Music*, 21.

4. Enclosure began in the late Middle Ages and continued until the nineteenth century, but during the seventeenth century, in between the Tudor and Hanoverian statutes, there was a brief period of "enclosure by agreement." During this interlude, land enclosure was seen by many to be in the best interests of all, a solution to England's problems with vagrancy and beggary and a means of regenerating agricultural production. See Frederick Jack Fisher, ed., *Essays on the Economic and Social History of Tudor and Stuart England* (Cambridge: Cambridge University Press, 1961); Joan Thirsk, *Agricultural Change: Policy and Practice* (Cambridge: Cambridge University Press, 1990); and Andrew McRae,

God Speed the Plough: The Representation of Agrarian England 1500–1660 (New York: Cambridge University Press, 1996).

5. Karen Edwards argues that responses to enclosure were "divergent" in the seventeenth century, that "conversion of the 'waste common' to arable was the least contentious of all the kinds of enclosure marking the period," and that "The depopulation of the country, or the fact that so many remained outside the enclosure, was the social ill that most worried contemporaries." "Eden Raised: Waste in Milton's Garden," in *Renaissance Ecology: Imagining Eden in Milton's England,* ed. Ken Hiltner (Pittsburgh: Duquesne University Press, 2008), 259–72, 265.

6. Edwards, "Eden Raised," 262.

7. Molly McClain argues that enclosure riots often represented a clash between aristocracy and gentry rather than between landowners and commoners per se. "The developments of the civil war years encouraged a sense of political independence among the Monmouthshire gentry. After the Restoration, local gentlemen no longer depended on great noblemen to provide them with political leadership. In fact, the county did not have a single resident peer" (119). Nigel Smith suggests that although enclosure had been going on for centuries, it was only as a result of the political and economic disruptions of the civil war that enclosure became part of the popular politics of the midcentury (*Literature and Revolution,* 320ff.).

8. See Christopher Hill, "The Religion of Gerrard Winstanley," in *The Collected Essays of Christopher Hill: Religion and Politics in Seventeenth-Century England* (Amherst: University of Massachusetts Press, 1986); Andrew McRae's chapter on agrarian communism in *God Speed the Plough*; and David Loewenstein, "Digger Writing and Rural Dissent in the English Revolution: Representing England as a Common Treasury," in *The Country and the City Revisited,* ed. Gerald MacLean, Donna Landry, and Joseph P. Ward (Cambridge: Cambridge University Press, 1999).

9. [E.G.], *Wasteland's Improvement; or, Certain Proposals Made and Tendred to the Consideration of the Honorable Committee appointed by Parliament for the Advance of Trade, and General Profits of the Commonwealth: wherin are some hints touching the best and most commodious way of improving the forrests, fenny-grounds and wast-lands throughout England* (London, 1653), 3. All quotations are from this edition.

10. Milton, "Proposalls of Certaine Expedients," in *Complete Prose Works of John Milton,* ed. Don M. Wolfe et al., 8 vols. (New Haven: Yale University Press, 1953–82), 7:338.

11. Edwards, "Eden Raised," 266–71.

12. Rachel Crawford, *Poetry, Enclosure and the Vernacular Landscape, 1700–1830* (Cambridge: Cambridge University Press, 2002), 54. A chart, intended to suggest that "the qualities that idealize the open-field system reflect those which derogate the enclosed system," is on 56.

13. For changes in the meaning of enclosure in popular politics, see William Carroll, "The Nursery of Beggary: Enclosure, Vagrancy and Sedition in the Tudor-Stuart Period," in *Enclosure Acts: Sexuality, Property, and Culture in Early Modern England*, ed. Richard Burt and John Michael Archer (Ithaca: Cornell University Press, 1994), 38. Changes in the meaning of enclosure in popular politics are discussed also in James L. Siemon, "Landlord, Not King: Agrarian Change and Interarticulation," in the same volume.

14. Thomas More, *Utopia*, ed. Edward Surtz, S.J. (New Haven and London: Yale University Press, 1964), 25.

15. McRae, *God Speed the Plough*, 3.

16. Crawford, *Poetry, Enclosure, and the Vernacular Landscape*, 12.

17. "The 'champain head' of Milton's Paradise is crowned by an 'enclosure green' (4.133–34); the two seem to be distinct areas but cannot in fact be distinguished. Milton deliberately combines the best features of private land and primeval wilderness; Eden is an "enclosure wild," which in the fallen world would be a contradiction in terms (9.543). In other poets Paradise is either diffused throughout the world or heavily gated and walled, an 'inclosure' in the strictest sense." James Turner, *The Politics of Landscape : Rural Scenery and Society in English Poetry 1630–1660* (Oxford: Blackwell, 1979), 127.

18. Edwards, "Eden Raised," 260.

19. According to Barbara Lewalksi, Milton is virtually alone in making this choice: "Rare if not unique in theological and literary representations of the Edenic paradise, Milton's garden is invulnerable to another sort of loss—regression to a wilderness state." "Milton's Paradises," in *Renaissance Ecology: Imagining Eden in Milton's England*, ed. Ken Hittner (Pittsburgh: Duquesne University Press, 2008), 15–30, 17.

20. Edwards, "Eden Raised," 260.

21. Karen Edwards claims that Eve's language here is political—"lopping and pruning are activities that demand a figurative reading, especially in light of the events of January 1649"—and points out that the same vocabulary is used by Gerrard Winstanley in his arguments for cultivating "waste" ground at St. George's Hill ("Eden Raised," 263).

22. John Rumrich, *The Matter of Glory: A New Preface to Paradise Lost* (Pittsburgh: University of Pittsburgh Press, 1987), 171.

23. Lewalski, "Milton's Paradises," 20.

24. The intellectual history of seventeenth-century materialism is well covered by Stephen Fallon, *Milton among the Philosophers: Poetry and Materialism in Seventeenth-Century England* (Ithaca: Cornell University Press, 1991); in John Rogers, *The Matter of Revolution: Science, Poetry, and Politics in the Age of Milton* (Ithaca: Cornell University Press, 1996); Roger Ariew, John Cottingham, and Tom Sorell, eds., *Descartes' Meditations: Background Source Materials* (Cambridge and New York: Cambridge University Press, 1998); and Lisa Sarasohn, *Gassendi's Ethics: Freedom in a Mechanistic Universe* (Ithaca: Cornell University Press, 1996).

25. Fallon, *Milton among the Philosophers*, 80.

26. Fallon, *Milton among the Philosophers*, 103.

27. Schoenfeldt, *Bodies and Selves*, 132.

CHAPTER 3

1. Thomas Jemielity argues that the *Dunciad* is structured as a mock-apocalypse and corresponds deliberately to each stage of a biblical apocalypse narrative: "Like its principal biblical model, Pope's book of Revelation presents the 'salvation history' of the dunces in a Genesis-to-Revelation framework—first introduced in the the *Dunciad* of 1728—that apes the same biblical panorama in the concluding book of the Christian scriptures." "'Consumatum Est': Alexander Pope's 1743 *Dunciad* and Mock-Apocalypse," in *"More Solid Learning": New Perspectives on Pope's* Dunciad, ed. Catherine Ingrassia and Claudia N. Thomas (London: Associated University Presses, 2000), 167. See also Thomas Jemielity, "A Mock-Biblical Controversy: Sir Richard Blackmore in the *Dunciad*," *Philological Quarterly* (University of Iowa, Iowa City) 74, no. 3 (1995): 249–77.

2. J. Philip Brockbank points to the Miltonic link in "The Book of Genesis and the Genesis of Books: The Creation of Pope's *Dunciad*," in *The Art of Alexander Pope*, ed. Howard Erskine-Hill and Anne Smith (London: Vision Press, 1979): "Pope's cosmic embryology is an internalized rendering of the ambiguous fecundity of Milton's Chaos" (195). Pope's dependence on *Paradise Lost* is discussed more generally in Barbara K. Lewalski's "On Looking into Pope's Milton," *Milton Studies* 11 (1978): 29–50.

3. For a brief account of the unorthodox aspects of Milton's theology, see Maurice Kelley's introduction to *De Doctrina Christiana* (trans. John Carey, ed. Maurice Kelley), section 4, "Creation," in *Complete Prose Works of John Milton*, ed. Don M. Wolfe (New Haven: Yale University Press, 1953–82), 6: 87–90.

All quotations from *De Doctrina Christiana* are from this edition. The *Complete Prose Works* will be abbreviated as *CPW* in following citations.

4. Cf. *De Doctrina Christiana*, 1.7, "Of Creation": "anyone who says, then, that 'to create' means 'to produce out of nothing,' is, as logicians say, arguing from an unproved premise" (*CPW*, 6:306). Milton explains the substance of creation thus:

> It is, I say, a demonstration of God's supreme power and goodness that he should not shut up this heterogeneous and substantial virtue within himself, but should disperse, propagate and extend it as far as, and in whatever way, he wills. For this original matter was not an evil thing, nor to be thought of as worthless: it was good, and it contained the seeds of all subsequent good. It was a substance, and could only have been derived from the source of all substance. It was in a confused and disordered state at first, but afterwards God made it ordered and beautiful. (*CPW*, 6:308)

5. John Rumrich, *Matter of Glory: A New Preface to Paradise Lost* (Pittsburgh: University of Pittsburgh Press, 1987).

6. Milton, *The Art of Logic*, in *CPW*, 8:234.

7. Stephen M. Fallon, "Paradise Lost in Intellectual History," in *A Companion to Milton*, ed. Thomas Corns (Oxford: Blackwell Publishers, 2001), 335.

8. John Rogers, *The Matter of Revolution: Science, Poetry and Politics in the Age of Milton* (Ithaca: Cornell University Press, 1996), 1.

9. Thomas Hobbes, *Elements of Philosophy* (1655), section 1, "De corpore," quoted in Rogers, *The Matter of Revolution*, 4. Of the vitalists mentioned above, Harvey and Cavendish were both royalists; Winstanley, Milton, and Marvell republicans (though of differing stamps). John Rogers, however, suggests that Harvey, who at first positioned the heart as the sovereign organ in the body, shifted to the more "democratic" view that each bodily element contributed equally and vitally to the operation of the whole, and finally attempted a republican reconciliation of the two positions during the interregnum period (*Matter of Revolution*, 18–22).

10. In their celebrated book *Leviathan and the Air Pump: Hobbes, Boyle and the Experimental Life*, Steven Shapin and Simon Schaffer offer a very sophisticated account of the relationship between Hobbes's anti-Puritan, antirepublican politics and his natural philosophy:

> As a treatise in civic philosophy *Leviathan* was designed to show the practices that would guarantee order in the state. That order could be, and

during the Civil War was being, threatened by clerical intellectuals who arrogated to themselves a share of civic authority to which they were not entitled. Their major resources in these acts of usurpation were, according to Hobbes, a false ontology and a false epistemology. Hobbes endeavored to show the absurdity of an ontology that posited incorporeal substances and immaterial spirits. Thus, he built a plenist ontology, and, in the process, erected a materialistic theory of knowledge in which the foundations of knowledge were notions of causes, and those causes were matter and motion. (19)

For a fuller exploration of their argument, see chapter 3, "Seeing Double: Hobbes' Politics of Plenism before 1660," and chapter 6, "Natural Philosophy and the Restoration: Interests in Dispute."

11. Fallon, "Paradise Lost in Intellectual History," 334.

12. Stephen Fallon writes, "Cudworth and More countered the threats to free will and theism that they perceived in mechanist philosophy by arguing for an animist universe." *Milton among the Philosophers: Poetry and Materialism in Seventeenth-Century England* (Ithaca and London: Cornell University Press, 1991), 54. Cudworth and More were the leading figures in the Cambridge Platonist movement, which reacted against Hobbesian mechanism in defense of free will. The movement had an impact on Milton's thought, as Fallon shows, but Milton also significantly departs from it, specifically in his rejection of the Platonist commitment to dualism. The vitalist whose thought is probably most closely aligned with Milton's was that of Henry More's pupil Anne Conway, who argues for a animatist, monist universe in *The Principles of the Most Ancient and Modern Philosophy* (1690). See Fallon, "Milton and Anne Conway," in *Milton among the Philosophers*, 111–36. For a fuller account of the philosophical attractions of vitalism, see Rogers, *The Matter of Revolution*, chapter 1.

13. Rumrich, *Matter of Glory*, 70.

14. *De Doctrina Christiana* is regarded as Milton's frankest theological statement, since it was not published in his lifetime. According to Barbara Lewalski, the text was composed between 1658 and 1674; see Lewalski's *The Life of John Milton: A Critical Biography* (London: Blackwell, 2000), 415ff.

15. *De Doctrina Christiana*, "Of Creation." Milton glosses this account with the remark that "all form—and the human soul is a kind of form—is produced by the power of matter" (*CPW*, 6:322).

16. For an account of Milton's unorthodox theology and politics, see John Rumrich, "Radical Heterodoxy and Heresy," in *A Companion to Milton*, ed.

Thomas Corns (Oxford: Blackwell, 2001). See also *Milton and Heresy*, ed. S. Dobranski and J. Rumrich (Cambridge and New York: Cambridge University Press, 1998), in particular Thomas Corns, "Milton's Antiprelatical Tracts and the Marginality of Doctrine." Christopher Hill offers a summary of the intellectual influences on Milton's radical theology and philosophy in *Milton and the English Revolution* (London: Faber & Faber, 1977), 233–41 ("Theology and Logic") and 324–33 ("Materialism and Creation"). See also Maurice Wiles, *Archetypal Heresy: Arianism through the Centuries* (Oxford and New York: Clarendon Press, 1996).

17. Rumrich, *Matter of Glory*, 71.

18. Sharon Achinstein argues that for Milton and his radical contemporaries, "the English Revolution was not a complete failure; . . . radical energies released there continued to fire politics and religious controversy in the Restoration; and . . . the literary activities of the radical sectarians merit attention for their complex engagement with political and otherworldly concerns. . . . [W]e can consider Milton's ongoing commitment to religious radicalism as his response to the agonies of the present." *Literature and Dissent in Milton's England* (Cambridge and New York: Cambridge University Press, 2003), 115. For a summary of Milton's radical politics in Paradise Lost see David Loewenstein, "The Radical Religious Politics of Paradise Lost," in *A Companion to Milton*, ed. Corns. See also Armand Himy, "Paradise Lost as a Republican 'Tractatus Theologico-Politicus,'" in *Milton and Republicanism*, ed. David Armitage, Armand Himy, and Quentin Skinner (Cambridge: Cambridge University Press, 1995), 118–34; Sharon Achinstein, "Milton and the Fit Reader: *Paradise Lost* and the Parliament of Hell," in *Milton and the Revolutionary Reader* (Princeton: Princeton University Press, 1994),177–223; and David Quint, *Epic and Empire: Politics and Generic Form from Virgil to Milton* (Princeton: Princeton University Press, 1993).

19. Lewalski, *Life of John Milton*, 442.

20. See, for example, Cedric Brown, "'This Islands Watchful Centinel': Anti-Catholicism and Proto-Whiggery in Milton and Marvell," in *English Literature 1650–1740*, ed. Steven Zwicker (Cambridge: Cambridge University Press, 1998), 165–84; and Nancy Lees Riffe, "Milton and Eighteenth-Century Whigs," *Notes and Queries* 11 (1964): 337–38.

21. Alexandre Koyre, "The Significance of the Newtonian Synthesis," in *Newtonian Studies* (Cambridge, MA: Harvard University Press, 1965), 3–24, reprinted in *Newton: Texts, Backgrounds, Commentaries*, ed. Bernard Cohen and Richard Westfall (New York and London: Norton, 1995), 60–61.

22. Koyre, "The Significance of the Newtonian Synthesis," 70.

23. Koyre, "The Significance of the Newtonian Synthesis," 70.

24. Rogers describes the philosophy of Milton's suggestion that matter is self-willed: "the vitalist process of material self-organization is the direct result neither of God's command nor of his vigilant and ongoing manipulation of an inert substance. The process by which 'order from disorder sprung' (3,713) was set in motion by an unrepeatable originary act that empowered the world's material mould to order itself; once the abyss has been impregnated with a self-activating *divina virtus*, the effective control over generation devolves on the now self-generating matter of chaos" (*The Matter of Revolution*, 14).

25. The doctrine of self-generative matter was adopted by political radicals such as the regicide Robert Tichborne because it offered what John Rogers calls "the promise of a metaphysical justification for political equality and self-determination" (*The Matter of Revolution*, 121). Doctrines of self-generation were adopted in 1648 by Van Helmont, who offered a theory of fermentation in *Ortus Medicinae*, and even by William Harvey, whose *De Generatione Animalium* (1651) argued that spontaneous conception was possible without direct contact with sperm.

26. Even in the case of humans, willful disobedience results in a "purgation" that imitates the purging of dregs at Creation:

> But longer in that Paradise to dwell, / The Law I have to Nature him
>   forbids:
> Those pure immortal Elements that know
> No gross, no unharmonious mixture foul,
> Eject him tainted now, and purge him off
> As a distemper.   (11. 48–53)

27. Arguments that would appear to separate Milton's philosophy from Pope's are in fact written into the *Dunciad*; Pope self-consciously adopts aspects of Milton's doctrine that we would expect him to repudiate. These are summarized by Barbara Lewalski: "[Milton's] unflinching recognition of evil as evil; his presentation of Chaos not only as the power of disintegration and disorder but also as the source and substratum of all creation, emanating originally from God; his conception of hierarchy as fluid and dynamic rather than fixed and static." "On Looking into Pope's Milton," *Milton Studies* 11 (1978): 47.

28. Aubrey Williams is the first critic to recognize the centrality of theater in the *Dunciad*; the theatricality motif is discussed in "A Theater for Worldlings," in *Pope's Dunciad: A Study of Its Meaning* (London: Archon Books, 1968), 87–112.

29. In one of the few essays exploring the parallel between Pope's Chaos and Milton's, J. Philip Brockbank points to this same affinity: "In a Rabelaisian rendering of Dulness's anti-creation, the 'Nectarous humor' that 'issuing flow'd'

from Milton's Satan . . . is transmuted into a kind of divine diarrhoea whose virtues refresh the energies of Curll and Lintot. In parody of the plenitude and fecundity of Milton's creation, the uncreating labour of 'purgings, pumpings, blankettings, and blows' lets the 'fresh vomit run forever green.'" "The Book of Genesis and the Genesis of Books: The Creation of Pope's *Dunciad*," in *The Art of Alexander Pope*, ed. Howard Erskine-Hill and Anne Smith (New York: Barnes and Noble, 1979), 199.

30. *Newton: Texts, Backgrounds, Commentaries*, 322.

31. Betty Jo Teeter Dobbs, "Newton's Alchemy and His Theory of Matter," *Isis* 73 (1982): 512–28, reprinted in *Newton: Texts, Backgrounds, Commentaries*, 322.

32. Pope, "Epistle to Lord Bathurst," line 116.

33. Swift, "The Bubble," 1–8.

34. Catherine Ingrassia, *Authorship, Commerce and Gender in Early Eighteenth-Century England* (Cambridge: Cambridge University Press, 1998), 4. For important accounts of the rise of public finance in England and its relationship to literary culture, see P.G.M. Dickson, *The Financial Revolution in England: A Study in the Development of Public Credit, 1688–1756* (London: Macmillan, 1967); James Thompson, *Models of Value: Eighteenth-Century Political Economy and the Novel* (Durham, NC: Duke University Press, 1996); Colin Nicholson, *Writing and the Rise of Finance: Capital Satires of the Early Eighteenth Century* (Cambridge: Cambridge University Press, 1994); and Sandra Sherman, "Credit, Simulation, and the Ideology of Contract in the Early Eighteenth-Century," *Eighteenth-Century Life* 19, no. 3 (1995): 86–102.

35. Pope, "Epistle to Lord Bathurst," 45–48.

36. Swift, "The Bubble," 120–24.

37. The conviction that a system of credit is based on a delusional misrepresentation of paper as money is at the heart of Pope's and Swift's skeptical satires on the South Sea disaster, and is anticipated by Locke, who during the recoinage crisis of 1695–96 held that English coins should be reminted to be worth their real value in weight of silver. In his essays on the coinage crisis, *Some Considerations of the Consequences of the Lowering of Interest and Raising the Value of Money* (1691) and *Short Observations on a Printed Paper Intitled, For Encouraging Coining Silver Money in England, and after for Keeping it Here* (1695), Locke ridicules the nation that "paper, in the form of bills of exchange, can effectively substitute for precious metal." Quoted in James Thompson, *Models of Value* (Durham, NC: Duke University Press, 1996), 56ff.

38. Ingrassia, *Authorship, Commerce and Gender*, 40.

39. *Human Ordure, Botanically Considered; The First Essay of the Kind, Ever Published in the World*. First printed in Dublin in 1733 by S. Powell for John

Watson, it was reprinted in London in the same year with an attribution by Dr. S——t. The pamphlet was subsequently reprinted (in London in 1748 and 1757). Not till the 1757 edition is the pamphlet attributed to Swift, and Swift's authorship is generally doubted.

40. For a full account of the pamphlet wars following the publication of the *Dunciad*, see Ingrassia, *Authorship, Commerce and Gender*, chapter 2, "Alexander Pope, Gender and the Commerce of Culture," 40–76, 63ff.

CHAPTER 4

1. Swift's excremental neuroses have been discussed most famously by Norman O. Brown, in "The Excremental Vision," in *Life against Death* (New York: Vintage Books, 1959). More recent accounts include Claude Rawson, "Swift's Poems," in *Order from Confusion Sprung: Studies in Eighteenth-Century Literature from Swift to Cowper* (London and Boston: Allen & Unwin, 1985), and Carol Houlihan Flynn, *The Body in Swift and Defoe* (Cambridge: Cambridge University Press, 1990). Classic histories of the place of excrement in Western culture are Norbert Elias, *The Civilizing Process* (1939), trans. Edmond Jephcott (Oxford: Blackwell Publishers, 1994), and Mary Douglas, *Purity and Danger: An Analysis of Concepts of Pollution and Taboo* (New York: Praeger, 1966). An important recent text is Alain Corbin's *The Foul and the Fragrant: Odor and the French Social Imagination*, trans. Miriam L. Kochan, Roy Porter, and Christopher Prendergast (Cambridge, MA: Harvard University Press, 1986).

2. Jonathan Swift, "A Description of a City Shower," in *The Complete Poems*, ed. Pat Rogers (Harmondsworth: Penguin Books, 1983), lines 61–63. All quotations from Swift's poetry are taken from this edition.

3. Kolnai, *On Disgust*, 53.

4. Robert Mahony, in *Jonathan Swift: The Irish Identity* (New Haven: Yale University Press, 1995), gives a full "critical heritage" of Swift's reception as an Irish spokesman and critic, from the eighteenth to the twentieth centuries. Discussions of the history and substance of Swift's attacks on Whig policies toward Ireland are in Mahony's first chapter, "Swift and George Faulkner: Cultivating Irish Memory"; in Oliver Watkins Ferguson, *Jonathan Swift and Ireland* (Urbana: University of Illinois Press, 1962); and in S. J. Connolly, "Swift and Protestant Ireland: Images and Reality," in *Locating Swift: Essays from Dublin on the 250ᵗʰ Anniversary of the Death of Jonathan Swift*, ed. Aileen Douglas, Patrick Kelly, and Ian Campbell Ross (Portland: Four Courts Press, 1998). An interesting collection on representations of the English colonial presence in Ireland

is *Representing Ireland: Literature and the Origins of Conflict 1534–1660*, ed. Brendan Bradshaw, Andrew Hadfield, and Willey Maley (Cambridge: Cambridge University Press, 1993).

5. Carole Fabricant draws attention to the sense in which Swift's interest in waste reflects the literal realities of early eighteenth-century Dublin, which "became a natural haven for abandoned refuse and for the human 'refuse' of a highly stratified class society." *Swift's Landscape* (Baltimore: Johns Hopkins University Press, 1982), 28. Fabricant points out that the glutted representations of waste and residue in Swift's writing reflect the literal status of Ireland as wasteland: "England's harsh economic sanctions, designed to protect her own clothing industry and to convert Ireland into a dumping ground for English manufactured goods, replaced potential prosperity with immediate hardship" (28).

6. Jonathan Swift, "A Modest Proposal," in *The Writings of Jonathan Swift*, ed. Robert A. Greenberg and William B. Piper (New York: Norton and Co., 1973), 504.

7. Lynn Festa, *Sentimental Figures of Empire in Eighteenth-Century Britain and France* (Baltimore: Johns Hopkins University Press, 2006), 158, 16.

8. Festa explores this relationship in the context of the transAtlantic slave trade; see "Of Price and Men," in *Sentimental Figures of Empire*, 155ff.

9. Makhail Bakhtin, *Rabelais and His World*, trans. Helene Iswolsky (Bloomington: Indiana University Press, 1984), 19.

10. "A Modest Proposal" (1729), in *The Writings of Jonathan Swift*, ed. Robert A. Greenberg and William B. Piper (New York: Norton, 1973), 504.

11. Rawson, *Order from Confusion Sprung*, 126.

12. Robert Phiddian recognizes the ambiguity of Swift's voice by noting that his parodies are deeply unstable, not often based in orthodox genres, spoken in a voice we might take to be Swift's own: "we cannot even rely on them to be wrong." *Swift's Parody* (Cambridge: Cambridge University Press, 1995), 17.

13. Claude Rawson, *God, Gulliver and Genocide: Barbarism and the European Imagination, 1492–1945* (Oxford: Oxford University Press, 2001), 186.

14. For a history of Swift's involvement in the Wood's Halfpence scheme, see Ferguson, *Jonathan Swift and Ireland*. For a more recent assessment, see Connolly, "Swift and Protestant Ireland."

15. Jonathan Swift, "A Letter to the Shop-Keepers, Tradesmen, Farmers and Common-People of Ireland," in *Swift's Irish Pamphlets: An Introductory Selection*, ed. Joseph McMinn (Gerrards Cross, Ulster: Colin Smythe, 1991), 60. All quotations are from this edition.

S. J. Connolly argues, however, that Swift's stance of beleaguered victimization in the *Drapier's Letters* is carefully constructed: "to claim that Ireland was in a state of 'slavery' was a wild exaggeration" (36). Connolly suggests that the Irish patriotic voice had much more influence than Swift implies (eager as he was to promote his own role as savior of the Irish): "When conflicts did occur, as in the Wood's Halfpence controversy of 1722–5 . . . what was made clear was the inability of the British government to have its way against the determined opposition of the Irish political nation" ("Swift and Protestant Ireland," 37).

16. Treatments of Swift's "economic" thinking about Ireland are in Patrick Kelly, "'Conclusions by no Means Calculated for the Circumstances and Condition of Ireland': Swift, Berkeley and the Solution to Ireland's Economic Problems," in *Locating Swift; and James Kelly*, "Jonathan Swift and the Irish Economy in the 1720s," *Eighteenth-Century Ireland* 6 (1991): 7–36.

17. "A Letter to the Shop-Keepers, Tradesmen, Farmers, and Common People of Ireland," 62.

18. Swift's representation of currency in the *Drapier's Letters* consciously reproduces the conservative, or mercantilist, position that money should embody wealth itself—should have an unfixed or literal value—and that it should not be understood merely as the measure or representation of wealth.

19. Catherine Ingrassia argues that paper credit disrupted traditional assumptions about property, wealth, and status in England: "'Descendents' not only leave their traditional family estates but potentially gamble or 'job' them away in the crowded confines of Exchange Alley. The geographic and ideological shift constricts and diminishes the male descendent by replacing the authority and identity of landed wealth with the anonymity of paper credit." "The Pleasure of Business and the Business of Pleasure: Gender, Credit and the South Sea Bubble," in *Studies in Eighteenth-Century Culture* 24 (1995): 193.

20. Festa, *Sentimental Figures of Empire*, 155. Cf. James Thompson's description of the way in which money generates systems of exchange and equivalence: "Unlike land, which is stable and inert, unchanging over time, immutable and trans-historical, money is associated with alchemy, with changability per se . . . money can turn everything into its opposite" (*Models of Value*, 71).

21. Catherine Ingrassia points out that anxieties about the status of the literary artifact were informed, and even set in motion, by the theorization of credit and abstract value taking place in the early eighteenth century. Swift's anxieties form part of a general recognition that literary value and commodity value are, in a sense, analogous: "Like a stock scheme, fiction was based on nothing 'real' or tangible; indeed it offered possibilities that may or may not be realized. Speculators in fiction or in finance must make an emotional and economic investment, they must exercise the power of fantasy in pursuit of immediate gratification;

they must use their imagination to envisage the outcome of the narrative implicitly being offered" ("The Pleasure of Business," 206).

22. Joseph Addison, *Spectator*, no. 3 (1711), in *Spectator*, ed. Donald F. Bond (Oxford: Clarendon Press, 1965), 1:14–17, 15. All page numbers refer to this edition.

23. "An Examination of Certain Abuses, Corruptions, and Enormities, in the City of Dublin," in *Swift's Irish Pamphlets*, 167–68.

24. Jonathan Swift, *A Tale of a Tub*, in *The Writings of Jonathan Swift*, 323.

25. Max Byrd remarks that "Just as Pope more or less consciously attacks something disruptive in the very nature of poetry, so Swift, with a clearer sense of his private temptations, attacks something to him insane in the very nature of religion." *Visits to Bedlam: Madness and Literature in the Eighteenth Century* (Columbia: University of South Carolina Press, 1974), 70.

26. Discussed in Philip Harth, *Swift and Anglican Rationalism: The Religious Background of* A Tale of a Tub (Chicago: University of Chicago Press, 1961), 44. Harth calls attention to John Tillotson's treatise on the subject, "Against Transubstantiation" (*Works*, 2: 447–48). Scholarship on the Anglican rationalist position has shown, however, that theologians would defend other divine mysteries, particularly the Trinity, even though they discredited transubstantiation. Stillingfleet and Tillotson, among others, "resorted to a distinction between the existence of a thing and the manner of its existence. We can understand the fact or existence of a mystery once it has been revealed, even though we cannot understand its manner" (Harth, 45).

27. For a history of theological and doctrinal disputes in the late seventeenth and early eighteenth centuries, see Isabel Rivers, *Reason, Grace and Sentiment: A Study of the Language of Religion and Ethics in England, 1660–1780* (Cambridge: Cambridge University Press, 1991), vol. 1.

28. See Harth, *Anglican Rationalism*; Gerard Reedy, "A Preface to Anglican Rationalism," in *Eighteenth-Century Contexts: Historical Inquiries in Honor of Philip Harth*, ed. Howard D. Weinbrot, Peter J. Schakel, and Steven E. Karian (Madison: University of Wisconsin Press, 2001).

29. *Paradise Lost*, 3.1–55, 7.1–39.

30. Traced in Mahony, *Jonathan Swift: The Irish Identity*, chapters 1 and 2.

31. Anon., *Human Ordure, Botanically Considered; The First Essay of the Kind, Ever Published in the World* (London, 1733), 7–8. All quotations are from this edition.

32. See Mahony, "The Early Biographers: Preserving Mixed Impressions," in *Jonathan Swift: The Irish Identity*.

33. Anon. *Reason against Coition: A Discourse Deliver'd to a Private Congregation* (London, 1732), 29. All quotations are from this edition.

CHAPTER 5

1. However, as Louis Landa explains in his edition of Defoe's *A Journal of the Plague Year*, this figure is not wholly reliable, based as it is on London's Bills of Mortality from the summer and autumn of 1665. Daniel Defoe, *A Journal of the Plague Year* (1969; Oxford: World's Classics, 1990), 279. All page numbers refer to this edition.

2. Paula McDowell argues that conversation, "uncontained orality," is figured as a form of contagion. "Gossip is an epidemic, inasmuch as it spreads disease. The citizens respond to the bills with excited "talk," but their overhasty orality causes further spreading of the contagion. The government responds to this "thoughtless Humour of the People" by publishing more would-be authoritative texts, giving out "printed Directions, spreading them all over the City." But these printed texts are ineffectual, for the erroneous bills have already done their damage." "Defoe and the Contagion of the Oral: Modeling Media Shift in *The Journal of the Plague Year*," *PMLA*, 121, no. 1 (2006): 86–106, 96.

3. Max Byrd points out that Defoe's accounts of London are marked by his characters' "feelings of alienation and anxiety" as they move through an "unplanned, privately controlled" urban sprawl. In other words, the model of the civic wasteland, described in my discussion of Pepys, Evelyn, and Dryden, persists in Defoe's writing. *London Transformed: Images of the City in the Eighteenth Century* (New Haven: Yale University Press, 1978), 24–25. Byrd suggests, moreover, that Defoe's classical antecedents for the *Journal* are descriptions of cities under siege: the *Iliad*, Thucydides' *History*, Lucretius' *De Rerum Natura* and the *Decameron* (30). The "disaster setting" of Defoe's texts is reminiscent of the descriptions of biblical wasteland literalized in the Great Fire.

4. Caroline Bynum, "Why All the Fuss about the Body? A Medievalist's Perspective," *Critical Inquiry* 22, no. 1 (Autumn 1995): 1–33, 24.

5. Kolnai, *On Disgust*, 56.

6. Bynum, "Why All the Fuss," 27.

7. Defoe, *A Journal of the Plague Year*, 59.

8. Cockayne, *Hubbub*, 189.

9. Cockayne, *Hubbub*, 181.

10. Cockayne, *Hubbub*, 216, quoting 8 George I (1735).

11. Giambattista Vico, *New Science* [Principles of The New Science Concerning the Common Nature of Nations], section 337, trans. David Marsh and ed. Anthony Grafton (London: Penguin, 1999), 122.

12. Joseph Roach, *Cities of The Dead: Circum-Atlantic Performance. The Social Foundations of Aesthetic Forms* (New York: Columbia University Press, 1996), 38.

13. Bynum, "Why All the Fuss," 3.

14. Cockayne, *Hubbub*, 157.

15. Roach, *Cities of the Dead*, 52.

16. John Vanbrugh, "Vanbrugh's Proposals for the Fifty Churches" (1711), quoted in Roach, *Cities of the Dead*, 52.

17. Rolls, *London's Resurrection* (London, 1668). The suburbs were, however, regarded as an uncontaminated area, free from the disease and contagion that sullied the city of London, both literally and figuratively. See Margaret Pelling, "Skirting the City? Disease, Social Change and Divided Households in the Seventeenth Century," in *Londinopolis: Essays in the Cultural and Social History of Early Modern London*, ed. Paul Griffiths and Mark S. R. Jenner (Manchester and New York: Manchester University Press, 2000), 154–75.

18. Anon. [Erasmus Jones], *Luxury, Pride and Vanity, the Bane of the British Nation: Wherein is shown the prodigality and profuseness of all ranks, and conditions* (London, 1736). It is interesting that the title of the pamphlet should choose the words "prodigality and profuseness" to describe the excesses of luxury—words that overlap with the teeming abundance of waste.

19. Peter Linebaugh, *The London Hanged* (Cambridge: Cambridge University Press, 1992), 9.

20. Bernard Mandeville, *An Enquiry into the Frequent Causes of Executions at Tyburn*, ed. Malvin R. Zirker (Los Angeles: Augustan Reprint Society, William Andrews Clark Memorial Library, 1964), 27. All page numbers refer to this edition.

21. Michel Foucault, *Discipline and Punish: The Birth of the Prison* (New York: Vintage Books, 1979), 45. Foucault observes that "a body effaced, reduced to dust and thrown to the winds, a body destroyed piece by piece by the infinite power of the sovereign, constituted not only the ideal, but the real limit of punishment" (50). The forced decomposition of the body, its visibly hastened disintegration, affirmed that the condemned person was both socially, and literally, waste matter.

22. Peter Linebaugh, "The Tyburn Riot against the Surgeons" in *Albion's Fatal Tree: Crime and Society in Eighteenth-Century England*, ed. Douglas Hay, Peter Linebaugh, John G. Rule, E. P. Thompson, and Cal Winslow (Harmondsworth: Penguin, 1977), 65.

23. Jonathan Sawday, *The Body Emblazoned: Dissection and the Human Body in Renaissance Culture* (London: Routledge, 1995), 3.

24. Joseph Roach argues that "at one time in European tradition, as in many other traditions world-wide, the dead were omnipresent: first, in the mysterious sense that their spirits continued to occupy places among the quick; second, in the material sense that medieval burial custom crowded decomposing corpses into hopelessly overfilled churchyards and crypts, whence they literally overflowed into the space of the living" (*Cities of the Dead*, 48). His position is supported by David Stannard, in chapters 1 and 5 of *The Puritan Way of Death* (Oxford: Oxford University Press, 1977), and by Claire Gittings, in *Death, Burial and the Individual in Early Modern England* (London: Croom Helm, 1984).

25. Sawday, *The Body Emblazoned*, 37.

26. Flynn, *The Body in Swift and Defoe*, 24. Flynn goes on, "Dead bodies, viewed for centuries as natural representations of the progress of life into death, suddenly signify all the lethal qualities of an increasingly complicated urban existence that inhibits, even prohibits, health" (24–25).

27. Mary Douglas, *Purity and Danger: An Analysis of Concepts of Pollution and Taboo* (New York: Praeger, 1966), 40. Douglas's chapter headings reinforce the overlap between the disposal of the body and the elimination of waste: "External Boundaries," "Internal Lines," "The System at War with Itself."

28. Richard Baxter, *The Saints Everlasting Rest; or, A Treatise of the Blessed State of the Saints in their Enjoyment of God in Glory*, ed. William Young (London: 1915), section 12.

29. Jonathan Dolimore, *Death, Desire, and Loss in Western Culture* (New York: Routledge, 1998), 187.

30. The pamphlet is probably by Thomas Nashe. For a history of the Marprelate controversy, see Kristin Poole, *Radical Religion from Shakespeare to Milton*, chapter 1, "Falstaff and the Drama of Martin Marprelate." For analysis of the Marprelate debates in the history of satire, and the particular significance of the attack on Presbyterians, see Nigel Smith, "Marprelate Revived," in *Literature and Revolution in England: 1640–1660* (New Haven: Yale University Press, 1994), 297–304.

31. See Gittings, *Death, Burial and the Individual*, and Martin Stannard, *The Puritan Way of Death*, chapter 5.

32. Death, with the doctrine of predestination, became a frighteningly solitary, alienated affair. Claire Gittings explains: "it was a more individualistic philosophy which emerged at the Reformation and one in which the dividing line between life and death, the living and the dead, assumed a far greater clarity" (*Death, Burial and the Individual*, 40).

33. Robert Bolton, *Mr Boltons Last and Learned Worke of the Foure Last Things* (London, 1635), quoted in Gittings, *Death, Burial and the Individual*, 46–47.

34. For a reading of artistic representations of perishable commodities and mortal beings, see Simon Schama, "Perishable Commodities: Dutch Still-life Painting and the 'Empire of Things,' " in *Consumption and the World of Goods*, ed. Derek Brewer and Roy Porter (London: Routledge, 1993).

35. Samuel Pepys, *The Diary of Samuel Pepys*, ed. Robert Latham and William Matthews (Berkeley: University of California Press, 2000), July 18, 1665.

36. Stephen Greenblatt, *Hamlet in Purgatory* (Princeton: Princeton University Press, 2001), 17.

37. *A Directory for the Publique Worship of God throughout the Three Kingdoms of England, Scotland and Ireland* (1644). This includes the reformed order for the burial of the dead from the years of the republic. Quoted in Gittings, *Death, Burial and the Individual*, 48.

38. John Bender points to the relationship in *Imagining the Penitentiary*, when he argues that in the *Journal* the whole of London has become a prison, unlike in the *Tour*, where some of London's prisons are singled out and attended to as individual, self-contained structures (72ff.).

AFTERWORD

1. Joseph Addison, *Spectator*, no. 69 (1711).

2. Festa, *Sentimental Figures of Empire*, 210.

3. Festa, *Sentimental Figures of Empire*, 212.

4. Festa, *Sentimental Figures of Empire*, 220.

BIBLIOGRAPHY

Primary Sources

Addison, Joseph. *The Spectator.* Ed. Donald F. Bond. Oxford: Clarendon Press, 1965.

Augustine. *City of God.* Trans. Henry Bettenson. Harmondsworth: Penguin Books, 1972.

Baxter, Richard. *The Saints Everlasting Rest; or, A Treatise of the Blessed State of the Saints in their Enjoyment of God in Glory.* London, 1650.

The Benefit of Farting Explain'd; or, The Fundament-All Cause of the Distempers Incident to the Fair Sex Inquir'd Into . . . Wrote in Spanish, By Don Fart in Hando Puff-Indorst . . . Translated into English . . . by Obadiah Fizle. London, 1722.

Blackstone, William. *Commentaries on the Laws of England.* 1766. Chicago: University of Chicago Press, 1979.

Brome, Alexander. *Bumm-Fodder; or, Wastepaper Proper to Wipe the Nation's Rump with, or Your Own.* London, 1660.

Calendar of State Papers, Domestic Series [of the Reign of Charles II]. Great Britain Public Records Office.

A Collection of Very Valuable and Scarce Pieces Relating to the Last Plague in the Year 1665. London, 1721.

Defoe, Daniel. *A Journal of the Plague Year.* 1722. Ed. Louis Landa. 1969; Oxford: World's Classics, 1990.

———. *A Tour through the Whole Island of Great Britain.* 1724–26. Ed. Pat Rogers. 1971; Harmondsworth: Penguin, 1986.

Dryden, John. *Astrea Redux*. 1660. In *The Works of John Dryden*. Ed. Edward
    N. Hooker and H. T. Swedenberg. 20 vols. Berkeley: University of Cali-
    fornia Press, 1956.
———. *Annus Mirabilis: The Year of Wonders 1666–1667*. In *The Works of
    John Dryden*. Ed. Edward N. Hooker and H. T. Swedenberg. 20 vols.
    Berkeley: University of California Press, 1956.
———. *An Essay of Dramatic Poesy*. 1668. In *Oxford Authors: John Dryden*.
    Ed. Keith Walker. Oxford: Oxford University Press, 1987.
———. *Absalom and Achitophel*. 1681. In *The Works of John Dryden*. Ed.
    Edward N. Hooker and H. T. Swedenberg. 20 vols. Berkeley: University
    of California Press, 1956.
———. *MacFlecknoe*. 1682. In *The Works of John Dryden*. Ed. Edward N.
    Hooker and H. T. Swedenberg. 20 vols. Berkeley: University of California
    Press, 1956.
[E.G.]. *Wasteland's Improvement; or, Certain Proposals Made and Tendred to
    the Consideration of the Honorable Committee appointed by Parliament for
    the Advance of Trade, and General Profits of the Commonwealth: wherin are
    some hints touching the best and most commodious way of improving the for-
    rests, fenny-grounds and wastelands throughout England*. London, 1653.
Evelyn, John. *Fumifugium; or, The Inconvenience of the Aer and Smoake of
    London Dissipated*. London, 1660.
———. *The Diary of John Evelyn*. Ed. E. S. de Beer. Oxford: Clarendon Press,
    1955.
Fielding, Henry. *Tom Jones*. 1749. Ed. John Bender and Simon Stern. Oxford:
    Oxford University Press, 1998.
Ford, Simon. "The Conflagration of London." 1667. In *London in Flames,
    London in Glory: Poems on the Fire and the Rebuilding of London*. Ed.
    Robert Arnold Aubin. New Brunswick: Rutgers University Press, 1943.
———. "London's Resurrection." 1669. In *London in Flames, London in
    Glory: Poems on the Fire and the Rebuilding of London*. Ed. Robert Arnold
    Aubin. New Brunswick: Rutgers University Press, 1943.
Gay, John. *Trivia; or, The Art of Walking the Streets of London*. 1716.
———. *The Beggar's Opera*. 1728. Ed. Bryan Loughrey and T. O. Treadwell.
    Harmondsworth: Penguin, 1986.
Grosley, Pierre Jean, *A Tour to London; or, New Observations on England, and its
    Inhabitants . . . Translated from the French by Thomas Nugent*. Dublin, 1772.
Hardy, Nathaniel. *Lamentation, Mourning and Woe, Sighed forth in a sermon
    . . . on the 9th Day of September Being the next Lord's Day after the Dismal
    Fire in the City of London*. London, 1666.

Harington, John. *Sir John Harington's A New Discourse of A Stale Subject,
     Called The Metamorphosis of Ajax.* 1596. Ed. Elizabeth Story Donno. New
     York: Columbia University Press, 1962.

Hooke, Robert. *Micrographia.* London, 1765.

*Human Ordure, Botanically Considered; The First Essay of the Kind, Ever Pub-
     lished in the World, By Dr. S——t.* London, 1733.

Jacomb, Thomas. *A Treatise of Holy Dedication, both Personal and Domestick,
     the latter of which is (in special) recommended to the citizens of London, upon
     their Entering into their New Habitations.* London, 1667.

[Jones, Erasmus]. *Luxury, Pride and Vanity, the Bane of the British Nation:
     Wherein is shown the prodigality and profuseness of all ranks, and conditions.*
     London, 1736.

Kenyon, J. P. *The Stuart Constitution: Documents and Commentary.* Cam-
     bridge: Cambridge University Press, 1986.

Locke, John. *Second Treatise of Government.* 1690. Ed. C. B. Macpherson.
     Cambridge, MA: Hackett Publishing, 1980.

The London Gazette, no. 24, February 1–5, 1665. London, 1666.

*Londons Flames Discovered by Informations Taken before the Committee, Ap-
     pointed to Enquire after the Burning of the City of London, and after the
     Insolency of the Papists, &c.* London, 1667.

Mandeville, Bernard. *The Fable of the Bees; or, Private Vices, Publick Benefits.*
     1724. Ed. F. B. Kaye. Oxford: Clarendon Press, 1924.

———. *An Enquiry into the Frequent Causes of Executions at Tyburn.* 1725.
     Ed. Malvin R. Zirker. Los Angeles: Augustan Reprint Society, William
     Andrews Clark Memorial Library, 1964.

Marphoreus [Thomas Nashe?]. *Martins Months Minde, That Is, A Certaine
     Report, and True Description of The Death, and Funeralls, of Olde Martin
     Marreprelate.* London, 1589.

Marvell, Andrew. "Last Instructions to a Painter." 1667. In *Andrew Marvell:
     The Complete Poems.* Ed. Elizabeth Story Donno. Harmondsworth: Pen-
     guin, 1985.

Milton, John. *A Masque Presented at Ludlow Castle [Comus].* 1637 (first pre-
     sented 1634). In *The Complete Poetry of John Milton.* Ed. John T. Shaw-
     cross. New York: Anchor, 1971.

———. *De Doctrina Christiana.* 1674. Trans. John Carey. Ed. Maurice Kelly.
     In *Complete Prose Works of John Milton.* Ed. Don M. Wolfe. New Haven:
     Yale University Press, 1953–82.

———. *Paradise Lost.* 1674. In *The Complete Poetry of John Milton.* Ed. John
     T. Shawcross. New York: Anchor, 1971.

Milward, John. *The Diary of John Milward, Esq., Member of Parliament for Derbyshire, September, 1666 to May, 1668*. Cambridge: Cambridge University Press, 1938.

Moore, Adam. *Bread for the Poor, and Advancement of the English Nation Promised by Enclosure of the Wastes and Common Grounds of England*. London, 1653.

More, Thomas. *Utopia*, 1516. Ed. Edward Surtz, S.J. New Haven and London: Yale University Press, 1964.

Pepys, Samuel. *The Diary of Samuel Pepys*. 1665–66. Ed. Robert Latham and William Matthews. Berkeley: University of California Press, 2000.

Pope, Alexander. "The Rape of the Lock." 1713. In *The Oxford Authors: Alexander Pope*. Ed. Pat Rogers. Oxford: Oxford University Press, 1993.

———. "Epistle to Lord Bathurst." 1728. In *The Oxford Authors: Alexander Pope*. Ed. Pat Rogers. Oxford University Press, 1993.

———. The *Dunciad*. 1742. In *The Oxford Authors: Alexander Pope*. Ed. Pat Rogers. Oxford: Oxford University Press, 1993.

Reason against Coition: A Discourse Deliver'd to a Private Congregation, By the Reverend Stephen M——, . . . To Which is Added, A Proposal for Making Religion and the Clergy Useful. London, 1732.

Rolls, Samuel. *London's Resurrection; or, The Rebuilding of London Encouraged, Directed and Improved, in Fifty Discourses together with a Preface, giving some account both of the Author and Works*. London, 1668.

Sprat, Thomas. *History of the Royal Society*. London, 1667.

Stillingfleet, Edward. *A sermon preached before the honourable House of commons at St. Margarets Westminster, Octob. 10. being the fast-day appointed for the late dreadfull fire in the city of London*. London, 1666.

Swift, Jonathan. *A Tale of A Tub*. 1704. In *The Writings of Jonathan Swift*. Ed. Robert A. Greenberg and William B. Piper. New York: Norton, 1973.

———. *A Proposal For the Universal Use of Irish Manufacture*. 1720. In *Irish Tracts 1720–1723 and Sermons*. Ed. Louis Landa. Oxford: Basil Blackwell, 1948.

———. *Letter IV to the Whole People of Ireland*. 1724. In *Swift's Irish Pamphlets: An Introductory Selection*. Ed. Joseph McMinn. Gerrards Cross, Ulster: Colin Smythe, 1991.

———. *A Letter to the Right Honorable Lord Viscount Molesworth*. 1724. In *Swift's Irish Pamphlets: An Introductory Selection*. Ed. Joseph McMinn. Gerrards Cross, Ulster: Colin Smythe, 1991.

———. *A Letter to the Shop-Keepers, Tradesmen, Farmers and Common-People of Ireland*. 1724. In *Swift's Irish Pamphlets: An Introductory Selection*. Ed. Joseph McMinn. Ulster: Colin Smythe, 1991.

———. *A Short View of the State of Ireland*. 1728. In *Swift's Irish Pamphlets: An Introductory Selection*. Ed. Joseph McMinn. Gerrards Cross, Ulster: Colin Smythe, 1991.

———. "A Modest Proposal." 1729. In *The Writings of Jonathan Swift*. Ed. Robert A. Greenberg and William B. Piper. New York: Norton and Co., 1973.

———. *An Examination of Certain Abuses, Corruptions and Enormities, in the City of Dublin*. 1732. In *Swift's Irish Pamphlets: An Introductory Selection*. Ed. Joseph McMinn. Gerrards Cross, Ulster: Colin Smythe, 1991.

———. *The Complete Poems*. Ed. Pat Rogers. Harmondsworth: Penguin Books, 1983.

A True and Faithful Account of the Several Informations Exhibited to the Honorable Committee Appointed by the Parliament to Inquire into the Late Dreadful Burning of the City of London. House of Commons, Committee to Enquire into the Burning of London. London, 1667.

Vico, Giambattista. *New Science [Principles of the New Science concerning the Common Nature of Nations]*. 1725. Trans. David Marsh. Ed. Anthony Grafton. London: Penguin, 1999.

Waller, Edmund. "Instructions to a Painter." London, 1665.

Ward, Edward. *The Second Part of the History of the London Clubs, Particularly, the Farting Club, the No-Nos'd Club, the Misers Club, the Atheistical Club; With A Comical Relation of the Devil in a Bear Skin*. London, 1709.

Wren, Christopher. *Parentalia; or, Memoirs of the Family of the Wrens*. London, 1750.

Secondary Sources

Achinstein, Sharon. "Milton and the Fit Reader: *Paradise Lost* and the Parliament of Hell." In *Milton and Revolutionary Reader*. Princeton: Princeton University Press, 1994.

———. *Milton and the Revolutionary Reader*. Princeton: Princeton University Press, 1994.

———. "Milton's Spectre in the Restoration: Marvell, Dryden and Literary Enthusiasm." *Huntington Library Quarterly* 59, no. 1 (1997): 1–29.

Agnew, Jean-Christophe. *Worlds Apart: The Market and the Theater in Anglo-American Thought, 1550–1750*. Cambridge: Cambridge University Press, 1986.

Allen, Rick. *The Moving Pageant: A Literary Source-Book on London Street Life*. London: Routledge, 1998.

Altick, Richard. *The Shows of London*. Cambridge, MA: Belknap Press, 1978.

Anderson, Warwick. "Excremental Colonialism: Public Health and the Poetics of Pollution." *Critical Inquiry* 21, no. 3 (Spring 1995): 640–69.

Appleby, Joyce Oldham. *Economic Thought and Ideology in Seventeenth Century England*. Princeton: Princeton University Press, 1978.

Apter, Emily, and William Pietz, eds. *Fetishism as Cultural Discourse*. Ithaca: Cornell University Press, 1993.

Ariew, Roger, John Cottingham, and Tom Sorell, eds. *Descartes' Meditations: Background Source Materials*. Cambridge and New York: Cambridge University Press, 1998.

Armstrong, Nancy, and Leonard Tennenhouse. *The Imaginary Puritan: Literature, Intellectual Labor, and the Origins of Personal Life*. Berkeley: University of California Press, 1992.

Aston, Robert. "Insurgency, Counter-Insurgency and Inaction: Three Phases in the Role of the City in the Great Rebellion." In *London and the Civil War*. Ed. Stephen Porter. Basingstoke: Macmillan, 1996.

Baine, Rodney M. *Daniel Defoe and the Supernatural*. Athens: University of Georgia Press, 1968.

Bakhtin, Mikhail Mikhailovich. *The Dialogic Imagination: Four Essays*. University of Texas Press Slavic Series, no. 1. Austin: University of Texas Press, 1981.

———. *Rabelais and His World*. Trans. Helene Iswolsky. Bloomington: Indiana University Press, 1984.

Bataille, Georges. "The Notion of Expenditure." In *Visions of Excess: Selected Writings, 1927–1939*. Ed. Allan Stoekl. Minneapolis: University of Minnesota Press, 1985.

———. "Death." In *The Bataille Reader*. Ed. Fred Botting and Scott Wilson. Oxford: Blackwell, 1997.

Beier, A. L., and Roger Finlay. *London 1500–1700: The Making of the Metropolis*. London and New York: Longman, 1986.

Bender, John. *Imagining the Penitentiary: Fiction and the Architecture of Mind in Eighteenth-Century England*. Chicago: University of Chicago Press, 1987.

Bernstein, Peter L. *Against the Gods: The Remarkable Story of Risk*. New York: John Wiley & Sons, 1998.

Black, Scott. *Of Essay and Reading in Early Modern Britain*. Basingstoke: Palgrave Macmillan, 2006.

Blackwell, Mark R. "The Two Jonathans: Swift, Smedley and the Outhouse Ethos." In *Locating Swift: Essays from Dublin on the 250th Anniversary of the Death of Jonathan Swift, 1667–1745*. Ed. Aileen Douglas, Patrick Kelly, and Ian Campbell Ross. Portland: Four Courts Press, 1998.

———, ed. *The Secret Life of Things: Animals, Objects and It-Narratives in Eighteenth-Century England*. Lewisburg: Bucknell University Press, 2007.

Bowers, Rick. "Sir John Harington and the Earl of Essex: The Joker as Spy." *Cahiers Élisabèthains* 69 (2006): 13–20.

Boyle, Frank. *Swift as Nemesis: Modernity and Its Satirist*. Stanford: Stanford University Press, 2000.

Braudy, Leo. "Unturning the Century: The Missing Decade of the 1690s." In *Fins de Siècle: English Poetry in 1590, 1690, 1790, 1890, 1990*. Ed. Elaine Scarry. Baltimore: Johns Hopkins University Press, 1995.

Brewer, John, and Susan Staves, eds. *Early Modern Conceptions of Property*. London and New York: Routledge, 1995.

Brockbank, J. Philip. "The Book of Genesis and the Genesis of Books: The Creation of Pope's *Dunciad*." In *The Art of Alexander Pope*. Ed. Howard Erskine-Hill and Anne Smith. New York: Barnes & Noble, 1979.

Brown, Laura. *Ends of Empire: Women and Ideology in Early Eighteenth-Century English Literature*. Ithaca: Cornell University Press, 1993.

Brown, Norman O. "The Excremental Vision." *In Life against Death*. New York: Vintage Books, 1959.

Burke, Helen. "*Annus Mirabilis* and the Ideology of the New Science." *ELH* 57, no. 2 (1990): 307–34.

Burt, Richard, ed. *Enclosure Acts: Sexuality, Property, and Culture in Early Modern England*. Ithaca: Cornell University Press, 1994.

Bynum, Caroline Walker. *The Resurrection of the Body in Western Christianity, 200–1336*. New York : Columbia University Press, 1995.

———. "Why All the Fuss about the Body? A Medievalist's Perspective." *Critical Inquiry* 22, no. 1 (Autumn 1995): 1–33.

Byrd, Max. *Visits to Bedlam: Madness and Literature in the Eighteenth Century*. Columbia: University of South Carolina Press, 1974.

———. *London Transformed: Images of the City in the Eighteenth-Century*. New Haven: Yale University Press, 1978.

Bywaters, David A. *Dryden in Revolutionary England*. Berkeley: University of California Press, 1991.

Carroll, William C. " 'The Nursery of Beggary': Enclosure, Vagrancy and Sedition in the Tudor-Stuart Period." In *Enclosure Acts: Sexuality, Property, and Culture in Early Modern England*. Ed. Richard Burt. Ithaca: Cornell University Press, 1994.

Certeau, Michel de. *The Practice of Everyday Life*. Trans. Steven Rendall. Berkeley: University of California Press, 1984.

Chakrabarty, Dipesh. "Open Space/Public Place: Garbage, Modernity and India." *South Asia* 14, no 1 (1991): 15–31.

Cockayne, Emily. *Hubbub: Filth, Noise and Stench in England*. New Haven: Yale University Press, 2007.

Combe, Kirk. "But Loads of Sh—— Almost Choked the Way." In *Texas Studies in Literature and Language* 37, no. 2 (Summer 1995): 127–64.

Connolly, S. J. "Swift and Protestant Ireland: Images and Reality." In *Locating Swift: Essays from Dublin on the 250th Anniversary of the Death of Jonathan Swift, 1667–1745*. Ed. Aileen Douglas, Patrick Kelly, and Ian Campbell Ross. Dublin and Portland, OR: Four Courts Press, 1998.

Corbin, Alain. *The Foul and the Fragrant: Odor and the French Social Imagination*. Cambridge, MA: Harvard University Press, 1986.

Corns, Thomas. "Milton's Observations upon the Articles of Peace: Ireland Under English Eyes." In *Politics, Poetics and Hermeneutics in Milton's Prose*. Ed. David Loewenstein and James Turner. Cambridge: Cambridge University Press, 1990.

Crawford, Rachel. "English Georgic and British Nationhood." *ELH* 65, no. 1 (Spring 1998): 123–58.

———. *Poetry, Enclosure and the Vernacular Landscape, 1700–1830*. Cambridge: Cambridge University Press, 2002.

Damrosch, Leopold, Jr. *The Imaginative World of Alexander Pope*. Berkeley: University of California Press, 1987.

Davidson, Jenny. *Hypocrisy and the Politics of Politeness: Manners and Morals from Locke to Austen*. Cambridge: Cambridge University Press, 2004.

Dickson, P.G.M. *The Financial Revolution in England: A Study in the Development of Public Credit, 1688–1756*. London: Macmillan, 1967.

Dillon, Janette. *Theatre, Court and City, 1595–1610: Drama and Social Space in London*. Cambridge: Cambridge University Press, 2000.

Dobranski, S., and J. Rumrich, eds. *Milton and Heresy*. Cambridge: Cambridge University Press, 1998.

Dolimore, Jonathan. *Death, Desire, and Loss in Western Culture*. New York: Routledge, 1998.

Doody, Margaret A. "Gender, Literature, and Gendering Literature in the Restoration." In *The Cambridge Companion to English Literature: 1650–1740*. Ed. Steven Zwicker. Cambridge: Cambridge University Press, 1998.

Douglas, Mary. *Purity and Danger: An Analysis of Concepts of Pollution and Taboo*. New York: Praeger, 1966.

Earle, Peter. *A City Full of People: Men and Women of London 1650–1750*. London: Methuen, 1994.

———. *The Making of the English Middle Class: Business, Society and Family Life in London, 1660–1730*. London: Methuen, 1989.

Edwards, Karen. "Eden Raised: Waste in Milton's Garden." In *Renaissance Ecology: Imagining Eden in Milton's England*. Ed. Ken Hiltner. Pittsburgh: Duquesne University Press, 2008.

Eilon, Daniel. *Factions' Fictions: Ideological Closure in Swift's Satire*. Newark: University of Delaware Press, 1991.

Elias, Norbert. *The Civilizing Process*. Trans. Edmund Jephcott. Oxford and Cambridge, MA: Blackwell, 1994.

Fabricant, Carole. *Swift's Landscape*. Notre Dame: University of Notre Dame Press, 1995.

———. "Speaking for the Irish Nation: The Drapier, The Bishop and the Problems of Colonial Representation." *ELH* 66, no. 2 (1999): 337–72.

Fallon, Stephen M. *Milton among the Philosophers: Poetry and Materialism in Seventeenth-Century England*. Ithaca: Cornell University Press, 1991.

———. "*Paradise Lost* in Intellectual History." In *A Companion to Milton*. Ed. Thomas Corns. Oxford: Blackwell, 2001.

Ferguson, Oliver Watkins. *Jonathan Swift and Ireland*. Urbana: University of Illinois Press, 1962.

Festa, Lynn. *Sentimental Figures of Empire in Eighteenth-Century Britain and France*. Baltimore: Johns Hopkins University Press, 2006.

Fischer, John Irwin, Hermann J. Real, James Woolley, eds. *Swift and His Contexts*. New York: AMS Press, 1989.

Fish, Stanley Eugene. *Surprised by Sin: The Reader in Paradise Lost*. 1967; Berkeley: University of California Press, 1971.

Fisher, Frederick Jack, ed. *Essays on the Economic and Social History of Tudor and Stuart England*. Cambridge: Cambridge University Press, 1961.

Flynn, Carol Houlihan. *The Body in Swift and Defoe*. Cambridge: Cambridge University Press, 1990.

Foucault, Michel. *The Order of Things: An Archaeology of the Human Sciences*. New York: Vintage Books, 1973.

———. *Discipline and Punish: The Birth of the Prison*. New York: Vintage Books, 1995.

Fox, Christopher, and Brenda Tooley, eds. *Walking Naboth's Vineyard: New Studies of Swift*. Notre Dame: University of Notre Dame Press, 1995.

Freud, Sigmund. *Civilization and Its Discontents*. Trans. and ed. James
    Strachey. New York: W.W. Norton, 1961.
Gattrell, Vic. *City Of Laughter: Sex and Satire in Eighteenth-Century London*.
    New York: Walker & Co., 2007.
Gittings, Clare. *Death, Burial and the Individual in Early Modern England*.
    London: Croom Helm, 1984.
Greaves, Richard L. *Enemies under Their Feet: Radicals and Nonconformists in
    Britain 1664–1677*. Stanford: Stanford University Press, 1990.
Greenblatt, Stephen. "Filthy Rites." In *Learning to Curse: Essays in Early Mod-
    ern Culture*. New York: Routledge, 1990.
———. "Remnants of the Sacred in Early Modern England." In *Subject and
    Object in Renaissance Culture*. Ed. Peter Stallybrass, Margretta de Grazia,
    and Maureen Quilligan. Cambridge: Cambridge University Press, 1996.
———. *Hamlet in Purgatory*. Princeton: Princeton University Press, 2001.
Griffin, Dustin. "The Beginnings of Modern Authorship: Milton and
    Dryden." *Milton Quarterly* 24, no. 1 (March 1990).
Griffiths, Paul, and Mark Jenner, eds. *Londinopolis: Essays in the Cultural and
    Social History of Early Modern London*. Manchester, 2000.
Habermas, Jurgen. *The Structural Transformation of the Public Sphere: An
    Inquiry into a Category of Bourgeois Society*. Trans. Thomas Burger and
    Frederick Lawrence. Cambridge, MA: MIT Press, 1989.
Haley, David B. *Dryden and the Problem of Freedom: The Republican Aftermath
    1649–1680*. New Haven: Yale University Press, 1997.
Harris, Jonathan Gil. "This Is Not a Pipe: Water Supply, Incontinent Sources,
    and the Leaky Body Politic." In *Enclosure Acts: Sexuality, Property, and
    Culture in Early Modern England*. Ed. Richard Burt. Ithaca: Cornell Uni-
    versity Press, 1994.
———. *Foreign Bodies and the Body Politic: Discourses of Social Pathology in
    Early Modern England*. Cambridge and New York: Cambridge University
    Press, 1998.
Harris, Tim. *London Crowds in the Reign of Charles II: Propaganda and Politics
    from the Restoration until the Exclusion Crisis*. Cambridge: Cambridge
    University Press, 1987.
Harth, Philip. *Swift and Anglican Rationalism: The Religious Background of "A
    Tale of a Tub."* Chicago: University of Chicago Press, 1961.
Heilbroner, Robert L. *The Worldly Philosophers: The Lives, Times, and Ideas of
    the Great Economic Thinkers*. New York: Simon & Schuster, 1986.
Henry, John. *The Scientific Revolution and the Origins of Modern Science*. New
    York: St. Martin's, 1997.

Hill, Christopher. "Heresy and Radical Politics." In *The Collected Essays of Christopher Hill: Religion and Politics in Seventeenth Century England.* Amherst: University of Massachussetts Press, 1986.

———. "The Religion of Gerrard Winstanley." In *The Collected Essays of Christopher Hill: Religion and Politics in Seventeenth-Century England.* Amherst: University of Massachusetts Press, 1986.

———. *The English Bible and the Seventeenth Century Revolution.* London: Penguin, 1994.

Himy, Armand. "*Paradise Lost* as a Republican 'Tractatus Theologico-Politicus.'" *In Milton and Republicanism.* Ed. David Armitage, Armand Himy, and Quentin Skinner. Cambridge: Cambridge University Press, 1995.

Hitchcock, Tim. "The Publicity of Poverty in Early Modern London." In *Imagining Early Modern London: Perceptions and Portrayals of the City from Stow to Strype, 1598–1720.* Ed. J. F. Merritt. Cambridge: Cambridge University Press, 2001.

———. *Down and Out in Eighteenth-Century London.* London: Hambledon & London, 2004.

———. "Literary Beggars and the Realities of Eighteenth-Century London." In *A Concise Companion to the Restoration and Eighteenth Century.* Ed. Cynthia Wall. Oxford: Blackwell, 2005.

Hooker, E. N. "The Purpose of Dryden's *Annus Mirabilis.*" In *Essential Articles for the Study of John Dryden.* Ed. Hugh Thomas Swedenberg. Hamden, CT: Archon Books, 1966.

Hoxby, Blair. *Mammon's Music: Literature and Economics in the Age of Milton.* New Haven: Yale University Press, 2002.

Hunter, J. Paul. *The Reluctant Pilgrim.* Baltimore: Johns Hopkins University Press, 1966.

———. *Before Novels: The Cultural Contexts of Eighteenth-Century English Fiction.* New York: Norton, 1990.

Ingrassia, Catherine. "The Pleasure of Business and the Business of Pleasure: Gender, Credit and the South Sea Bubble." *Studies in Eighteenth-Century Culture* 24 (1995): 191–210.

———. *Authorship, Commerce and Gender in Early Eighteenth-Century England: A Culture of Paper Credit.* Cambridge: Cambridge University Press, 1998.

Jardine, Lisa. "Encountering Ireland: Gabriel Harvey, Edmund Spenser, and English Colonial Ventures." In *Representing Ireland: Literature and the Origins of Conflict 1534–1660.* Ed. Brendan Bradshaw, Andrew Hadfield, and Willey Maley. Cambridge and New York: Cambridge University Press, 1993.

———. *Ingenious Pursuits: Building the Scientific Revolution*. London: Little, Brown, 1999.

Jemielity, Thomas. " '*Consummatum Est*': Alexander Pope's 1743 *Dunciad* and Mock-Apolcalypse." In *"More Solid Learning": New Perspectives on Pope's Dunciad*. Ed. Catherine Ingrassia and Claudia N. Thomas. London: Associated University Presses, 2000.

———. "A Mock-Biblical Controversy: Sir Richard Blackmore in the *Dunciad*." In *Philological Quarterly* 74, no. 3 (1995): 249–77.

Jenner, Mark. "Luxury, Circulation and Disorder: London Streets and Hackney Coaches c.1640–c.1740." In *The Streets of London: From the Great Fire to the Great Stink*. Ed. Tim Hitchcock and Heather Shore. London: Rivers Oram Press 2003.

———. " '"Nauceious and Abominable'? Pollution, Plague and Poetics in John Gay's Trivia." In *Walking the Streets of Eighteenth-Century London: John Gay's Trivia*. Ed. C. Brant and S. Whyman. Oxford: Oxford University Press, 2007.

Jose, Nicholas. *Ideas of the Restoration in English Literature, 1660–71*. Cambridge, MA: Harvard University Press, 1984.

Kishlansky, Mark. *A Monarchy Transformed: Britain 1603–1714*. Harmondsworth: Penguin, 1997.

Klein, Lawrence E. "Politeness and the Interpretation of the British Eighteenth Century." *Historical Journal* 45, no. 4 (2002): 869–98.

Klinck, Dennis. "Shakespeare's Richard II as Landlord and Wasting Tenant." *College Literature* 25, no. 1 (1998): 21–34.

Knoppers, Laura Lunger. *Historicizing Milton: Spectacle, Power, and Poetry in Restoration England*. Athens: University of Georgia Press, 1994.

Kolnai, Aurel. *On Disgust*. Ed. and intr. Barry Smith and Carolyn Korsmeyer. Chicago: Open Court, 2004.

Kristeva, Julia. *Powers of Horror: An Essay on Abjection*. Trans. Leon S. Roudiez. New York: Columbia University Press, 1982.

Langford, Paul. "The Uses of Eighteenth-Century Politeness." *Transactions of the Royal Historical Society* 12 (2002): 311–31.

Lee, Jae Num. *Swift and Scatological Satire*. Albuquerque: University of New Mexico Press, 1971.

Lewalski, Barbara Kiefer. "The Tyburn Riots against the Surgeons." In *Albion's Fatal Tree: Crime and Society in Eighteenth-Century England*. Ed. Douglas Hay, Peter Linebaugh, John G. Rule, E. P. Thompson, and Cal Winslow. Harmondsworth: Penguin, 1977.

———. *Paradise Lost and the Rhetoric of Literary Forms*. Princeton: Princeton University Press, 1985.

———. "On Looking into Pope's Milton." *Milton Studies* 11 (1978): 29–50.

Linebaugh, Peter. *The London Hanged*. Cambridge: Cambridge University Press, 1992.

Loewenstein, David. "Digger Writing and Rural Dissent in the English Revolution: Representing England as a Common Treasury." In *The Country and the City Revisited*. Ed. Gerald MacLean, Donna Landry, and Joseph P. Ward. Cambridge: Cambridge University Press, 1999.

———. "The Radical Religious Politics of *Paradise Lost*." In *A Companion to Milton*. Ed. Thomas Corns. Oxford: Blackwell, 2001.

Low, Anthony. *The Georgic Revolution*. Princeton: Princeton University Press, 1985.

Lupton, Julia Reinhard. "Mapping Mutabilitie: Or, Spenser's Irish Plot." In *Representing Ireland: Literature and the Origins of Conflict 1534–1660*. Ed. Brendan Bradshaw, Andrew Hadfield, and Willy Maley. Cambridge and New York: Cambridge University Press, 1993.

Mackie, Erin. *Market à La Mode: Fashion, Commodity, and Gender in the* Tatler *and the* Spectator. Baltimore: Johns Hopkins University Press, 1997.

Mahony, Robert. *Jonathan Swift: The Irish Identity*. New Haven: Yale University Press, 1995.

Maley, Willy. "How Milton and Some Contemporaries Read Spenser's *View*." In *Representing Ireland: Literature and the Origins of Conflict 1534–1660*. Ed. Brendan Bradshaw, Andrew Hadfield, and Willy Maley. Cambridge and New York: Cambridge University Press, 1993.

Manley, Lawrence. *Literature and Culture in Early Modern London*. Cambridge and New York: Cambridge University Press, 1995.

———. "Of Sites and Rites." In *The Theatrical City*. Ed. David Smith, Richard Strier, and David Bevington. Cambridge and New York: Cambridge University Press, 1995.

McClain, Molly. "The Wentwood Forest Riot: Property Rights and Political Culture in Restoration England." In *Political Culture and Cultural Politics in Early Modern England*. Ed. Susan Amussen and Mark Kishlansky. Manchester: Manchester University Press, 1995.

McDowell, Paula. "Defoe and the Contagion of the Oral: Modeling Media Shift in *The Journal of the Plague Year*." *PMLA* 121, no. 1 (2006): 86–106.

McKellar, Elizabeth. *The Birth of Modern London: The Development and Design of the City 1660–1720*. Manchester: Manchester University Press, 1999.

McKeon, Michael. *Politics and Poetry in the Restoration: The Case of Dryden's Annus Mirabilis*. Cambridge, MA: Harvard University Press, 1975.

———. *The Origins of the English Novel 1600–1740*. Baltimore: Johns Hopkins University Press, 1987.

McRae, Andrew. *God Speed the Plough: The Representation of Agrarian England 1500–1660*. New York: Cambridge University Press, 1996.

Nokes, David. *Jonathan Swift, a Hypocrite Reversed: A Critical Biography*. Oxford and New York: Oxford University Press, 1985.

Nussbaum, Martha. "'Secret Sewers of Vice': Disgust, Bodies and the Law." In *The Passions of Law*. Ed. Susan A. Bandes. New York: New York University Press, 1999.

Ogborn, Miles. *Spaces of Modernity: London's Geographies 1680–1780*. New York: Guilford Press, 1998.

Orlin, Lena Cowen, ed. *Material London, ca. 1600*. Philadelphia: University of Pennsylvania Press, 2000.

Paster, Gail Kern. *The Body Embarrassed: Drama and the Disciplines of Shame in Early Modern England*. Ithaca: Cornell University Press, 1993.

———. "The Epistemology of the Water Closet: John Harington's *Metamorphosis of Ajax* and Elizabethan Technologies of Shame." In *Material Culture and Cultural Materialism in the Middle Ages and the Renaissance*. Ed. Curtis Perry. Turnhout, Bel. Brepols, 2001.

Patey, Douglas Lane, and Timothy Keegan, eds. *Augustan Studies: Essays in Honor of Irvin Ehrenpreis*. Newark: University of Delaware Press, 1985.

Phiddian, Robert. *Swift's Parody*. Cambridge and New York: Cambridge University Press, 1995.

Pocock, John Greville Agard. *Virtue, Commerce, and History: Essays on Political Thought and History, Chiefly in the Eighteenth Century*. Cambridge and New York: Cambridge University Press, 1985.

Poole, Kristin. *Radical Religion from Shakespeare to Milton: Figures of Nonconformity in Early Modern England*. Cambridge: Cambridge University Press, 2000.

Poovey, Mary. *The History of the Modern Fact: Problems of Knowledge in the Sciences of Wealth and Society*. Chicago: University of Chicago Press, 1998.

Porter, Roy. *Patients and Practitioners: Lay Perceptions of Medicine in Pre-Industrial Society*. Cambridge and New York: Cambridge University Press, 1985.

———. *Disease, Medicine and Society in England, 1550–1860*. London: Macmillan, 1987.

———. "Cleaning up the Great Wen: Public Health in Eighteenth-Century London." In *Living and Dying in London.* Ed. W. F. Bynum and Roy Porter. London: Wellcome Institute, 1991.

———. "Consumption: Disease of the Consumer Society." In *Consumption and the World of Goods.* Ed. John Brewer and Roy Porter. London and New York: Routledge, 1994.

———. *London: A Social History.* London: Hamish Hamilton, 1994.

Quint, David. *Epic and Empire: Politics and Generic Form from Virgil to Milton.* Princeton: Princeton University Press, 1993.

Raitt, Suzanne. "Psychic Waste: Freud, Fechner and the Principle of Constancy." In *Culture and Waste: The Creation and Destruction of Value.* Ed. Guy Hawkins and Stephen Muecke. Oxford: Rowman & Littlefield, 2002.

Rawson, Claude Julien. "The Injured Lady and the Drapier." *Prose Studies* 31 (1980): 15–43.

———. *Order from Confusion Sprung: Studies in Eighteenth-Century Literature from Swift to Cowper.* London and Boston: Allen & Unwin, 1985.

———. *God, Gulliver and Genocide: Barbarism and the European Imagination, 1492–1945.* Oxford and New York: Oxford University Press, 2001.

Real, Hermann Josef. *Securing Swift: Selected Essays.* Bethesda, MD: Academica Press, 2001.

Reedy, Gerard. "A Preface to Anglican Rationalism." In *Eighteenth-Century Contexts: Historical Inquiries in Honor of Philip Harth.* Ed. Howard D. Weinbrot, Peter J. Schakel, and Stephen E. Karian. Madison: University of Wisconsin Press, 2001.

Rivers, Isabel. *Reason, Grace and Sentiment: A Study of the Language of Religion and Ethics in England, 1660–1780.* Vol. 1. Cambridge: Cambridge University Press, 1991.

Roach, Joseph R. *Cities of the Dead: Circum-Atlantic Performance.* New York: Columbia University Press, 1996.

Rogers, John. *The Matter of Revolution: Science, Poetry, and Politics in the Age of Milton.* Ithaca: Cornell University Press, 1996.

Rogers, Jonathan. "We Saw a New Created Day: Restoration Revisions of Civil War Apocalypse." In *The English Civil Wars in the Literary Imagination.* Ed. Claude Summers. Columbia: University of Missouri Press, 1999.

Rogers, Pat. *Grub Street: Studies in a Subculture.* London: Methuen, 1972.

Rumrich, John. *The Matter of Glory: A New Preface to Paradise Lost.* Pittsburgh: University of Pittsburgh Press, 1987.

———. "Radical Heterodoxy and Heresy." In *A Comparison to Milton*. Ed. Thomas Corns. Oxford: Blackwell, 2001.

Said, Edward W. *The World, the Text, and the Critic*. Cambridge, MA: Harvard University Press, 1983.

Sarasohn, Lisa. *Gassendi's Ethics: Freedom in a Mechanistic Universe*. Ithaca: Cornell University Press, 1996.

Sawday, Jonathan. *The Body Emblazoned: Dissection and the Human Body in Renaissance Culture*. London: Routledge, 1995.

Schama, Simon. "Perishable Commodities: Dutch Still-Life Painting and the 'Empire Of Things.'" In *Consumption and the World of Goods*. Ed. Derek Brewer and Roy Porter. London: Routledge, 1993.

Schoenfeldt, Michael. "Fables of the Body in Early Modern England." In *The Body in Parts: Fantasies of Corporeality in Early Modern Europe*. Ed. Carla Mazzio and David Hillman. New York: Routledge, 1997.

———. *Bodies and Selves in Early Modern England*. Cambridge: Cambridge University Press, 1999.

Scott-Warren, Jason. "The Privy Politics of Sir John Harington's *New Discourse of a Stale Subject, Called the Metamorphosis of Ajax*." *Studies in Philology* 93, no. 4. (Fall 1996): 412–42.

Seidel, Michael. "The Restoration Mob: Drones and Dregs." *Studies in English Literature 1500–1900* 12 (1972): 429–43.

Shapin, Steven. *Leviathan and the Air-Pump: Hobbes, Boyle, and the Experimental Life: Including a Translation of Thomas Hobbes,* Dialogus physicus de natura aeris *by Simon Schaffer*. 1985; Princeton: Princeton University Press, 1989.

———. *The Scientific Revolution*. Chicago: University of Chicago Press, 1996.

Sharpe, Kevin, and Steven N. Zwicker, eds. *Politics of Discourse: The Literature and History of Seventeenth-Century England*. Berkeley: University of California Press, 1987.

Siemon, James R. "Landlord, Not King: Agrarian Change and Interarticulation." In *Enclosure Acts: Sexuality, Property, and Culture in Early Modern England*. Ed. Richard Burt. Ithaca: Cornell University Press, 1994.

Sinfield, Alan. "*Poetaster*, the Author and the Perils of Cultural Production." In *Material London ca. 1600*. Ed. Lena Cowen Orlin. Philadelphia: University of Pennsylvania Press, 2000.

Smith, David, David Bevington, and Richard Strier, eds. *The Theatrical City: Culture, Theater, and Politics in London, 1576–1649*. Cambridge and New York: Cambridge University Press, 1995.

Smith, Nigel. *Literature and Revolution in England, 1640–1660*. New Haven: Yale University Press, 1994.

―――. "'Making Fire': Conflagration and Religious Controversy in Seventeenth-Century London." In *Imagining Early Modern London: Perceptions and Portrayals of the City from Stow to Strype, 1598–1720*. Ed. J. F. Merritt. New York: Cambridge University Press, 2001.

Stallybrass, Peter, and Allon White. *The Politics and Poetics of Transgression*. Ithaca: Cornell University Press, 1986.

Stallybrass, Peter, Margretta de Grazia, and Maureen Quilligan, eds. *Subject and Object in Renaissance Culture*. Cambridge and New York: Cambridge University Press, 1996.

Strasser, Susan. *Waste and Want: A Social History of Trash*. New York: Metropolitan Books, 1999.

Strauss, Leo, and Joseph Crospey, eds. *A History of Political Philosophy*. Chicago: University of Chicago Press, 1987.

Thirsk, Joan. *Agricultural Change: Policy and Practice*. Cambridge: Cambridge University Press, 1990.

Thomas, Claudia N. "'Writing Nonsense': Pope, Rabelais and the Fair." In *'More Solid Learning': New Perspectives on Alexander Pope's Dunciad*. Ed. Catherine Ingrassia and Claudia N. Thomas. London: Associated University Presses, 2000.

Thompson, James. *Models of Value*. Durham, NC: Duke University Press, 1996.

Todd, Dennis. *Imagining Monsters: Miscreations of the Self in Early Modern England*. Chicago: University of Chicago Press, 1995.

Trotter, David. *Cooking with Mud: The Idea of Mess in Nineteenth-Century Art and Fiction*. New York: Oxford University Press, 2000.

Turner, James. *The Politics of Landscape: Rural Scenery and Society in English Poetry 1630–1660*. Oxford: Blackwell, 1979.

Twyning, John. *London Dispossessed: Literature and Social Space in the Early Modern City*. Basingstoke: Macmillan, 1998.

Uglow, Jenny. *Hogarth: A Life and a World*. London: Faber & Faber, 1997.

Veblen, Thorstein. *A Veblen Treasury: From Leisure Class to War, Peace, and Capitalism*. Ed. Rick Tilman. Armonk, NY: M. E. Sharpe, 1993.

Wall, Cynthia. *The Literary and Cultural Spaces of Restoration London*. Cambridge and New York: Cambridge University Press, 1998.

―――. *The Prose of Things: Transformations of Description in the Eighteenth Century*. Chicago: University of Chicago Press, 2006.

Watt, Ian. *The Rise of the Novel*. Berkeley and Los Angeles: University of California Press, 1965.

Weinstein, Rosemary. "New Urban Demands in Early Modern London." In *Living and Dying in London*. Ed. W. F. Bynum and Roy Porter. London: Wellcome Institute, 1991.

Wiles, Maurice. *Archetypal Heresy: Arianism through the Centuries.* Oxford: Clarendon Press, 1996.

Williams, Aubrey L. *Pope's* Dunciad; *A Study of Its Meaning.* Hamden, CT: Archon Books, 1968.

Williams, Guy R. *The Age of Agony: The Art of Healing, c. 1700–1800.* 1975; Chicago: Academy Chicago Publishers, 1986.

Williams, Raymond. *Marxism and Literature.* Oxford: Oxford University Press, 1977.

Winn, J. A. *Dryden and His World.* New Haven: Yale University Press, 1987.

Wyrick, Deborah Baker. *Jonathan Swift and the Vested Word.* Chapel Hill: University of North Carolina Press, 1988.

Zizek, Slavoj. *The Sublime Object of Ideology.* Trans. Jon Barnes. London and New York: Verso, 1989.

Zwicker, Steven. *The Arts of Disguise: Politics and Language in Dryden's Poetry.* Princeton: Princeton University Press, 1984.

———. *Lines of Authority: Politics and English Literary Culture 1649–1689.* Ithaca: Cornell University Press, 1993.

INDEX

abjection, 3–12; and abundance, 42, 43; and ambiguity, 11, 54–55; confusion of the abject and the valuable, 16, 91, 94–95, 96; and the confusion of life and death, 11; desire for the abject, 54; disgust and social exclusion, 10; the human body as abject, 10, 105–6, 113; Kristeva and, 54; memorial function of literary, 108; in Milton's works, 42, 43, 54, 58, 62; in Pope's work, 17; Protestant theology and, 107; in Swift's works, 10, 15–16, 17, 91, 94, 101, 105–6, 108; in Ward's works, 14; writing and the preservation of, 17

abstraction: of literary waste, 5; of value linked to paper credit or debased currency, 46, 84–85, 93–96, 163nn19–21

abundance. *See* excess

Achinstein, Sharon, 158n18

Addison, Joseph, 17, 87, 96–97, 100, 137–43

alchemy, 65, 83, 85; credit as alchemical transformation, 84–85, 96–97, 163n20

alienation of the individual, 16, 23–25, 41, 165n3; doctrine of predestination and, 167n32

ambiguity: abjection and, 11, 54–55; exchange and uncertainty of value, 10–11; of putrefaction, 7–8; of relationship between waste and value, 43, 54–56, 162n12

ambivalence: toward death or the corpse, 118–19, 132, 134–35; and disgust, 54; Eve's ambivalence toward Edenic excess, 53–55

Anglo-Dutch War, Second, 27–30

animate matter, 70; animist materialism in Milton's works, 69–71, 74, 84, 85, 86, 90; "it-narratives," 17; literary creation as the creation of, 73–74; in Pope's works, 73–74

Annus Mirabilis (Dryden): apocalyptic narrative in, 27–28, 30–35, 39, 41; commerce in, 28–35, 138; and the containment of waste, 42; greed as subject in, 34–35; *Paradise Lost* and, 42; as political poem, 28–30, 32, 35; and wasteland as literary landscape, 16, 26–28, 34, 41

apocalypse: as commercial failure in Dryden's works, 28, 30–35; millennialism and, 150n11; Milton's theology and transformative power of, 70–71; mock-apocalypse and the *Dunciad*, 80, 87–89, 90, 92, 155n1; religious narrative as frame for Great Fire of London, 18–19, 23, 32, 39–40; and resurrection or regeneration, 70–71, 92; Swift's use of flood imagery, 91–92; and unregenerate chaos, 87–89, 91–92; and wasteland as site of judgment, 19

Austen, Jane, 5